RODEO IDAHO!

by

LOUISE SHADDUCK

First Edition
10 9 8 7 6 5 4 3 2 1

ISBN: 1-886609-25-X

About the cover:
Jay Faulkner of Gooding was a mainstay as a steer wrestler with the University of Idaho Rodeo Team. The cover picture shows Jay getting a hammerlock on the horns of the steer before his feet touched the ground. Jay was a member of the team for the school years of 1992–1994. He returned to the University to complete his degree and rodeoed again. The photo was taken during the 1994 spring rodeo at Washington State University. *Photo courtesy Steve Maki.*

Book Production by
Tamarack Books, Inc.
PO Box 190313
Boise, ID 83719-0313
1-800-962-6657

Printed in the United States of America

Dedication

To that unknown young man in Pocatello who sat for several hours during a 1993 book signing in Willard Peterson's little shop, The Walrus and The Carpenter. He observed the comings, goings, and conversations of those purchasing books. As the signing was winding down, he said, "You know what your next book just *has* to be, don't you? It *must* be on Idaho rodeo. Idaho is a rodeo state and Idaho deserves a book on rodeo."

Well, it wasn't the next book, but his comment, "Idaho deserves a book on rodeo," never completely left my mind. I hope he still visits the book stores and somehow this book will reach his hands, eyes, and heart. And he will feel that Idaho got what it deserved.

Table of Contents

Vernon Oliver, father of the many-time world champion calf roper
Dean Oliver. In this 1920 snapshot, Vernon poses with his handsome
saddle horse, "Old Nick," and the family dog.

Foreword

by

Dean Oliver

That fellow in Pocatello who told Louise Shadduck that Idaho is a rodeo state is right. Whether we are riding and roping in the rodeo arena or working to put it on, or one of the thousands of Idahoans attending the contest and show, we are a part of something that grows bigger every year. It seems to me that I have been at it all of my life, but there were a few years there when I was a little kid before I realized that being a cowboy was what I wanted to do. Many of the readers of this book have read or heard the stories of how my brother and I would sneak out of the house after everyone was asleep at night and highjack the neighbor's calves to practice roping. There is quite a bit about me in the book, but I will tell you a little more of who I am and maybe of how I got that way.

I was born on November 17, 1929, just a few days after the big stock market crash that was a signal for the Great Depression. It was a rough time, but it was the time that I learned to work hard at whatever I did, whether it was farm work or practicing for rodeo. My father, Vernon, and mother, Vester, came west from Missouri. We had horses and they became just a natural part of our lives. Here is a 1920 picture of my dad and his horse called "Old Nick." You can tell that dad thinks he is quite a horse.

When I was six or seven, we moved to Burley. There were lots of horses there and I guess that began my interest in riding. The next move was to Nampa and we lived in a house right next to the Snake River Stampede grounds, where I was to ride and rope so many times I can't count them. One of the things I am proud to be doing now is serving as a member of the Board of Directors of the Snake River Stampede.

I am also one of the five members of the Grievance Committee for the Professional Rodeo Cowboys Association. The Grievance Committee is made up of old-timers such as cowboys and stockbreeders. We listen to anyone who has a grievance against the PRCA and we settle as often for the person making the complaint as we do the organization we represent. We've got to stick up for what is right against the wrong. I have always felt that way. I'm the kind of man who doesn't believe that the people who work hard to make a living should be supporting those who are perfectly able to work but don't. I believe in giving to those who are disabled.

Lots of good things are happening to rodeo; that is why it is growing so fast. Some like to say that rodeo is "lousy," but if that is true, it is because lousy people make it that way. All in all, there are a lot of good people and our new generation is more lenient than we have been. We have fine young people entering rodeo every year, and believe me, they work hard and are very good at riding, roping, and wrestling steers, and even clowning. A lot of that is what this book is about.

It is sixty-three years since the PRCA was organized when a bunch of cowboys refused to take part at the Boston Garden Rodeo unless they were guaranteed fair prize money and more fairness in judging. Even then, the cowboys were trying to make rodeo a better sport. That group stayed together and called themselves the Cowboys' Turtle Association, feeling they had been as slow-moving as turtles in organizing. All this is getting ahead of the Oliver family story.

My dad learned to fly and got his private pilot's license. He flew hunters into the Chamberlain Basin in our Idaho wilderness. On February 2, 1940, dad and his friend, Guy Givens of Givens Hot Springs, were hunting coyotes from the plane. They were flying near Arco and a snowstorm came up. They hit a mountain and both were killed. Dad was only thirty-nine at the time, and there were all of us (my brother, Vernon Dale, and I, and our five sisters, Ruth, June, Juanita, Kay, and Donna) and our mother were left without him. It was a hard blow, but we all did what we could to help out.

We learned to make decisions and trust our judgments. That came in handy, too, when snap judgments are necessary in the rodeo arena, particularly in my specialty of calf roping. I learned while doing it, learning to adjust as something goes wrong, like running down the rope after lassoing the calf.

Mother started selling real estate. I could help a little bit, but more as she got older. I quit school after the ninth grade and worked on a ranch in Oregon. When I was fifteen, I decided I wanted to be a cowboy, and was about twenty-one when I started to rope. I was working on a dairy farm in Meridian for one hundred and fifty dollars a month, when I went to the Kuna Rodeo and won seventy dollars in the roping contest. I couldn't help but compare that seventy dollars for one contest with the one hundred and fifty dollars it took me a month to earn at hard farm work. Right then, I knew what I was going to do with my life.

Luckily, I met and married Martha Reizenstein, who had moved to Idaho with her parents, seven sisters and two brothers from Bridgeport, Nebraska. We worked together to make a living and give me the chance to compete in rodeo. We have five daughters, Sheryl, DeAnn, Nikki, and the twins, Kelli and Karla. The girls rode our horses, and Nikki rides and has her own horse which she raised from a colt. She broke it to ride and goes to the cow cuttings now. Jim Roeser gave her a stud and I gave the mare from which she got the colt.

In the late 1980s, we bought seventy acres, and rent two hundred more, of irrigated land at Greenleaf in Canyon County. We have a hundred and fifty head of Hereford-Angus, a crossbreed dark red animal of good size. They have really nice calves which we sell to the cattle sales yards.

I still teach calf roping at the College of Southern Idaho in

Twin Falls and the College of Idaho [Albertson College] in Caldwell. The current crop of rodeoers is really good. They tend to business and see it as an occupation. We don't see much partying in rodeo anymore. While the purses grow larger every year, it is now possible to make a million dollars in one year, where it used to take an entire career to come close to that. The costs are also just too high for cowboys to drink and carouse and then expect to be winners. The National Finals just continue to get better and better. The future looks very good.

Acknowledgments

Any attempt to historically record Idaho happenings from early days up to and including current activities, requires help from many sources, i.e. newspapers, films, photos, magazines, letters, books, other writers, persons interested or active in the subject. In the case of RODEO IDAHO! or "Yippee Ti Yo," all of the above and many more were of inestimable help.

I am indebted to hundreds in and out of Idaho. Many of them are included in the chapters as participants, officials in clubs and associations dealing with rodeo, or members of the families of cowboys and cowgirls. Others suggested sources from which or who turned out to have a wealth of information. After more than three years, helpful acts are still coming in as this book goes to press. To all of them I give deep thanks. Particularly to Kathy Gaudry, publisher of Tamarack Books, for her early enthusiasm for the subject. Just talking about it, before word one was on paper, she declared it "my best book." She endured many delays with grace and understanding. My thanks, also, to the world's greatest calf roper Dean Oliver, who took the time for interviews in person and by telephone, as did his good wife, Martha, and for steering me in the right direction to others in the sport. Even more, thanks for his Foreword to the book.

Most especially, do I thank longtime friend and sister press woman Joy Beckman of Weiser, Mann Creek, and Boise. Over the years our friendship has included her family and many joyful (pun intended) experiences. When I asked Joy for suggestions, she made contacts, interviewed rodeo activists, and collected much history and pictures of the Adams and Washington county rodeo. She sent such good notes and outlines that the writing was easy. Of unusual help was Pam McClary of Boise and Colorado

Springs through her association with the Cowgirl Hall of Fame, in digging out information on Bonnie McCarroll and other women riders, and she was the first to steer us to Bonnie's friend Freita Halsted; and thanks also to Pam's dad, Jim McClary of Boise. Diana Richman, who answered a cry for help and within a matter of days located sources and material that had eluded us. To the amazing Vearl Crystal, a cowboy patriot who serves his country, the sport of rodeo, and has an inborn talent to be a friend and helper. May his tribe increase. A special tip of the Stetson to Fred and Thelma Ramey of Salmon and Cougar Gulch, Idaho pioneers who watched rodeo grow from small roundups in Salmon River country to the extravaganzas of today; Gail Ward, Beth Mack, Karen Crystal, Charles and Betty McLain, Harold and Jean Smart, Jim and Sally Howell, Don Bich, Judy Bright, Dennis Charters; to the quartet of Archie Gookstetter, Gil Yates, Tony Moen and Les Williamson, who diligently worked digging up material on the building of early-day rodeo in North Idaho; Karen MacDonald, to Pete Wilson and his "coffee buddies" in Bonners Ferry; George Russell, Muggs Bentley, Jack and Fran Soltman, Eugene B. Wilson, Pat and Juanita O'Maley, Lydia Justice Edwards, Margaux Edwards, Parker Woodall, Alann and Mali Krivor; Penny Armstrong, Idaho office staffs of U.S. Senators Larry Craig and Dirk Kempthorne; Bill Deal, Gib Keithly, Linda Morton-Keithley, Elaine Bacon, Bonnie Delyea, Joe Dobson, Mary Jane and Ben Dobson, Charles B. Dowdy, Jr., Carol MacGregor, Marty Peterson, Tim and Rita Roeser, Bud and Mike Roach, Colen H. Sweeten, Jr., Henry Gotz, Merci Day Nickerson, Mike Bullard, Brian McCrea, Pete Hohman, Coeur d'Alene Chamber of Commerce, Salmon *Recorder-Herald,* Challis *Messenger,* Ruth Lightfoot Aram, Avery L. Shadduck, Kiantha Shadduck, Douglas Miller, Howard and Joan Allen, Jerry Gee, Jerry Elder, Arlene and Helen Pischner, Linda Davidson, Steve Maki, Reed and Marilyn Hansen, Myrtle Churchill; North Idaho College, University of Idaho, Boise and Coeur d'Alene libraries; Avis Thompson; Pat and Heidi Acuff, Rosalea Moore, Betty

McLain, Kay and Joan Nelson, Diane Richman, Steve Ruppel and the North Idaho College computer service.

Every author should have a friend like David Little, who was a mainstay during the writing about his father, *Andy Little, Idaho Sheep King*. When asked for information on rodeo in the Emmett Valley, David jumped into his pickup and drove many miles to talk to old friends as he retraced roads followed when actively participating in and promoting of rodeos during the days when it was large in his life. Those contacts brought many more. Eva Armitage remained of much help through the four books in ten years; David Walker and Oscar Steinley for finding photos, Chris Holloway, Midge Kristin, Marsha Skinner, Helen McMullen, Dorothy Boxleitner, Paul Boxleitner, Nola Higley, Mike Mitchell, Sandy Shoemaker, Judge Dan Eiseman, Paul Nettleton, J. Dressen and St. Maries Chamber of Commerce, Velma Morrison, Evelyne Jensen, Howard and Joan Allen, Melvin and Rama Griffeth, Nelda Williams, Diane Garcia, Chris Thompson, Joe Jordan, Patsy Jordan Storey, Penny Armstrong, Marianne Love, Valle Novak, Debbie Russell, Sheila Richards, Belva McCullough, Frankie Dougal, Debbie Reynolds, Peg Paulsen Ellibee, Midge Kristen, Ann Upchurch Lunceford, Earl and Judy Lunceford, Audrey Eldridge and the Idaho Cowboys Association, Bob Christensen, Guy Cash, Jr., Charles Dowdy, Jr., Jack and Fran Soltman, Eugene B. Wilson, Dr. James Y. Lea, Bill and Joan Hust, Carol S. Fort, Jane Daniels, Nancy Stratford, Clen and Emma Atchley and, finally warm thanks to that supportive five who became staffers at times needed: Don Sausser, Holly Cooley, Don Riley, Brianne Hill and, to speed up the windup, David Moseley.

Thanks, troops, and if I have missed any of you, just toss a lariat my way and give a hard yank.

Louise Shadduck
Lyondale Landing on
Lake Coeur d'Alene

November 20, 2000

Introduction

How "Yippee Ti Yo!" Began

After eating the dust of thousands of cattle herded for mile after mile around and over the hills and mountains, across the rivers, beyond the ranges and plains, to the railheads for shipping to the markets, the early day cowboys needed some R and R. There was the needed rest and lots more of recreation when the riders from several trail herds arrived at the same time in the little clapboard cow towns.

For unwinding at the end of the long drive, the riders chose to pit the skills of riding and roping by the better riders from one group against the top men of another. It was what they did best, and fellow riders were eager to put considerable money on their champs. The bets placed, it didn't take long to determine who was the winner on the bucking bronc, at roping a steer, or winning a race.

From the railhead, small town and neighborhood contests grew into today's roundups, rodeos, stampedes, and frontier days. There will always be arguments of "we were first" on where and when the initial rodeo was held, yet yesterday's pitting of skills at the railhead towns and neighborhood events bear small resemblance to the stampede spectaculars of today. The core competitions: bareback, bronc, and bull riding, calf roping, and steer riding remain the main events. Barrel racing, team roping, wild cow milking, and others have been added as rodeo grew and prospered. In later years, as the larger towns and cities contracted for the animals and acts, special entertainment has been added.

In the United States, Prescott, Arizona claims "the World's Oldest Rodeo," beginning in 1888 and continuing for more than

one hundred years. Others claim the first was in Pecos, Texas.
And, in 1897, Cheyenne, Wyoming gave birth to Frontier Days,
which has become a lusty giant, offering high purses, and attracting thousands. In Idaho, Nampa made its entry into the rodeo
world in 1906 with a July bucking contest. Official rodeos
followed.

One year after Idaho became a state in 1890, the little town
of Eagle Rock changed its name to Idaho Falls. In 1908, a community fair was held and Buffalo Bill's Wild West Show performed riding and racing with cowboys and Indians. Buffalo Bill
Cody had been a scout and Indian fighter before hitting upon the
idea of his Wild West Show, which swept the country, Canada,
and Europe. In 1922, the Idaho Falls Fair added an Indian relay
race with twelve horses taking part. In September, 1912, the first
full-fledged rodeo was named the War Bonnet Roundup and

Rodeo warm-up at the Kootenai County Fairgrounds, August 5, 1960.
Courtesy of Oscar Steinley.

began an annual event that is still going on. Many of Idaho's other villages and towns followed. The sport has become so popular that bleachers and grandstands fill early. Rodeo fans are willing waiters. Western wear has become so fashionable, even with those who have never ridden a horse, that it could appear to a non-rodeo participant that the shows are put on by cowgirls and cowboys for others just like them. It is big business in Idaho and, indeed, all of America. "Rodeo is the only original American sport," is an oft-quoted aphorism. For many, it has become a profession and Idaho champions are among that lot. The world itself is from the Spanish for "roundup," just as "la reata," has been Americanized to "lariat."

All of Idaho's larger towns, many smaller ones, and a few villages hold an annual rodeo. Cowboys and cowgirls ride the circuit in Idaho, many other states, and Canada to vie for purses large and small, hand-tooled saddles and big silver belt buckles. The original cowboy, who rode the ranges, handled the cattle, and drove the herds to the railheads, would be astounded at how the legend of his western life has magnified, strengthened, and endured. The fact is that the rip-roaring era of the cowboy was just a glitch on the computer of life and grew from the cowboy's need for play after days of hard work and boredom.

Ken MacDonald of Bonners Ferry, one of the four MacDonald brothers who put Boundary County on the Inland Empire rodeo map, pauses for a picture at the chute in 1968.

Ken MacDonald shows his fine steer-riding style on "Short Fuse" at the 1970 rodeo in Republic, Washington.

From the Panhandle Tip

BONNERS FERRY

It is fitting that the Wild Horse Trail crossed the Kootenai River near the present site of Bonners Ferry. Men who rode or drove horses from Walla Walla to the British Columbia gold fields in the 1860s called themselves prospectors, but were among the first genuine cowboys.

Horses and riders began an active role in the area shortly after 1859 when old Chief Abraham and his Kootenai tribal braves took members of the International Boundary Commission for a canoe ride down the Kootenai River. They camped for the night where the town would be. Soon the Pony Express riders in the Star Mail Service used the site for rest stops and overnight stays en route to the Wild Horse Mines in Canada.

Bonners Ferry is the largest town and the county seat in Boundary, taking its name from the forty-eight mile width at the tip forming the international boundary with Canada. The new county was created by an act of law January 23, 1915, and was sliced from the northern part of Bonner, which earlier had been carved out of Kootenai County.

There have been rodeos in Boundary County for many years, but records of those days are kept only in memory. Old timers such as Fred Meddock, Renne Wickstrom, and others took their large repertoire of rodeo stories with them when they died. Fred's stories included those of rodeos with the Indians participating.

Among the tough competitors from Boundary County are the four MacDonald brothers, Jim, Ralph, Dan, and Kenny, bareback, bronc, and steer riders; Marv Cook, bareback rider; Guy Patchen, roper; Bob Robertson, roper; Phil Sweet, current award winning bareback and bull rider.

1

Roy Glauner, described by Karen MacDonald as "one of the real old timers," was nominated for the National Cowboy Hall of Fame. Another was Homer Holcomb, a renowned rodeo clown who has a plaque and photo in the Hall of Fame. Homer carried the marks of being "all crippled up" in his later years. He operated a restaurant called "Holcomb's Round-up" east of Moyie Springs. The walls were covered with pictures taken during his illustrious career as a clown and bullfighter. Many a cowboy was grateful that Holcomb's clowning had spared him from serious injury.

The MacDonald cowboys were born to Donald "DJ" and Amelia MacDonald, along with seven other children. Dan and Kenny did a lot of rodeoing, while Jim and Ralph participated to a lesser degree. Kenny's earliest rodeo memory is from 1947 when Jim was a contestant and neighbor Bill Wickersham broke his leg trying to ride a saddle bronc. The Saddle Club sponsored several rodeos in following years. Rodeos were sporadic in Bonners Ferry because of water over the arena whenever the Kootenai River, either by seepage or flooding, reached that level. In 1948, the city, rodeo grounds, and the arena were all flooded and the arena required complete rebuilding.

Guy Patchen is retired as a calf roper but still team ropes with his son, Guy Arthur. He remembers that local stock owners organized the Kootenai Valley Rodeo Association and provided animals for the events in 1953 through 1955.

The following two years, stock was provided by Ring and Hutsell of eastern Washington for the professional RCA rodeos held in the fall, due to earlier high water. Canada's Charlie Harrison brought in his string for the 1958 show.

Bob Schall of Arlee, Montana, brought a variety of bucking stock for 1959 and 1960. They were big and tough and provided plenty of excitement. The Kootenai River Rodeo Association joined with the Boundary County Fair Board to handle behind-the-scenes work through 1960.

The 1960 show created such a love of rodeo competition in Kenny MacDonald it lasted beyond 1982 when he retired from a successful career. He rode bareback broncs and bulls. His brother Dan started out in bareback but switched to become a successful saddle bronc and bull rider. Kenny's wife, Karen, remembers that they worked during the week, packed the car, and took off "pretty consistently every weekend for twelve years to rodeo in other places." He has trophies and silver buckles from many wins. His favorite buckle was the first he won in bareback at Eureka, Montana in 1963. The first championship buckle came the same year for bareback in western rodeos sponsored by the Shaw Rodeo Association.

Describing the Smelterville rodeos in 1965 and 1967 as "rootin', tootin'" events, he won his first all-around in bareback and bull riding and came home with two buckles and a large trophy. Kellogg old-timer Ray Noyen, Shoshone County Commissioner for many years, remembers that the Sheriff's Mounted Posse sponsored rodeos in 1964, 1965, and 1967 in conjunction with the Lions Club's Frontier Days. Kenny's biggest all-around cowboy win was the Grangeville Border Days in 1968.

The bunch of wild horses, contracted for by the Sphar Brothers in Sandpoint from the Bud Kramer Ranch in Miles City, Montana, nearly obliterated the bucking chutes and arena during the 1961 and 1962 rodeos. Jim McGowan brought his stock to town from Republic, Washington, 1964 and 1965. The Rodeo Association was ready to hand the reins on to a younger group and 1965 was their last year of sponsorship. Rodeo died out for a year and the Selkirk Saddle Club rallied and took over in 1967. The Saddle Club and Jim McGowan then sponsored the successful Kootenai River Rodeo for the next fourteen years. After a layoff, rodeo started again in 1991.

In more recent years, stock has been supplied by Conway/Kitchen of Browning, Montana. The Snake River Rodeo contractors provided the rough stock for the "Old Timers Rodeo" in 1982. Entrants were to be over forty to compete and three of the MacDonald brothers, Ralph, 47, rode a bull; Dan, 45, rode a saddle bronc; and Kenny, 41, rode bareback and a bull. Guy

Dan, one of the four wild-riding MacDonald brothers from Bonners Ferry, is hanging on as "Fandango" pulls a real twister at the 1963 Riggins Rodeo.

Patchen and Bob Robertson, in their fifties, team roped. When told that "Forty-one isn't old," Kenny retorted, "We were old all right, but the bulls weren't."

C&C Rodeo Company of Washington has provided the stock during the past few years.

A well-known horse-loving family for several decades was that of Frank and Mary Brown of Bitterwind Ranch near Bonners Ferry. The Browns kept about one hundred horses at the training ranch. Their son, Frankie, was a jockey who raced thoroughbreds throughout the West. A daughter, Leslie, won awards in both cutting and barrel racing. When eighteen and a 1983 graduate of Bonners Ferry High School, Leslie won the district championship for cutting at Lewiston and competed in cutting and barrel in the Idaho Rodeo competition finals at Filer. She was named Panhandle Rodeo Queen for Sandpoint and made guest appearances at the Bonners Ferry and Coeur d'Alene rodeos.

SANDPOINT

Sandpoint and Bonner County are two of the reasons Idaho has always been known as horse country. The Indians traded horses with the mountain men, the explorers, and trappers. Many of the early settlers came by horse and wagon. Thus, horses and men and women made history together. It was nearly a century and a half after David Thompson, the famous explorer, fur trader, and mapmaker arrived in 1809, that people and horses teamed to bring about rodeo.

Genuine cowboys were living the life long before rodeo arrived. One of those, Harold Tibbs, was a horseboy before growing into a cowboy and had yet to meet the bucking kind. "To tell the truth, as long as I can remember, I wanted to be a cowboy," Tibbs said. He likes the wide open spaces of the West and any kind of a horse. For him, life has been extremely good. A relative of champ rider and 1951 and 1955 world all-around cowboy Casey Tibbs, Harold was born in 1916 at Sheridan, Montana, near Virginia City, where both his parents were schoolteachers. When he was five years old they were living in Outlook, Washington and he made friends with a milkman who delivered with a team and horses. "Whenever the milkman had his gentle horse, he would let me drive," Tibbs remembers.

His parents were the moving kind and lived in many places. As a teenager at San Bernadino California, Harold found a nearby riding academy and volunteered to take "dudes" out for rides. He likes people and made friends. The next move was to Lewiston where his parents added to their teaching studies at the Normal School. It was Harold's good fortune that they rented a house from Idaho Cavalry guard captain, S. Robert Lowe, who moved into the basement. He asked Harold to ride and exercise his gentle horses.

Next they moved to Copeland in Boundary County where the parents taught in a two-room school. Tibbs crossed the Kootenai River to bring horses back on the ferry and then was permitted to ride.

Soon they moved to Bonners Ferry where his mother taught at several country schools and he graduated from the eighth grade at Meadow Creek School. They next moved to Rupert, about which he said, "There were lots and lots of riders in Rupert. Every vacant lot had a horse staked." A move back to Bonners Ferry brought his 1934 graduation from high school. Young Tibbs was befriended by Simon Francis, the Kootenai Indian interpreter. When Francis learned that Harold had a passion for horses, he let him exercise his horse away from the reservation. This he did for three summers. The only order was to bring the horse back once a week to be checked out. The quarter horse "Dan" was developed to run a quarter of a mile in fast time.

While being interviewed in the attractive home he and his wife have north of Sandpoint, Harold looked out the window and quietly said, "I wish I had that horse now. He was quite a horse. He could be mean at times and gave me a bad time, but I could handle him. As a matter of fact when Simon Francis came to get me, he was driving an old Star automobile and had one leg in a cast. He didn't say how he broke his leg and I found out later that "Dan" had reared straight up and over backward, landing on Francis' leg. He didn't tell me until later that he rode from Bonners Ferry to Copeland to show folks how well he could ride."

The longer the old Indian and the young boy were friends, the more Harold Tibbs learned about the life of Simon Francis. The Indian interpreter told the cowboy how he became the one who breached the language barrier between the Whites and the Indians. The story goes that another Indian was killed and the

father of Simon Francis was blamed for it, although he was inno-
cent. His father could not stand the humiliation that was heaped
upon him by those who did not know, nor cared to find out the
truth. He managed to procure enough hemlock to drink it and
die. It was eventually learned that a renegade called "Whiskey
Jim" was guilty of the murder. It was during the time of humiliation that Simon Francis' father took him across the Canadian line
where he learned to read and to write and from that experience
became the interpreter for the tribe.

**Excitement builds in rodeo fans as they watch Jerry Elder showing fine
form atop a dirt churning bull. Jerry is the son of Lisa and the late Billy
Elder and has traveled widely throughout the country to rodeos.
Injuries curtailed his steer riding, but he remains in close touch with
horses. Now living in Blanchard, he is a traveling ferrier, shoeing
horses for a number of northern Idaho ranchers.**
Courtesy of Mike Bowman.

Tibbs was so eager to become a full-time cowboy that he had decided to drop out of high school. "I would not have finished had I not overheard comments of my brother and three sisters, all of whom were honor students, wondering and worrying about me. Along with the pleading of my mother, it was enough to convince me that I should get that diploma. On the day of graduation from Bonners Ferry High School in 1934, I had my suitcase packed and as soon as I had the diploma in hand, I left for Madison County. A friend had gone there a year before to work on the Millard Easter Cattle Ranch. I spent the next three years riding seven horses in the mountains and herding five hundred head of cattle, roaming over forty-two thousand acres," Tibbs reminisced.

He was given a furnished cabin out on the range and was up before daylight every day to herd. He came back to the cabin about noon for a meal which he described as, "Mostly canned beans, tomatoes, fruit, along with bacon and venison."

The range was in beautiful country, at twelve thousand feet elevation, with a valley floor of five thousand feet. "After several winters of that wind starting up at the North Pole and roaring all the way down to the South Pole, turning around and coming back with thirty-five degrees below zero, I decided enough was enough," Tibbs said.

He went back to Bonners Ferry during the Depression years and rented horses so that he and another cowboy could go into the logging business. Tough luck accompanied a new job during which he had a leg snapped while wrapping a chain around a log. His leg caught in between the tree and the chain. In telling of his rescue by Jack Chapel, "A big kid built like a gorilla, all legs and arms, picked me up like I was a little child and ran down the hill to a cabin where a young couple was living. Lucky for me, the man there was Andy Darnell, who had been a nurse in a Los Angeles hospital. He made splints of small boards and bound up my leg. He picked up me and the cot and carried us to his pickup and drove for a half hour to the Bonners Ferry Hospital. Again, he hoisted his load and took me right into the waiting room and asked for a doctor. Doctor Edwards was out of the hospital and Andy shouted, 'If we don't get a doctor right now I'm going to tear this place apart.' Doctor Bowell showed up right away.

"I had just paid $3.98 for a pair of knee high rubber boots and I was wearing both my pairs of jeans because it was winter and still cold. Doctor Bowell was cutting up the leg of the jeans and when he got to the boots, I said, 'Wait a minute now doc, those cost me $3.98.' Andy Darnell stepped up and held my legs while the doctor pulled the boots off. I was seven weeks in the hospital and infection set in. Lucky for me, my uncle J.O. Murphy of Aurora, Illinois, a railroad doctor, was willing to use his medical train pass and was allowed to take a look at me. He arrived in the late evening and the next morning had X-rays taken. They showed that the broken bones had slipped and were starting to shorten. My foot was turning black, so my uncle put me in a temporary cast and took me on the train back to the Aurora hospital. It was 1939 and sulfa drugs had just come out. I had pneumonia and my leg was running a steady stream of puss. My uncle started pulling on my leg a little bit everyday and finally had it straightened out. I got out of the hospital in July but was in a cast for two years. That was pretty tough for an active cowboy."

His parents separated and in 1940 his mother moved to Sandpoint. He left Bonners Ferry to be with his mother. Before leaving he purchased a horse and stabled it in Sandpoint at a riding barn at the end of Boyer Avenue, to ride in the evenings. He worked at logging for his brother and at a body shop. He was hired by the tool department at Farragut Naval Training Station during the construction of that massive center in the early days of World War II.

In 1954, Harold married Virginia Halter, who had three children by a previous marriage. Marianne (Love), Kevin, and Mike are as dear to him as the children he and Virginia had. Barbara and Laurie, both teachers, and Jim, an architect in

Kalispell, Montana, are all graduates of the University of Idaho. All six remain fascinated by stories that Tibbs tells of his life as a cowboy.

Senft's 1942 Rodeo

Tibbs well remembers the 1942 rodeo produced by brothers Ed and Dick Senft at the Sandpoint ballpark, using snow fences to separate the crowd from the horses. The next year the rodeo was moved to Senft property off the Baldy Mountain Road just north of the Great Northern Railroad. "It was a rousing success. Farragut Naval Training Station sailors with rodeo experience competed and the crowds ballooned. They brought in riders with followings from the outside and one of the most impressive things I have ever seen was the Flathead and Kootenai Indians coming into the arena to do native dances. They were wearing bells and feathers and were fine looking people," said Tibbs.

In the earliest days of rodeo in Sandpoint, there were no chutes for the saddle broncs. All the animals were brought out at one time and an excited crowd watched the saddling in the center of the arena. The spectators screamed approval as each rider

Opening the Sandpoint rodeo during World War II.

mounted his horse. Volunteer labor rebuilt or repaired and painted bucking boards, chutes and readied the arena each year.

In the late forties, after World War II, Ira Cave put on rodeos in northern Idaho, eastern Washington, and western Montana. Riding and bucking stock were in great demand for the local farm and ranch boys who participated. T.T. McGhee, who knew stock from mane to tail, went to the area of St. Ignatius and Hot Springs, Montana, buying and trading horses. He drove them down the Clark Fork River Highway (old Highway 10) and would also hire local boys to ride them. The McGhees had a breath-taking ranch in Hidden Lakes out of Sandpoint. Patty Harkey said, "That beautiful ranch is now a beautiful golf course." T.T.'s sons Floyd and Thornton were cattle buyers and Floyd later furnished stock for rodeos.

Among local area rodeo riders were the Tenney brothers, Heber and Rex of Bonners Ferry, ropers. Scotty Bagnell was credited with being among the best of rodeo clowns and bull riders. Jakey Johnson was another stock contractor in the 1950s.

Myrtle Churchill and her two boys were living at Newport and drove to Sandpoint in 1950 for two events. The Kids Rodeo on the Fourth of July and the main event on August 22 and 24. Myrtle enjoyed rodeo as much as the boys did and vowed that from then on they would never miss one. She remained true to her promise and soon became a valued officer of the rodeo association. In 1977, Myrtle was named Grand Marshal in recognition of the willing and mighty assistance she had given when a need arose. She was director of the food booth, parade chairman, and member of the horseback drill team and for several years secretary of the committee.

It had been awhile since the Senft-sponsored rodeos and people of the area were itching to get back in the arena or the bleachers. Calling the new organization the Panhandle Rodeo Association and forming a partnership with the Sandpoint Lions Club, a dozen supporters got together during the winter of 1973 to name officers to spearhead plans for putting on the best rodeo

Early rodeo at Dick Senft's grounds, Sandpoint.

in many years in 1974. They invited the Horse Association to
join them. A colorful, talented, and likable truck driver for Priest
River's Merritt Brothers Lumber Company, Arnold Roberts, was
named president. He was also president in 1974 and 1975.
Along with driving truck, Arnold used his fine voice to sing with
his four-piece country and western band called "The Bull
Shippers." During the original meeting it was mentioned there
was no money. Arnold tossed down a ten dollar greenback and
suggested the others do the same thing. All were quick to join.
Rodeo came back to Sandpoint with a one hundred and twenty
dollar poke. Enthusiasm was high and soon volunteers were
aboard for the many jobs needed to put the sport show together.
Among the several outstanding rodeo stars at the early shows
was Don Gay, champion bull rider.

Gary Spurgeon was president in 1976 and again in 1983.
The rodeo continued to be a big part of the area's summer entertainment and volunteer help was steady.

Mali and Alan Krivor, now of Coeur d'Alene, talk yet of the
excitement of being among the volunteers when real estate
dealer Ken Brown was president in 1977 through 1979. Ken put

his sales ability to work in recruiting helpers to pick up rocks on the arena grounds, repair the chutes and many other tasks. Both Mali and Alan worked on publicity and promotion. Patty Spurgeon Harkey remembers the "colorful and fancy" programs that were produced. The upbeat and eager mood of the committee was infectious and everyone wanted to help. Myrtle Churchill, Herb and Jean Offerman, Duke Peterson, and many others were volunteers for years. Bobbie Crousore, a winning barrel racer was also queen.

Bob Davidson of Sagle was president in 1980 and 1981. Darrel Keegan of Sandpoint followed in 1982 and Gary Spurgeon again in 1983. Patty Spurgeon Harkey, who was the only woman at the original planning meeting and took the minutes for several years, was president during 1984 and 1985. Merrill Martin, who was in rodeo as a young man, was president in 1986. Truck driver Allen Countryman was the last president for the association's final rodeo in 1987. Since then the rodeos have been held in conjunction with the Bonner County Fair.

Joe Kelsey was the stock contractor for the first few years and Sonny Riley of the "Flying J" and the Snake River Rodeo Company furnished the stock later. Patty Starkey said, "They both worked closely with the committee for several years to keep rodeo going." Patty said that John Porter of Super Drug Store was one of the great supporters for junior rodeo and the big show.

Duke Peterson

Valle Novak, Sandpoint's longtime and respected reporter-writer, interviewed "old-timer" Duke Peterson before the 1983 rodeo. He remembered riding in the early fifties. Peterson worked with cattle most of his life and when herding as a boy, knew he wanted to be a saddle bronc rider. Roping also became a specialty and he won a number of prize silver belt buckles. "But not much money," he observed, "because top money for three days of bronc riding amounted to about $125."

From age ten, he helped on the ranch with the job of riding colts. He learned early that one of the most important rules in breaking horses was to rear back in the saddle. "At six years I rode six miles to the school bus stop, rain or shine. I left my horse with a neighbor and rode him back at night.

"Winter times were busy as we broke horses then. The snow was deep and it didn't hurt so badly when a horse threw you. When I was eleven or twelve, we went to brandings, followed by a big barbecue. One time we rounded up all the cows and rode 'em. That was really wild and I have a scar to show where a wild old cow threw me into a barbed wire fence." From those days before high school, during the week Peterson rode colts to herd about two hundred cattle. He managed to buy three wild horses and used them to practice roping. Whenever there was a weekend rodeo anywhere in the area, he attended. "They didn't have high school rodeos in those days, but once in awhile I sneaked into a Rodeo Cowboys Association show and picked up pointers."

Back in the 1940s, Peterson took part in some exhibitions and told of his dad and a partner riding the same bull, one on the front end and the other backwards holding on to the tail. "So, one time, I tried it on the rear end. Of course, I got tossed over the hind end of that bull. Man, that was rough. I was sure spittin' that green tobacco."

In 1953, Peterson said a makeshift rodeo was held when the community couldn't find any stock for bull riding. "There were a lot of dairies in the area, so we gathered a bunch of twenty-five or thirty dairy bulls to do a show. They were the worst bulls I'd ever seen and they were mean. Man, they'd fight." In the 1950s, Peterson suffered a punctured lung and three broken ribs when thrown by a big and mean bull. He was in the hospital for a while.

In 1955, Peterson referred to "trading in his spurs for a wedding ring." He and wife Ethel became the parents of three sons, Jim, Bob, and Bill, all of whom inherited their dad's love of rodeo. They became active riders. Peterson coached a high school rodeo team for seven years. He also served as an assistant to neighbor and trick rider Shirley Jones.

Clint Harkey

Bullriding was the favorite sport of Clint Harkey of Sagle. Unlike Peterson, he did not have a background of working with cattle and horses. Serving in the U.S. Coast Guard and stationed at Galveston, Texas, he and some buddies decided to attend a rodeo. He became so carried away with the atmosphere of skill, strength, and excitement that he rode a bull, and later a bareback bronc. That did it. He was hooked.

Bareback and bull riding became his favorite competitive events. "I just wanted to ride the horse," he told writer Valle Novak, "and there was always so much to remember in saddleback riding, bringing your legs forward, toes out, and spurring." Harkey liked to ride in corduroy pants because they stick to bull's hide. Jeans are too slippery and the early Brahmas were mean and tough to ride, because the hide slipped.

Harkey recalled losing several of his back teeth when he got hung up on a bull that had thrown him. "I couldn't get my hand free and was dragged and tossed for awhile. I finally jerked my hand free, but landed beneath the bull which then stepped on my face and jaw. I was in the hospital for awhile."

That memory brought up the value of a good rodeo clown. "When a cowboy is being dragged and tossed, like I was, that is where the clowns are really needed to lure the bull away. The clown that day was off on his timing somehow, which is why a good clown is worth his weight in gold." Good clowns have literally saved the lives of bull and bronc riders. "They go right in there and fight the bull, climb on his back if necessary to get the rider free."

Steer wrestling is also called "bulldogging" and requires speed, agility, physical strength, and size. Dropping from a rocketing horse onto a galloping steer and throwing him to the ground, is showing how skill overcomes weight and gristle. The cowboy is permitted a "hazer" to help him line up the charging steer. It is the job of the hazer to place the steer and horse in good position before the rider dismounts. Time is called when the rider throws and turns the steer's head so that it and all four feet are in the same direction.

Popular suppliers of stock for the Sandpoint rodeos in those days were Walter "Sonny" Riley of the Flying Five Ranch located on the banks of the Snake River at Pomeroy and Donny Hutsell of Ritzville. They owned a hundred horses for saddle and bareback riding, forty crossbred Brahma bulls, bulldogging steers, and calves. Hutsell and Riley were kept on the jump with an itinerary taking in Prineville, Pendleton, and Union, Oregon; Toppenish, Walla Walla, Moses Lake, and the high school finals in Yakima, Washington; Reno, Nevada; Sandpoint and Sun Valley, Idaho. Then, they took a short rest before heading for the Cow Palace in Oakland, California.

ATHOL

Today's *real* "Bat" Masterson lives at Athol, Idaho. He wears muttonchop sideburns, leather vest and chaps, and has the look of a man who has spent most of his life outdoors. He also has an amazing history which includes breaking horses for the U.S. Army's Cavalry, being an outfitter and guide, a horse-shoer, served as a medic in Vietnam, been shot out of a helicopter, and he won rodeo contests in many places. He is related to the original Bat Masterson, a celebrated gunfighter who, at the age of twenty-two, was elected sheriff of Ford County, Kansas, the seat of which was Dodge. Idaho's Bat Masterson was born in Kalispell, Montana June 20, 1948, one of the nine sons and three daughters born to Verna and Lee Masterson. Bat can't remember a time when he wasn't acquainted with horses.

His grandfather, Frank Masterson, and father, Lee, raised horses for the Cavalry's remote station at Fort Riley, Kansas. At one time his father used Wild Horse Island on Flathead Lake in Montana to raise a herd of fifteen hundred horses, with some of them being shipped to Reno. All of the children of Verna and Lee Masterson learned to ride at an early age and most of them still do. In 1959, the Masterson family moved from Montana to

Bat Masterson grabs leather at the Garwood Rodeo.

Brunner Road in Athol and started logging for DeArmond/Idaho Forest Industries. The boys, with the exception of Willy and Pat, are still working as loggers for Idaho Forest Industries, Regulus, and Potlatch. One brother, Clark, was killed near North Idaho College in 1969, when he was struck by a log falling off a truck.

Rarely using his given name of Murray, he prefers the nickname of Bat. He managed to work or study where he could be near horses. Even though he moved from Athol to Seattle to attend school part-time while working for Boeing, he rode bareback at least four days a week and learned to shoe horses.

An accommodating type of horseshoer, he now travels from ranch to ranch to do the shoeing. He graduated from high school in 1966 and a year later, at age nineteen, signed on for active duty with the U.S. Navy at Camp Pendleton. While there, he trained horses in off hours. He had brothers in the Army Reserves. As a Marine corpsman, Bat flew to Vietnam. He vividly remembers when, at one stage of war, the Vandergrift combat helicopter landing on top of an evacuation hospital, was shot down by rocket fire and burned. Bat served as a medic to care for injured corpsmen. When they were in the jungle, he told servicemen that if they needed a medic. to fill their lungs and yell "Bat," because the Vietnamese had become wise to the word "Medic," and killed several medics when they appeared in response to the call.

Bat was out of the service in 1978 and has never been far from a horse since. He rodeoed, contested in bronc riding, bucking horses, and team roping. He was in the money in such spots as Seattle, Spokane, Salinas, and San Diego. Neither has he been far from doing whatever he could do to encourage young people to learn to ride and participate in rodeo.

Bat Masterson and Sam Scheu of Athol, each riding the traditional Nez Perce tribe's Appaloosa horses, as they team-rope at the Garwood arena.

In 1978, he established the Bat Masterson Ranch of Athol where he has thirty horses, encourages kids to practice on the ranch, and does team roping with his son and other young riders. Bat says, "Rodeo does a lot of good things. Our involvement in Junior Rodeo has been very positive for the kids. It is structured and they learn well. We have reached this stage in rodeo where participants can actually make a living at Open Toe rodeos." Bat's son, Jake, at age twenty in June 2001, started rodeo riding when twelve. He graduated from Timberlake High School at Spirit Lake in 1999 and is riding on the Junior Circuit. As could have been anticipated, Jake can also shoe horses and the money that he earns from that is going to help him work his way through college. Earlier he rode in Open Toe shows and gained his professional license as a pro rider in March, 1999. Previously, he was named "Rookie of the Year" in a contest with others from central and eastern Washington and northern Idaho in 1996. Jake started rodeoing in the mutton bustin' division when he was five. He moved on to barrel racing, pole bending, goat tail tying, and now wants to do roping. He likes timed events and plans to remain in rodeo.

His sister, Shanda, is fourteen and likes to show her beautiful white Arabian stallion "Tizfire." The first year in which she
showed Tizfire she won twenty ribbons in several different
classes.

Father Bat has guided backcountry rides which include the
North Fork of the Clearwater and Goose Creek. He yearly plans
pack trips for about seventy-five Camp Fire Girls. The trips take
five days with no more than ten youngsters and two counselors
at a time. They ride everyday and live in tents at night. One of
the base camps, Beaver Lake Ranch, is provided by Idaho Forest
Industries. Bat Masterson and others like him are reasons why
rodeo and riding gain strength each year.

GARWOOD

Several years back, NBC-TV sent a television photographer
to Garwood to televise the New Year's Day horseback ride, which
has become somewhat famous and certainly entertaining.
Someone who did not enjoy sitting in front of the television and

**The New Year's Day non-couch potatoes rebel with a trail ride
in the hills beyond Garwood and Athol
(while others watch football on the television).**

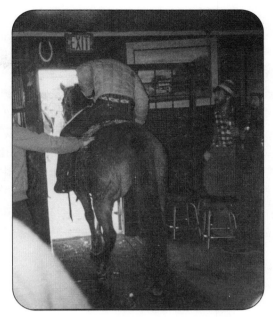

A cowboy stops by the Garwood Saloon to greet his friends on New Year's Day. This custom made national news after an edict that no horses would be allowed in the saloon on any day. NBC-TV commentator Tom Brokaw said he wondered if the rule said "No horse . . . nor any part thereof will be permitted. . . ."

watching football games on New Year's Day originated the idea of a two-hour horseback ride, culminating with a "ride through" the saloon from the front door out the back. As the festivities became more interesting and dangerous, followed by the fear that some rider or horse could actually be hurt, changes were made. No longer were the riders to remain mounted and shoot a little pool as they stopped halfway through the saloon.

Earl Magnus, who used to rope at the arena, came up with the idea of such a ride in 1973. A few telephone calls was all it took. An average of at least one hundred riders attend each year. The mounted party leaves at noon from the tavern and makes a loop onto Hudlow Road for a ridge ride of two hours. On the return, the front and back doors are opened and the riders and horses go through the tavern. In the "good old days," several hesitated in the main room and shot pool from horseback. The national television broadcast ended with the comment that the locals were beginning to worry lest someone be injured during the festivities and "Perhaps the day has arrived when no horse, nor any part thereof, will be admitted in the saloon."

At one time, Garwood was only a crossroads en route to
Rathdrum or Sandpoint. At that time Sam Wiseacre put up a
small sign. It contained two messages on the one board:

"Entering Garwood"
"Leaving Garwood"

With the rapid influx of newcomers during the past decade,
there are now many more residents in and near Garwood. About
fifty years ago, in a partnership venture, Sioux Wallace and
Wayne Darwood bought the Garwood tavern and in the same
year built an arena for the residents who wanted to practice and
participate in rodeo.

When Wayne Darwood moved to northern Idaho from
Twisp, Washington, he operated the Hayden Inn, known formerly
as the Smokehouse, at Hayden Lake. He also guided pack trips
for hunters into the backcountry. As a cowboy, he wanted to
become an excellent team roper, and he did. Cowboy friends
with whom he rode were Mort Castleton, Bob McMurray, and
Rocky Hilding.

Other friends Steve Delano and Dean Duncanson, plus a
number of volunteers started to work on April 16, 1985, on the
arena and grandstand which he and partner, Sioux Wallace,
wanted to build for the rodeo people. Thirty-five area residents
volunteered to help. The work ran so fast and smoothly that they
were ready for an all-day rodeo and family show on Memorial
Day weekend. By 1986 there were bleachers to hold one hundred and fifty. A gymkhana with team roping is held on a
Saturday and junior events for the kids are Sunday. A full blown
Labor Day Rodeo is held every year.

One year in the early 1990s, there were five rodeos held at
the Garwood arena. Wayne organized the Shriners' Club, junior,
summer, and fall rodeos. Generous cash prizes, ribbons, and trophies are awarded through many community workers. Fine saddles and silver belt buckles have been included. Nearly one

hundred girls and boys are entered in the various competitions. There have been as many as thirty-two youngsters in the mutton bustin' event alone. Two or three times each year a junior rodeo is held from nine in the morning until six in the evening. These rodeos continued from 1987 until 1994, "When the junior rodeo kids grew up," Darwood said.

Bob Smith of Chilco, now living in Sandpoint, and Al Landsgard of Rathdrum organized the Junior Drover Rodeo Club for youngsters. Bob Thompson of Chilco came to Idaho from South Dakota in 1975 and worked for Louisiana Pacific Lumber Corporation in Post Falls. He participates in team roping and won a silver buckle at the 1982 Garwood show with his stepson, Dwight Oberland. He also team roped with Wayne Magnus. In order to improve roping skills, he attended World Champion Dean Oliver's calf roping school at Caldwell. He remembered well the way that Dean taught roping, all the while standing on his feet, while the calves were turned out one at a time to race at him head-on. "Dean never missed. He would stand solid and send the loop of his rope dead ahead around the head of the calf." Thompson last participated in the Garwood Rodeo in 1996. He was sixty-one at the time.

Bill Flag, Wayne Darwood, Joe Muskgrove, and Bill Schoener (left to right) at the Garwood Arena.

COEUR d'ALENE

In 1878, when Oscar Canfield drove the first herd of Fort Sherman-bound cattle over Mica Flats and down the winding dirt road of Mica Hill, it never occurred to him that he was making history as a cowboy. He had a contract with the United States Army to provide beef for the soldiers at Fort Sherman and he did it with the gear he had at hand, a riding horse, a saddle, and bridle. Much the same trappings are used more than one hundred years later by rodeo cowboys and girls. It is likely that Oscar was a role model for his son, Sherman, who later became an outstanding bronc rider. *(See Chapter 4.)*

The Canfields were the first civilian settlers in Coeur d'Alene, building a large home at the west foot of the mountain named Canfield in honor of the hospitable Ann and Oscar. They entertained General William Tecumseh Sherman at dinner during his inspection tour of Fort Sherman and, learning that the highest mountain in the area did not have a name, the General suggested "Canfield." From Oscar's reality cowboying and his son's success as a bronc rider, the name Canfield became a part of western history.

From the rip-roaring cattle drive days, the cowboy legend grew to today's colorful rodeos and stampedes held in many Idaho towns and cities. Most are held in conjunction with the county fairs and the mix draws thousands of people. Many years were required and great volunteer effort expended to grow the North Idaho Rodeo from humble beginnings to the jam-packed and colorful shows of today.

In the 1930s, saddle maker Sam Theis' home and adjoining large flat field overlooked Fernan Lake. One day while looking at the lake and field, he had an idea that it would be a fine spot for a rodeo and set to work.

Sam called upon his friend Archie Gookstetter and several other interested horsemen to prepare an arena. In the summer of 1938, he telephoned a Plains, Montana friend, Ray Bryant who had bucking horses and riders, and asked him to ride on over the hills and mountains and put on a rodeo. Sam told Ray he could

The late W.J. Burns catches the moment on camera while Archie Gooksetter remains atop a writhing, wild bronco, and Lloyd Hull watches from his horse.

have the money from the show, and it was a deal. Plains is north of Missoula, and Ray and six riders herded about thirty bucking stock over the mountains to Fernan Lake.

Eighty-seven year old Archie Gookstetter, well-known horseman, has an amazing memory and quickly recalled the enthusiastic turnout for the first Fernan Rodeo. "I was pickup man for Bryant." Other local riders included Jim Messerly and Lloyd Hull. Later, all three rode in several events at the Coeur d'Alene Rodeo.

A number of riders wanted to own Theis saddles because they "sat well." When Sam did something, he did it as well as it could be done. So, when he decided to make saddles, he wanted to learn from the best in the business. Ellis Upchurch, at nearby Dishman, Washington, whose sister, Ann Upchurch Lunceford, still lives at Atlas, was the expert. "Ellis could build a saddle to fit the horse," Ann Lunceford said. "He loved everything about leather and working with it. His tooled designs on the saddles were works of art."

Ann told of their childhood on a working cattle ranch outside Prescott, Arizona, ranging from four to five hundred head of
beef cattle. It was while riding the range that Ellis discovered that
saddles could be much better fashioned to fit both horse and
rider. "He was riding in rodeos by that time," his sister said, "and
became unhappy with any saddle that did not fit the horse carrying it. He particularly wanted a fine and attractive saddle for
rodeo use. He learned all about saddles while riding the range
and in rodeos. One day the idea flashed into his mind that he
would become a saddle maker."

When the Upchurch family moved north, Ellis opened his
shop in Dishman and sought the best hardwood available for the
trees or framework. He then fit the saddle to conform to the back
of each particular horse, much as a tailor or dressmaker fits the
clothing to an individual.

Upchurch was the first man to whom Sam Theis turned
when he wanted to learn to be a saddler. He learned so well that
a Sam Theis saddle became as well-known as an Upchurch. Sam
knew that another saddle builder, Ray Holes of Grangeville, had
earned a worldwide reputation and clientele. He talked Ray into
teaching him the processes he used. He then spent another training week at the Hanley Saddle Shop in Pendleton, where most of
the cowboys riding in the legendary Roundup bought saddles. All
of the workers were superb toolers and carved designs on each
saddle.

The shop where Sam plied his trade is now a part of the
Fernan lakeside home of Rosalea Elder Moore, where the saddle
shop was remodeled into a bedroom. Her grandchildren and several "shirt-tail" relatives became rodeo riders and fans. The Theis
residence is owned by Pat and Heidi Acuff and their small son,
Colby. Many fine homes now fill the area where the first rodeo in
the county was held. North Idahoans still cling to the saddles they
bought years ago from Sam and Ellis. In September 1998, Archie
Gookstetter sold several Theis saddles back to Sam's son,
Charles. Other owners include Gil Yates, Virginia Burns, Pat

**Colby Acuff lives with his parents, Pat
and Heidi, on the Fernon Lake property
once owned by Sam Theis, one of the
great saddle makers of his day. Colby is
riding one of Sam's saddles and many
an adult envies him as they are now a
collector's prize.**

Acuff, Rachel Rosenberger and Barbara Renner, who directed
the Kootenai County Fair and Rodeo for years. Archie keeps one
of his in the entry porch at his home near the head of Fernan
Lake. The saddle, other tack, trophies and photos permit those
who enter to know, "This is the home of a cowboy."

From the Fernan rodeos there was need to find larger quarters. Berndt L. "Happy" Frandsen was working for the state highway department in 1939 and with his friend Joe Hill, both active
in Veterans of Foreign Wars Post 889, approached Archie and
asked his help in building a rodeo arena and racing track on the
site of the old Coeur d'Alene Mill grounds at the north face of
Tubbs Hill. The VFW was seeking sanction from the Rodeo
Cowboys of America (RCA) to sponsor an official event in 1940.
Permission granted. Archie worked with Al Copeland and Louis
Keck while William "Bud" Howard brought in machinery and
levelled the land. The attendance was large and sponsors thought
the arena and grounds were an ideal place for rodeo, but the gate
receipts fell short of expenses by three thousand dollars.

Local cowboys were happy with the prize money. Riding a
fiery horse called "Three Ways to Hell," Spencer Simmons of

Huetter won first in bronc riding. Second was Archie Gookstetter on "Huetter Special" and he nailed the first place in calf roping. Al Stevens of Huetter won second. Archie won the three quarter mile race with Richard Simmons second. Bob Kelly of Kelly's K-Bar Ranch on Fernan Road won bareback riding with Beryl Cole second. Other winners included Lloyd Hull and John Porter.

Despite Pearl Harbor's bombing by the Japanese on December 7, 1941, the VFW sponsored a larger rodeo the next September 6 and 7. Some of the best cowboys in the West competed. Oral Zumwalt and Bee Hinton won in bulldogging and Hinton added to his prize money in calf roping. A popular entertainment was Ruby Kelly's trained trick horse "Billie" holding the United States flag in her front hooves. A riding club had been formed but was disbanded for the duration. Family and neighborhood riding exhibitions were arranged and more people were buying, grooming and riding horses as a "gasless" pleasure. As soon as the war ended, talk of bigger rodeos resumed. Barbara

Rodeo has long been a part of Coeur d'Alene life. A cowboy looks over the arena from Tubbs Hill at the old Mullan Park Rodeo Grounds.
Courtesy of the Museum of North Idaho.

Renner remembers attending several rodeos at an arena in back of the Lariat Club on Government Way in the early 1950s.

In June 1948, well-known horse trainer at Hayden Lake, Rachel Rosenberger said that the time had come and organized the Hayden Lake Riding Club. The first officers were Clive Roberts, president, and Carl Klein, vice-president, advancing to the presidency the next year. Mrs. Don (Vera) McDonald was secretary and Mrs. W.W. Robinson treasurer. Sam Theis succeeded Rachel, president in 1950. Now incorporated as the Kootenai County Saddle Club, Rachel and Brig Allred were successor presidents. The club was growing by leaps and jumps while promoting more and better riding trails and bringing first-rate horse shows to the area. Talk began of expanding activities.

Patty Rosenberger of the Hayden Lake Riding Club was rodeo queen in 1958 as a representative of the Hayden Lake Riding Club. She is riding "Flicka," the beautiful white-stockinged horse upon which "nearly every kid in the area had learned to ride," according to Patty's mother, Rachel, who taught them.

With the enthusiasm that only a sixteen year old can display, Jeannette Miles, elected president in 1954 and rodeo queen the next year, visited the County commissioners and asked for the use of a small building at the fair grounds (it is now the cafe) and they said, "It's yours." Three groups were formed: Sheriff's Posse, Possettes, and Junior Posse. A number were active in bringing the rodeo to fruition. Bob Miles was president in 1955 and the first rodeo was held August 6 and 7.

Rodeo Committee members sit tall in their saddles. Left to right, Gil Yates, Sam Keeter, Jack Martin, and Rodeo Chairman Jim Messerly.
Courtesy of Gil Yates.

Volunteerism went into high gear. Sam Keeter designed and Saddle Club members built the rodeo plant. Riders took part in parades in Rathdrum and Coeur d'Alene, Harrison Old Timers picnic, and Hayden Days. Proceeds from the rodeo went to the Grandstand fund.

Club presidents, vice presidents and rodeo queens during the next five years included: Sam Keeter, Don English, and Barbara Woolsey, 1945; Dave Dietz, Smokey Koss, and Susan Nelson, 1957; Sam Keeter, Gil Yates, and Patty Rosenberger, 1958; Gil Yates, Sy Thompson, and Patty Rosenberger, 1959; Les Williamson, Bob Carlson, and Marge Howard, 1960; and in 1961, Les Williamson was president and Gena Gilmore queen.

Promotion took many forms and one in particular garnered a large crowd and publicity. Several of Coeur d'Alene's business and professional men traded business suits for rodeo regalia and tried their hands, feet, and posteriors at bucking broncs, steer wrestling, and calf roping for introductory acts to the rodeo.

Breakfasts, dances, travel to nearby communities to extend invitations, became annual events.

Queens in attractive suits and hats, riding handsome and spirited horses, added a lot of glitter and pizzazz. Before the Professional Rodeo Cowboys Association took charge with contracted producer and stock, the queens included: Jodi

Above: At one of the earliest rodeos held with the North Idaho Fair, Shirley Carter Jones of Hayden Lake is elevated by her horse and the fact that she is the Queen. Her princess attendants are Linda Gupstill, left, and Deena McFarland McLain, daughter of Bob and Gerri McFarland of Sandpoint.
Courtesy of Virginia Tibbs.

Left: Jamie Dee Kimball, daughter of Karen and James Kimball of Dalton Gardens, prepares her roping gear and gets ready to perform as Queen of the North Idaho Rodeo. Jamie Dee was an outstanding rider and traveled throughout the area many days to promote rodeo and the fair.

Williamson, Gail Atiles, Jeanni Phay, Patty Rosenberger, Jill Pifer, JoAnne Brueggeman, Chris Graham, Nancy Kellmore, Sue Risley, Tanna Richmond, Leann Palmer, April Jones, Sherry Pitner, Tracy Moen, Sherry Washburn, Karri Booth, Beth Booth, Gena Peterson, Helen Pischner, Cindy Funke, Jamie Kimball, Vicky

Helen Pischner, daughter of Arlene Pischner and Don Pischner, is an accomplished rider and in 1938 reigned over the North Idaho Fair and Rodeo at Coeur d'Alene. With her are Senior Princess Cindy Funke, left front, and Junior Princess Kim Rehard, right. The girls traveled throughout the Inland Empire to promote the rodeo and encourage the even-younger girls to experience the enjoyment that comes from riding.

Coeur d'Alene Rodeo Queen Tracy Moen and Princess Gena Peterson pose for a photo before the annual Lions Club Parade.

Schorzman, and Shawna Flom. Many of the queens and princesses were excellent riders and in 1976, Princess Candy Rorscheib joined with the 1974 Princess Kathy Lamb to compete in team roping.

The first professional show, sanctioned by the Rodeo Cowboys Association, was in 1959. Harley Tucker, well-known stock contractor for the RCA was also the producer.

The labor force was beefed up with three new families joining the club each month. When work party chairman Jim Messerly asked for help with repairs, the Lions Club offered to trade a work party at the arena for one at the Coeur d'Alene golf course. Record numbers turned out for each place and rodeo continued to be a cooperative effort.

The exchange of labor was carried on. In 1967, after years of diligent work and donating thousands of dollars from the rodeos to building the grandstand and bleachers, the Saddle Club gave up sponsorship. The Lions Club stepped forward to continue rodeo. During the interim year a rodeo association was formed to take the reins, but found it difficult to secure support for such a large undertaking. A number of the members also belonged to the Lions Club and asked the latter to take over.

Doug Schedler, Lions president, wasted no time in urging the club to do so. "Rodeo has a place here and we have an opportunity to assist and to expand it. We should underwrite the expenses of rodeo on a sustaining basis." They did, with unanimous approval. Strong and lasting friendships within the Saddle and Lions clubs brought about continued support from both groups with non-members volunteering help.

Night rodeo was the next step. When Gil Yates learned of a Spokane service station wanting to sell large night-lights, he drove over, purchased the lights and delivered them to the rodeo grounds. Les Williamson climbed the poles and set the bulbs in place. Night rodeo was born. Others began building an additional fifteen-hundred bleacher seats to add to the twelve hundred in the grandstand. The Silver Beach workshop of Joe Brueggeman was opened to the workers who drilled steel angle-iron supports, painted bleacher seats, operated drills, wrenches, hammers and wielded brushes. They canceled club meetings to have more time on the bleachers. When rodeo time arrived, they dressed in western gear, sold tickets, handed out programs and operated parking lots. One Lady Lion remarked, "What they do for rodeo," and promptly lined up her own crew to handle the food booth.

The arena was transformed as Rodeo Royalty, their friends and families, and even stock contractor Joe Kelsey, joined the Lions to help. Brueggeman, Yates, and Williamson spearheaded the tedious task to pick up rocks and smooth the grounds. An even more amazing effect was that they were back at it the next year and the next.

The United States was hoisting satellites to the heavens in 1963 when a unique group of women riders borrowed the sound, but not the spelling, to form the Saddleites. Ranging in age from ten to seventy, these women added a touch of style and sparkle to what they had been doing as trail riders and show par-

Dick Conrad was assistant drill master of the popular Saddlelites Precision Team.

Virginia Burns of Dalton Gardens proudly poses with her horse. Virginia has been an inspiration to young women and girls learning to ride.

ticipants. Vonne Witter, Virginia Burns, Claudia Steinley and Barbara Renner recruited other women riders from northern Idaho and eastern Washington for a precision drill team. They gifted their horses with white bridles and reins, decorative brown saddle blankets, white and orange pompoms, and girded the animals with tiny lights. From the first night show, they dazzled the audiences with precision drills.

Tight discipline was adhered to and practice was not to be missed. The results were that they never placed lower than second in competition at parades, horse shows, and rodeos throughout the Northwest. George and LaVonne Witter were drillmaster and captain. From 1963–1985, the Saddleites staged drills for the Omak Stampede, Spokane's Diamond Spur,

Lewiston Roundup, Cheyenne Frontier Days Stampede, and
many others.

World Jamboree of Scouts at Rodeo

Boy Scouts from 122 countries, reaching from Argentina to
Zambia, from Botswana to Tahiti, and from British Antigua to the
Seychelles, most of who saw an authentic championship Wild
West Rodeo did so for the first time on August 4, 1967. They
were taking part in the XII World Jamboree of the Boy Scouts at
Farragut State Park on the shores of Lake Pend Oreille when the
national Elks Lodge made the generous gift of transporting all
14,000 Scouts to the Kootenai County Rodeo.

Buses hauled half of the Scouts at a time to each of two
rodeos. Regardless of country, the boys responded with yells of
"Yippee" and "Let 'er buck" in no time at all as bareback, bronc,
and bull riders competed for the prize monies. The dean of
America's clowning, the sad-faced Emmett Kelly, inspired laugh-
ter from all over the world. The western film and television star
Rex Allen kept the show moving as master of ceremonies.

In 1990, the North Idaho Fair held its first Professional
Rodeo Cowboy Association sanctioned rodeo. Many of the
nation's best-known riders, such as Dean Oliver, Deb
Copenhaver, Larry Mahan, and others appeared. Kelsey Rodeo
was the stock contractor for most of the Coeur d'Alene area
rodeos in the 1950s, 60s, and 70s. The late Joe Kelsey and his
son, Sonny, were in the area so often they made many close
friends. Beard Rodeos is the most recent supplier of stock. Roping
and steer wrestling are the popular events.

From the contestants, the top twenty cowboys in each event
go on to compete in the National Finals held the first week in
December in Las Vegas. Several of the champions have competed at the North Idaho event since it was established in 1920.
They have included Dan Morton, all around-cowboy in 1997;
Clint Corey, number one runner-up; and Fred Whitfield, world
champ calf roper.

But the kids, the youngsters, the small-fry in boots and jeans were the ones who put the "Yippee" in the yells that filled the arenas in early-day rodeo. Somehow, those kids seemed to know, right from the get-go, that being cowboys and cowgirls was as much a state of mind as a career. While few of them made it a profession, it is also true that few of them have gotten it out of their systems. Nor did any cluster of kids ever have a stronger support group of parents and friends.

Earl Lunceford

Earl Lunceford has a favorite saying: "A good day is not a good day, unless you are riding a horse." He can be found doing just that at the magnificent horse ranch he and his wife Judy own and operate along Fernan Road east of Coeur d'Alene. Judy says, "He usually rides three different horses each day." The horses seem to know they are living in horse-heaven surroundings and as they look at those who are viewing them, there isn't a hanging head in the herd. The ranch, nestled between two treeclad mountains is a part of the old dude ranch established many years ago by Earl's maternal grandparents, John W. and Jeanette Fortin Kelly. Their daughter, June, married Earl Lunceford Sr., and they are the parents of Earl Jr. and his sister, Linda Poole.

There was no way Earl Lunceford could escape being involved with horse raising, riding, and rodeo, and he gave no sign of wanting to. Despite the fact that he spent much of his early adult and mid-life in medical engineering, invention, research, development, designing and organizing new companies, and becoming a super-salesman of medical products on a worldwide basis, he never forgot his experiences as a boy taking part in Junior Rodeo and riding on his Granddad's ranch.

Earl likes to compete and he likes roping, particularly team roping. An active member of the American Quarter Horse and the U.S. Team Roping associations, he has teamed with Charlie Huber of Glendive, Montana and with Wayne Magnus. He ropes regularly with John Miller of Arizona, a nephew of the late great rodeo champion Ben Johnson.

George Richmond

In the attractive eleven-acre Hayden Lake home of George
and Alberta Richmond, shelves of polished trophies and awards
leave no doubt that a rodeo performer lives there. They attest to
the riding and roping prowess of George Richmond. Smiling photos of three generations are visible. The grassy acres are the site
for horse training classes.

The trophies for steer and calf roping, bareback riding and
all-around cowboy are second in importance to Richmond. First
is Alberta who married him in June of 1945, on what he
describes as "the luckiest day of my life." She was a "cute school-
teacher" he met while stationed at Remount Fort Robinson,
Nebraska, during World War II.

He was born in February 1920, to Lon and Lila Richmond
on a ranch at Stetler, Alberta. He always had a horse. When two
and one-half, he rode a workhorse. Later, he chose his own colt
and at seven, rode six miles each way to school in a little town
called Delia. His mother taught him until the second grade.
Richmond recalls the rugged blizzards when his Dad or a neighbor would arrive at school with quilts and heated bricks to take
him home.

When eight, he saw a Tom Mix movie with the cowboy trick
roping. He knew he wanted to be a roper, got a lariat and began
a lifetime of practice. The family moved to Hilter, Montana,
where his Dad worked on a ranch with the Fitzgerald brothers.
"The brothers were saddle bronc riders and wanted me to
become one, too," Richmond said. "When I was fifteen, I went to
an amateur rodeo in Stanford, Montana and entered the contest.
I didn't get bucked off, but sure didn't win anything."

He returned to roping. At seventeen, while working in
Nevada, he entered a rodeo at Lemoille, south of Elko, and won
second in calf roping.

Richmond's parents were "depressioned out" of Montana,
sold their animals and equipment and moved to Nevada, where
his Dad became manager of a ranch near Elko. He worked for

his Dad and practiced roping, bought an old car with a single-axle trailer and started entering Nevada's amateur rodeos. In 1942, at twenty-two, he began three years and nine months duty in the United States Army, still working with horses.

Fort Robinson, known as "Remount," was part of the regular Army similar to the Cavalry, because of the buying and training of thousands of horses and mules. Richmond was assigned the Veterinary Corps. The mules were trained as pack animals for such mountainous areas as Italy and Burma where American forces were battling.

The fort was located in the historic area where the Indian Chief Crazy Horse, one of the last of the Indian holdouts, was held captive in an old log cabin on what became the fort parade ground. He was without food or water for three days and was killed while allegedly making an escape.

In the Army at Remount was trick roper Vernon Goodrich, a cowboy sidekick of the late great Monty Montana, who recently died at age eighty-six. Richmond also became a friend and went to the Madison Square Garden Rodeo in 1955 with Deb Copenhaver, Post Falls, who won the World Championship in saddle bronc riding. Idaho cowboys looked great that year, with Dean Oliver of Boise and Kuna, handed the champion calf roping trophy and taking seventh spot as all-around cowboy.

Richmond was on the fort's jumping team formed by Colonel Sager, veterinary department head. He had the idea that he could put his roping horse in with the others for rodeo. "I built a practice calf roping place on the base and bought some calves and trained that horse for roping. When the jumpers took part in rodeos, so did the roping horse." On June 22, 1944, winners at the Alliance Rodeo included Corporal Richmond who took second in calf roping and bareback riding and a twenty-five dollar purse for all-around cowboy.

When the fort was decommissioned, Richmond was a hired to help disband stock. Then, on to the rodeo circuit. That rodeo can be "darned near a disease" is shown in the writings of the

Richmond's daughter, Jeanne Northfield. In the January 27, 1962, issue of *Prorodeo Sports News,* she recorded a hilarious story of a plane trip her dad and a couple of other cowboys took to rodeos in the days before flying became an ordinary event. It is amazing what three cowboys will do to get to a rodeo.

George is recalling: "One pretty wild trip, working Red Lodge (Montana) and Cody (Wyoming) on at the same time. Don Harrington, Jimmie Cooper and I were flying along with the pilot. They'd start the show at Cody about an hour before the rodeo at Red Lodge. Theoretically you could rope at Cody and then jump in the plane and hop to Red Lodge. And the airport at Red Lodge was right alongside the rodeo grounds, so you could jump out, have your horse ready, and rope your calf.

"That was all fine except we bucked quite a headwind going to Cody. I noticed the gas gauge on this plane when we got back in and said to the pilot, 'Looks like we are low on fuel.' He said, 'Oh no, we've got another tank—we have plenty.'

"Well, we got about half-way back to Red Lodge, and that thing sputtered and died over some rough country. The pilot couldn't get her started again. He circled around and miraculously found a little hayfield in the hills. We sat her down. There was a fellow haying in the next little field and he had a barrel of gas on a wagon for his tractor. It wasn't airplane fuel, but we talked him into selling us some. We put some gas in that plane, and she started up on it.

"So we all filed in and this guy revs her up to everything he's got and we tear down this bumpy old field. But a big irrigation ditch was looming and he hadn't got up enough speed to get off the ground. So he puts on the brakes and swerves and missed the ditch.

"Cooper was sitting the best in the roping at Red Lodge, so the pilot decided if Harrington and I just stayed off the plane, maybe he could get her off the ground. And he did—he gunned her and just barely cleared the irrigation ditch and finally got her in the air, and went on.

"Harrington and I talked the farmer into taking us about twenty miles to the nearest airport. The pilot was to come back and pick us up there. We got to the airport, and waited and waited. This is almost unbelievable, but as he landed the plane at Red Lodge the landing gear gave way. So they slid in on her belly.

"He finally got another plane and picked us up and flew back to Red Lodge. By that time it was getting real late in the evening. The rodeo was over and they'd turned out our calves. And I'll never forget—Bill Linderman was the president of the RCA (Rodeo Cowboys Association), and he went to John Tunacliff, the stock contractor, and got the judges and the timers and they got the cattle in and let us rope our calves, and we placed."

As Jeanne wrote, "It is amazing what a cowboy will do to get to a rodeo. Amazing to everyone except another cowboy, that is. He's too busy making it to the next one."

Early in his career, he and Alberta went to a little rodeo in Laramie, Wyoming, where he "won quite a bit of money." He saved enough from rodeoing to take two roping horses and a "little bitty house trailer and truck" and set out on the circuit. In 1946, George won the calf roping title and all-around cowboy at Ellensburg.

By 1950, they were able to buy a small ranch near Whitehall, Montana, which they sold at a profit and leased a ranch at Park City, Montana, putting their money into cattle. The timing was bad and before they got the cattle to the ranch, the bottom fell out of the market and "we were worse than broke." In 1956, they sold for what they could get and were deep in debt. Friends suggested they file for bankruptcy, but they didn't think it was the right thing to do. Alberta, an active Christian, said, "With the Lord's help we eventually paid the money back, but it was a long road."

In 1959, George became a Christian and is a member of the Cowboy Chapter of the Fellowship of Christian Athletes. He is open and direct in his belief. Excerpts from his testimony in the

Circuit Rider, February 1982, contain: "I was raised with no religious training of any kind and even though I believed there was
a God, I had no knowledge of the Bible or the fact that Jesus was
sent to earth to save all mankind.

"My wife had accepted Jesus as a teenager but we did not
attend church for several years after we were married. After we
began to have a family she looked for a church. We were living
on a Montana Ranch with about three miles of dirt road, almost
impassable when it rained . . . she insisted on going in our old car
regardless of the road, and then to the evening service too. I
thought she was becoming a religious 'fanatic' and I began to
rebel. Eventually I did start attending church part time . . . but it
didn't seem to have much effect on me."

Financial problems accompanied the depressed cattle prices
and the added pressure was hindering success at roping, and
George admitted to "having a big helping of self-pity." He credits
becoming an active Christian to seeing the "many blessings" he
had. "My greatest time of growth and learning to rely on the Lord
was when I became involved in the planning and building of a
new Friend's Church here at Hayden Lake. Our little church was
overflowing with three services each Sunday and parking was
limited."

George was impatient and thought financing could be raised
easily and building started. "But God knew the timing," he said,
"and everything fell into place when it was right." Their family
includes two daughters and two sons, Joan Anne Nielsen, 52,
Mukilteo, Washington, has a son, Michael, 21, who rides in some
horse shows; and Jeanne Northfield, 47, and her children, Toby,
18, Elizabeth, 16, and twin sons, John and Matthew, 13. Lee, 48,
has two daughters, Mary Richmond Brown (Chris) of Post Falls,
accomplished horsewoman who rides in English events; and
Lynn, 18, western rider who takes part in team and breakaway
roping.

Son David, 43, has three children, Brander, 16; Lacy, 14;
and Victoria, 13. Lee and David both became fine ropers and

were in many rodeos. Granddad George describes Lynn as a "truly talented roper," and she has accompanied him to shows and rodeos as a participant.

No story of the Richmonds could be complete without mention of the renowned horse which virtually became a member of the family. The registered Quarter Horse, "Sunday Glory," was a sorrel gelding with lots of dash and flash. Richmond first saw Sunday Glory at a practice arena Sedona, Arizona. His "cow savvy" told him that the long-legged two-year-old was a winner and offered to buy him, but the owner kept the horse.

George Richmond of Hayden at the Pendleton Roundup in 1963 with two of his most prized possessions: "Sunday Glory" and the Dryer Memorial Trophy.

After the Richmonds moved to a ranch in Columbus, Montana in 1951, Rhodes wrote that he would sell Sunday Glory for five hundred dollars. George sent back a down payment of one hundred dollars, writing he would pick up the horse the next summer. He did so between roping contests in Ogden and Salt Lake.

Richmond took a good look back at the ranch and said "My first thought was that he wasn't worth the time and gasoline it took to get him. He showed good breeding in his conformation, but his disposition was pretty much bronc. He had a lot of buck in him and when he came undone, I started looking for a good place to land." Wet blankets were used to cure a horse inclined to buck and he rode Sunday Glory for miles around the ranch and in the fall used him in roping calves.

Idaho's Cowboy Master Dean Oliver beat out George and Sunday at the Rigby Rodeo calf roping the next spring. Coming in second to Oliver, Richmond decided Sunday needed practice then and there, but hadn't taken the time to tightly cinch his saddle. The result was that Sunday and Richmond parted company when the saddle slid as Sunday bucked. The following night at Rigby, Sunday Glory was less than glorious and repeated the bucking process. It was back to the wet blanket. George finally changed Sunday Glory from a bucking horse to one smartly carrying his rider into the proper roping position. Richmond and Sunday became a formidable team, averaging a second spot in 1958 at the National Western in Denver and in January 1960, third. In May they won the roping contest at Edmonton, Alberta. There were other awards on the circuit in the United States and Canada.

When the Richmonds moved to Hayden Lake, Sunday Glory went along. He died at twenty-eight and is buried behind the horse barn, near the riding school where he had been a feature. There were one hundred head of calves, later sold at auction, used in roping. The schools were held two weeks each summer between 1962 and 1967. One lad drove from Ontario, Canada, and, after reading an ad in a rodeo magazine, three boys came from Hawaii. Fifteen to eighteen camped on the ranch. Many went on to become rodeo performers.

Other ropers admired Sunday and often used him in competition. It is rodeo custom that the winning rider of a borrowed horse gives a fourth of the award to the owner. The Richmonds continue to live an active and contented life with the children and grandchildren frequent visitors. Interest in rodeo remains strong.

Jim Johnson

"I thought I did fine, because I didn't get killed," grunted thirty-eight year old Jim Johnson as he scrambled from the ground after his first steer ride. And added, "But I didn't last eight seconds." Jim is the kind of a guy who will do almost anything if it is a challenge. When Greg Orr, an employee and twenty years younger than Jim, challenged him to enter the steer-riding event in the1985 rodeo at Garwood, Jim couldn't resist. Nor did he give up after the first fall. He tried it again and again, all day long. While the young stripling Greg won his ride, Jim was being walked on by a bull. He suffered spinal bruises, but refused to give up. He kept at it despite breaking a wrist in 1995 and in 1996, another bull walked on his right leg two times. There was no break, so Jim lumbered up vowing he'd ride that critter yet.

Jim's wife Patty said, "He was black from the hip all down his leg. It took him twenty minutes to get to the bathroom the next morning and he was in extreme pain. When it took a full month to recover, I thought he would forget rodeo. But no, he was back in 1997. It must have been a miracle year, because he had no injuries."

In 1998, news photographer Bonnie Hudlet snapped a classic shot of Jim and the cutline beneath told the story: "Jim Johnson of Hayden flies through the air during his last ride as a professional bull rider."

Jim has high praise for the bullfighting clowns as he told of his experience when the bull threw him off. "I was starting to get up and still in a crouch when the bull pivoted around and came dead-ahead for me. In one continuous motion, the clown jumped

**Jim Johnson of
Coeur d'Alene waits
for his turn to bull
ride at the 1998
North Idaho Rodeo.
He was dubbed the
"oldest professional
bull rider in the
Northwest—and
arguably in the
nation."**

completely over me and landed with one foot on the animal's head. That got the bull's attention and stopped him while I got away. If it weren't for the clown bullfighters, rodeo would be a lot tougher. Their job is much more dangerous than that of the cowboys."

Greg and Jim told of the contest for the clown bullfighters at the National Finals in Las Vegas each year. "They are actually encouraged to jump lengthwise over the bulls and the more physical contact they have with the animal the greater points gained."

Jim says he took up parachuting to break his fear of heights. He took up bungee jumping, water skiing, and big game hunting for the challenge and was charged from fifteen feet by a black bear at one time. "There are a few things I haven't done yet but I want to water ski while being pulled by a plane," he says, "but so far I haven't found a pilot who will do that." He wants to run with the bulls in Pamplona, Spain and would like to have a helicopter land him on top of a balloon. "Some ask if I have a death wish, and I tell them 'No. I have a life wish.' Life is an adventure and I don't want to miss that. As I have gone along, not really thinking of what came next, but doing what looked interesting as it came along. I thank God everyday for my health and know that

I have another day. Just to be free is a great feeling and I have fulfilled a lot more than I ever thought I would." When Jim tells of his life, it is with excitement. Patty says, "He needed to do rodeo. There is something inside him that is fulfilled when he jumps right into the middle of these experiences. Our kids have enjoyed watching him." But, Jim and Patty discourage daughter, Jennifer, 25, and son, Terry, 26, from entering rodeo. "It is a dangerous sport," the parents agree.

Jim was fifty on November 16, 2000, and while he and Patty discourage their children, Jim says there is nothing to compare with the "rush" that comes from rodeo. "If everything I've ever done in my life, including the intimate things, were put together in one big shot of adrenaline, you'd have the thrill of rodeo."

He has praise for the continuing growth in rodeo, larger crowds and clowns and announcers attracting an increasing number of professionals, and a genuine love for the smaller shows such as Garwood and Rockford. "Tom Addis and Dodge have done great things with sponsorship of so much American rodeo," he said. Greg Orr started his own arena at Rockford and chuckles as he reports, "I let Jim ride free."

Pro-West Winners

Two Idahoans were winners in the Pro-West Rodeo Finals at the Kootenai County Fairgrounds in September 2000. Brent Herre of Caldwell won first in bull riding, and Randy Rauenzahn of Post Falls placed fourth in bareback riding.

ST. JOE COUNTRY

Planners would be hard put to find a more picturesque spot for a rodeo than the Benewah County Fairgrounds situated near the St. Joe River at St. Maries. The arena was carved out from the rolling hillside above the river and the overflow crowd at the rodeo find good seats on the hill. The bleachers hold about two hundred and fifty, and an equal number sat on the grassy slope. An equal number attended the second day and are ready for the 2001 show.

In 1999, assessing the desire and need for a rodeo in the
Benewah, a citizens group formed an association and holds the
event every Labor Day weekend in conjunction with the annual
fair and Paul Bunyan Days. Hard-working and rodeo-wise Suzy
Harpole Epler, vice-chairman of the fair board, was asked to be
chairman of the rodeo committee. She put her organizational skills
to the task and gives lots of credit for the successful rodeos in
1999 and 2000 to volunteer workers. To realize the extent of her
own dedication and sense of responsibility to the community is to
know that much of her planning was done from a hospital bed. If
such an injury can be thought of as apropos, it is interesting that
she received her broken back when she was bucked off her
favorite quarter horse "A.J." while taking part with a group of her
young 4-H club members in a horse show at nearby Princeton.
She was flat on her back in a hospital bed. One week was at the

**Kevin Burgess of Dalton Gardens manages to stay on top of a furious
bull. The bravest cowboys of all, the rodeo clowns, are serious as they
prepare for action.**

hospital, where she did as much rodeo planning as possible, and then took the bed home with her where she lay for another three weeks. She is still wearing a back brace but is no complainer.

Volunteers include Eddie Epler, Bill Tharp, Doug and Mark Harpole, Dick and Sharon Imes, Dave Ressor, Caryl Haskell, and Linda Whitehead. They wanted to do it right so sought and received sanction from the Pro-West Rodeo Association. Glen Harriman's Northern Cross Company of Omak, Washington, provided the stock of thirty bucking horses, more than twenty steers and thirty calves.

One hundred and forty signed up to rope calves, team rope, steer wrestle, ride bulls, saddle broncs and bareback, along with breakaway roping and barrel racing. Locals and events include Mike Waits, bull and bareback riding; Donna Cummings, breakaway; Julie Schwanz, riding barrels; Greg Berquist rode bulls. Tharp is an award winning calf roper and took part in that event.

Success crowned both the 1999 and 2000 events. "When we started we didn't even have a loading ramp," Chairman Suzy Epler said. "Now we not only have the ramp, but we own five bucking chutes, stripping chute, roping chute, and have bought heavy duty panels. We have done so well that we are now encouraging junior and high school rodeo."

It had been nearly thirty years since the St. Maries-Harrison area held a rodeo, when in October 1998 several friends got together and put on what one worker said was a rollicking one. "It didn't pay for itself, but, what the hey, it was a lot of fun," she said. Some planned to give it another go, but when the debits and credits were added, the debits won.

Ireta and Dale Remsburg were the arrangers and were helped by volunteers Sandy Shoemaker, Maxine and Lori Christensen, Tom and Natalie Christensen and others. "They knew expense was involved and were willing to take the risk. It was quite a risk and when the income was balanced against the outgo, Ireta and Dale hocked their truck to pay the riders," Sandy said. Something of the costs involved include the portable arena rented from Lewiston and six bucking chutes from Missoula. Trailers, panels and watering troughs and labor to install were donated. Bleachers came from the Kootenai school and the hay from Pete Nemeth's land where the rodeo was held.

Helen Lee, who lives on lake acreage "up the Benewah" and raises purebred sheep, was asked to donate twelve of the animals for the kids to ride in their mutton bustin' contests. Glen Harriman of Omak, Washington, was the stock contractor. Seventeen-year-old Scottie McTeer was the rodeo queen and also won first place in bull riding. Contests were in team roping and breakway, bronc and bareback riding, goat tying, and pole bending. In the latter event, the riders weave in and out among six poles. Riders came from southern and northern Idaho, eastern Washington and Montana.

On Saturday more than three hundred attended and Sunday afternoon there were about one hundred. Sandy Shoemaker summed it up as "A good rodeo. A little stressful because of the financial situation, but still a good rodeo."

Scottie McTeer, girl bullrider, placed first at the St. Maries Rodeo, September 12, 1998. *Courtesy of Sandy Shoemaker.*

Roundup Territory

LEWISTON
The Snake River Roundup

State Senator and rancher, Harry Wall, liked rodeo and everything about it. He enjoyed telling funny stories related to rodeo. One of his favorites was of the time he and good buddy A.L. "Bud" Alford, publisher of the *Lewiston Tribune,* drove to Pendleton for that highly rated roundup. Bud's newspaper was off the press about two o'clock in the morning and they left shortly after. Both were convivial types and had been known to take a drink or two on such festive occasions. Arriving happy in Pendleton and in broad daylight, they found a motel room, dropped their gear, and went to the rodeo grounds. There they joined other sociable fans, enjoyed the rodeo, and the following hours-long party.

In early morning, they found their way to the motel and fell into bed and sound asleep. In the morning, Harry awakened, shaved, and spruced up. As he entered the bedroom, Bud was struggling to awaken, balled his fists and rubbed them into the eyesockets, looked all around the room, and repeated the drill. After a few moments, Harry laughed and said, "What's the matter? Don't you know where you are?" Bud peered at him from half-closed eyes and replied, "No, I don't," hesitated and added, "and seeing *you* here doesn't help one damned bit."

Harry had arrived in Lewiston as a tire representative and fell in love with the town on the very first day. He asked the desk clerk at the handsome old Lewis and Clark Hotel for directions to a hotcake cafe a few blocks distant. It was early morning, the sun was shining, and everyone he encountered greeted him with a cheery "Hi," "Hello," or "How are ya?" At first, he was sure they mistook him for someone else. By the time he reached the cafe and was greeted as a regular, Harry knew Lewiston was the friendliest place he'd ever been and vowed that he'd live there one day. That day was not long in coming, and he became a wheat rancher, married the beautiful Mildred Pulpher who owned and operated the movie theaters.

Shortly after Harry had moved to Lewiston from Cleveland, Ohio, he was invited to become active in a number of projects, and the annual rodeo was his favorite. One year he was asked to pickup one of the judges as he arrived on the plane. The fellow had been one of the best of the bronc riders and Harry met him in the tiny airport on the hill above the town. The cowboy walked down the plane steps, spied Harry and said, "OK, c'mon let's go."

Muggs Bentley of Grangeville slips from his saddle onto the back of a galloping steer. C.R. Boucher, on his well-trained Quarter Horse, hazes for Bentley at the Lewiston Roundup, 1955.

Harry asked, "Don't you want to wait for your suitcase?" With a startled look, the guy said, "What suitcase? I didn't bring one. I'm only gonna be here three days!"

Harry's friendly nature and modulated voice not only helped in electing him to the Idaho state senate, but he was asked to announce the annual roundup, which he did for several years.

In his comments to the 1956 gathering, the eight annual, his voice boomed over the microphone, with: "It is only a little over one hundred years since the first covered wagon trains pushed west from the Missouri River, out into the great adventure to open new frontiers, to build a great empire within our nation. Today, every man, woman, and child knows this empire by two small words, 'the West.' To build that empire took courage and hard work. Only the strong survived.

"The games they developed are a true creation of their ruggedness. When the Pony Express rider, the plainsman, the frontiersman, and the cowboy had a little time for recreation, they had no modern tools nor cathedrals of sport, so it was necessary that they develop their own games with what they had at hand—their horses, their cattle, their stock. yes, who could ride the toughest horse, who could twirl a rope from a running horse down onto a running steer, stopping him in the best time. Thus, were the games of the cowboys born. Rough, tough games, just as young America was rough and tough.

"Today our frontiers are no more. But we can relive here in this arena the winning of the West by playing and contesting again those truly national games of the great American cowboy. It is with this thought that the Lewiston Roundup Association now presents the eighth annual Lewiston Roundup and they give it to you western! Let 'er buck!"

In Lewiston, the Roundup is the longest running community event. The business and professional women who make up the board of directors donate many days of work each year to keep the Roundup among the best in the West. The across-the-river neighboring town of Clarkston, Washington, is supportive, and many of the participants make their homes there. Warren Fuller, 78, of Clarkston was the Grand Marshal in 1998, but he had won his Idaho spurs by moving with his family to Lucile when he was five and attending school at Cow Creek and White Bird. Several of the board members have been among the Roundup announcers and the honor of Grand Marshal has saluted many old-timers who have served the community well.

Marty Peterson, a Lewiston product who is now special assistant to the president of the University of Idaho at the Boise Center, reminisced about the fine announcers at the Stampede: "The one thing that I do see at modern rodeos that is nearly on a par with the Lewiston Roundup of about forty years ago (1958) is the arena announcing. Jim Tallman on a horse with a wireless microphone is superb. Now, if he just had the voice of the great Cy Taillon, another rodeo legend, he would be as close to perfect as one can be."

Marty came to love rodeo because of the town's renowned roundup. He always refers to the internationally known announcer Cy Taillon as "the great Cy Taillon." It can be assumed that all Lewiston Roundup aficionados felt the same, for the man with the beautiful baritone voice had been announcing in that city straddling the Clearwater River for about thirty years when he died of cancer in April, 1980.

Cy was born in the Midwest and arrived in Montana, which he claimed as home even though spending little time there after hitting the rodeo big time. he had planned to become a bronc rider, but early-on an injured shoulder dashed that dream. There were other dreams realized, one leading to another: piano player in a Great Falls music store, member of a dance band, radio programs announcer, and announcer for livestock shows and fairs.

Numerous announcers have appeared over the years and include Randy Corley, former rodeo contestant who was three-time world champion rodeo announcer with a schedule that covered more than two hundred performances a year. S.J. Zoop Dove of New Mexico, four-time Dodge National Circuit Finals

Rodeo announcer, has been invited back to Lewiston for several years. His joking with the audience and the cowboys and cowgirls, as well as ribbing the clowns and barrelmen, makes him one of the family. Another consistent Lewiston (and a number of other rodeo towns) performer is Kelly Hughes of State Line, Idaho, and his Border Patrol dance band. They have played with Waylon Jennings and produced several albums.

Marty went on to say that he always looked at the Lewiston Roundup as the way rodeos should be. "While I never saw Jackson Sundown, I did see perhaps the second greatest of them, all, Casey Tibbs, in Lewiston. And other greats like Jim Shoulders, Harry Charters, and Deb Copenhaver. Also, those outstanding stock contractors, the Christiansen brothers and Kelsey Mumaugh. And legendary horses like War Paint and bulls like the Snowman."

World Champion bronc rider Jackson Sundown always insisted upon using his regular old range saddle when he competed in rodeos. In this picture, in front of a fine teepee, he is shown in full native dress. Note the beautiful beadwork, collar, and neckpiece on his carefully groomed horse. *Courtesy of Eugene Wilson.*

Deb Copenhaver of Post Falls relaxes in the saddle, a complete change of style from riding in the famed Lewiston Roundup as a champion. *Courtesy of Oscar Steinley.*

In a story about the "glitch that caused the grins," Marty told of the master calendar of more than five hundred events published in 1989 by the Idaho Centennial Commission, for which he served as vice chairman. "And in all of that, there was one glaring typo. It was in Challis or Mackay, but it was supposed to be the little 'britches' rodeo. Oh well, the typo gave them national coverage on Paul Harvey."

From the first rodeo on September 26, 27, and 28, 1935, the Lewiston Roundup has been a success and by 1949, ranked fourth in its class and reached tenth in the United States. Ratings were made according to the amount of money paid the winning contestants. Businessman Robert Wright came up with the idea of a rodeo to provide a major autumn event. He said he would underwrite production costs, an organizational meeting was held, and the work and enjoyment began. First president was A.L. Grover and Dorothy Brock was first queen. The community liked the idea and volunteers helped prepare for a fun-filled event including a kangaroo court to fine those not wearing western gear, dance hall saloon with gambling, chuck-wagon breakfast, and horse races. Schools and business closing for an afternoon of rodeo added to the excitement and support. The ticket line was several blocks long on opening day.

The Nez Perce tribe, from whom the county got its name, is instrumental in attracting many to the event from the early years on. They establish an encampment with tepees and extend an open invitation to the tribal dancing. Many members of the tribe don colorful native attire enhanced with beautiful beadwork and appear in the annual Saturday afternoon parade. In earlier days, they performed an encampment parade to commemorate special occasions for the tribe.

Many out-of-state greats are listed on the Lewiston Roundup Honor Roll of Champions such as Toots Mansfield, Bill and Bud Linderman, and Casey Tibbs. Reaching back to 1939, the Idaho

Kenny Stanton of Weiser is one of the outstanding winners at the Lewiston Roundup. This 1969 picture of his performance at the National Finals in Oklahoma City shows his winning style.

champs who have won at Lewiston (some of them several times and in different categories) include: Harry Charters, Bob Robinson, Dean Oliver, Kenny Stanton, Mike Beers, Burrel Mulkey, Deb Copenhaver, Jim Roeser, Royce Smith, Daryl Hodbey, Jeff Copenhaver, Dee Pickett, Tim Fuller, and Darrell Sewell. Listed as Women Professional Barrel Racers are Kay Davis and Brenda Tyler.

WINCHESTER

"Rodeo was a big part of my best early teenage years," says Brenda McCann who is even yet, after many years, secretary for the Craig Mountain Arena Association at Winchester. Brenda is typical of residents of the little town that was named for the rifle-of-choice at a citizens meeting in 1900. Most of them are willing volunteers and help to make rodeo a success. She is an enthusi-ast and her statements have a vocal exclamation point at the end of each sentence. "Rodeo is the number one spectator sport and bull riding is the fastest growing sport in the USA in terms of con-testants learning it."

Brenda, who spearheaded the effort to build new rodeo grounds in 1995, gives full credit for her own rodeo success to Roy Tommelson of Lapwai Creek Road in East Lewiston. He was a legend in his own time and won a reputation as a cougar hunter along with his work in rodeo. He was her teacher and mentor, and devoted further time to "haul all to the area Junior Rodeos during the late 1950s." As a result, she won prize money enough to buy all her school clothing and supplies and "to have a ball going to all the rodeos." She was dubbed the "Young Casey Tibbs" because she was never bucked off a steer during three summers of riding. During her steer riding days, she did suffer three major back injuries. Now Brenda says she and her husband "raise horses and grandkids, do horse training, and personally enjoy trail riding."

Although Brenda doesn't encourage her grandchildren to do rodeo, she is enthusiastic about their learning to ride. She wanted an arena nearby for that purpose and for Winchester to have a two-day rodeo with different riders each day during the Fourth of July weekend. Those were reasons for getting a volunteer group together six years ago and their efforts brought about five acres of rodeo grounds on the northwest boundary of the old Winchester City Park. The property was owned by Floyd Welborn. Officers of the active non-profit Craig Mountain Arena Association are Walt Weber, president; Mike McCann, vice-president; Brenda McCann, secretary; and Janell Willson of Reubens, treasurer. Gary Willson is the arena director. There is a purse of five thousand dollars shared by the winners.

John and LaDawn Ely of the Bar X Ranch in Asotin, Washington, are the professional rodeo stock providers, who produce the event. They truck twenty bulls, sixteen bucking horses, and sixteen saddle broncs to Winchester. They are the son and daughter-in-law of John Ely, Sr., who has had years of rodeo experience.

One of the open rodeo winners is Jason Patterson, for bull riding. Younger contestants are included in the adult rodeo and compete in junior breakaway, calf and steer riding, and junior barrel racing. Four central Idaho rodeo associations make use of the Winchester arena.

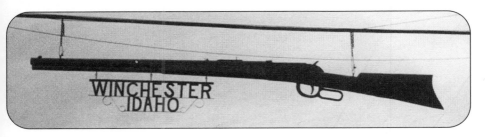

Rodeos on Home Ground

Along Salmon River and the adjoining cow country, the name Robie will always be associated with one of the biggest "home ground" rodeos in Idaho history. The daddy of the young men who put on shows that attracted thousands was Edward William Robie. His influence, example and exciting frontier history were indelibly impressed upon his children, grand and

The Robie homestead nestled among fruit trees along the Salmon River near Lucile, Idaho. Legendary rodeos were held on the mesa above the Robie home. Note the growth of the fruit trees that were mere seedlings when the family first moved into their house.

great-grandchildren. That influence was to such an extent, and to display the Robie pioneer spirit, a part of his life is being shared.

He had heart problems, but as much as possible, Edward William Robie, put it out of his mind and continued to live life to the fullest. On the morning of February 20, 1889, with an appearance of good health he left the family ranch on Salmon River for what he considered a short trip. It was no secret that he liked horses, and was on his way to a horse sale at the Bouffard residence on Skookum Chuck Creek. He never made it. That afternoon Tony Gordon, returning from the sale, found Robie's body, partially covered by snow, lying in the trail.

A called-coroner's jury found that he died from a heart attack. Place of death was listed as Salmon River, Freedom, Idaho. The post office called Freedom was at the mouth of Slate Creek and had a stockade, likely built by the settlers during the Indian wars. The Robie history is a fascinating one and gives an understanding of the family which provided the first Salmon River Rodeo. A second lieutenant in the Union Army, First Missouri Engineers, Robie moved to Idaho Territory and started mining on the Salmon River in the late 1880s or early 90s. He and his partners mined only from May to October. He spent the winter of 1872–73 in Idaho City and the following winter at White Bird. In the spring, he packed blankets and food on his back, and headed for the home mine. It took five to six days for him to walk the hundred plus miles. Snowshoes were needed for half that distance.

He and his partners hired six or seven Chinese to work the successful strikes. Each was paid fifty dollars a month with board and room. High quality gold brought them seventeen dollars an ounce and they soon cleared the mine of debt.

In a letter dated January 28, 1877, Kamiah, Idaho Territory, he answered many questions asked by his niece, Adda M. Brown, Georgetown, Madison County, New York. Robie wrote that he was a government sub-agency employee on the Nez Perce

Reservation at Kamiah, fifty miles above the Lapwai agency headquarters on the Clearwater River. "You want to know . . . if there is anyone else living here. Well, there are plenty of people such as they are. Five white men, three women and four children all told, and three or four hundred Indians, how is that? We have a church, schoolhouse, gristmill, saw-mill, carpenter shop, black smith shop, and a farm. Our school teacher and farmer are married men and have families. The Rev. Mr. Fee is teacher and his wife is matron. They have two girls. There were three but one of them went to Oregon last fall to attend school. Mr. Redfield is a farmer. He has a wife and two little boys. Then we have a lady teacher, Miss McBeth (one of the two McBeth sisters, historical teacher-missionaries to the Nez Perce). She has a school by herself and teaches theology. Peter Stagg is an engineer, and an old sailor and a German. G.W. Sharp is a blacksmith, a discharged soldier, and hails from Jersey. As for myself, I run the gristmill, sawmill and carpenter shop and make myself generally useful for a thousand dollars a year. Now you know all of us. We are all good people and have to 'walk the scratch' while we are here and set an example for the Indians to follow.

"We have preaching three times every Sunday. Mr. Fee preaches in the morning and some of the Indians in the afternoon and evening. Five of Miss McBeth's scholars are studying for the Ministry but none of them have been ordained yet. They preach in the Nez Perce language. I go to hear them sometimes. I can tell what they say but don't know what they mean. I only know a few words of the language but I like to hear them sing which they all do old and young. The house is always crowded and you would laugh to see the congregation. Some sitting on the seats and some on the floor and I expect they like the floor the best, and the Papooses tied onto boards standing up around the crowd."

Edward Robie and widow Isabella Benedict were married in 1879. Her husband was killed by the Indians and during the same raid she was captured and then released. She and her four children moved into the Robie home. They had four children, Emily (Chamberlin), Edward Victor, William, and Alice (Russell). In 1888, they lived on a large ranch on Salmon River where they set out a variety of fruit trees. They had many head of cattle and horses and Edward and his partner continued their mining operations. To manage the cattle and horses required the skills of genuine cowboys, which the family had.

The story of the Robie and Russell families was told by former instructor and associate dean of engineering at the University of Idaho George Robie Russell, one of the most native of white-skinned Idahoans. His father, Ralph, was raised on a place on Swamp Creek between Joseph and Enterprise, Oregon, "just over the mountains to the west." He moved to Pittsburgh on the Oregon side of the Snake River in 1904. Ralph courted Alice Robie and they were married in 1914 and made their home at Spring Camp north of Joseph and near Boles. The house where Alice was born in 1880, four miles north of Slate Creek, is still

A Robie Ranch Rodeo bareback rider waves away his pick-up man. Hundreds sit on the corral fence and watch the cowboy toughing out a jolting bronc ride.

Dan MacDonald of Bonners Ferry rides in the 1965 rodeo in Weippe.

there and now owned by son George who often makes extended visits.

This was the place where Bill Robie decided he would put on a rodeo and "so he just went up on the hill and scraped out a rodeo ground." Brothers Ben "Peck" and Ralph worked with Bill and the telling of it sounds simple: "They advertised and people just showed up. Lots of people would come," George said. The advertising was done by printing and handing out information fliers, posters for windows of businesses in nearby villages and towns, newspapers and word-of-mouth. It was effective and hundreds arrived by horseback, buggy and automobile. The cars were used to form a fence around the arena. "The rodeos were in the late thirties, likely 1938 and 1939," George said, "with thousands attending and it's interesting that so many still talk of them."

One of Idaho's earliest and largest rodeos was held at the Robie Ranch
near Lucile. Hundreds of people traveled miles to witness the event.
Early-day automobiles and wagons line the corral.

In 1938, cars parked up against the corral fence on the large Russell
family ranch. *Courtesy of Ronald Mahurin of Slate Creek.*

The Sewells and 7U Ranch

Anyone who approaches the White Bird area 7U Ranch of Bob and Kathryn Sewell immediately knows that here live a couple of real westerners. First there is a sign; "A Cowbelle Lives Here" and another proclaiming "Beef is Good." The Sewell's attractive home at the top of a rolling hill above Elfers Creek is full of history. The creek is named for Henry "Granddad" Elfers, who was killed during the Indian War.

The Sewells had been wanting a cattle brand. They found it when they drove south to visit her brother, Glen Wyatt, who was working on the Rollie Hawes' big dairy ranch at Three Creek in Owyhee County. As they drove up they saw a huge barn with an equally whopping 7U brand painted on the top. They liked it and found there were no restrictions to using it for their ranch.

The Sewells are real old-timers and Kathryn's grandad, Frank Wyatt, ran cattle between the Salmon and the Snake Rivers with headquarters at Deer Creek. His cattle browsed upon the Joseph and Boles Plains, then all open grazing. Wyatt first came into the country in the early 1870s from Independence, Missouri, before the homesteaders started arriving. His son and her father Edward was determined to live in Idaho and at age fourteen started west. He took off from Missouri on the train, but somewhere along the line he joined a cattle drive on the old Chisholm Trail. He stopped in Montana to work for a cattle outfit. As soon as he had earned money enough, he moved on for Idaho. Edward homesteaded on Wolf Creek on the Snake River. Kathryn remembered that her dad raised a "little dab" of hay. He raised cattle and his brand was the bow and arrow. His nickname became "Bow." He married Mattie Crooks, daughter of Jacob and Victoria Crooks, early pioneers on the Camas Prairie. It was on Deer Creek that Kathryn was born. She has a sister Margaret Rose living in Lewiston.

Bob Sewell's grandfather, Addison D. Sewell, came to the West and settled in the Willamette (Oregon) Valley. From there the family went to Pullman and in 1893, moved to Slate Creek in Idaho and the following year on to Cow Creek. Their son Ward was born in 1890, one of five boys. Earl became a cattleman. Two sons died when small and Hubert died at age twenty-four. Bob was born to Ward and Della Smith Sewell on July 19, 1920. Bob and Kathryn were married on July 17, 1940. They are the parents of Gary of Pendleton; Eileen (Uhlenkott), Fenn; Darrel, Clarkston; and Edward Bow (named for his Grandfather and goes by the name of Bow).

Gary and Darrel are team ropers and Bow is a calf roper. Bob has ridden in many events with his sons and Eileen served as a timer at numerous rodeos. Kathryn worked as rodeo secretary at Riggins for years and each has been honored as Grand Marshal.

Both remember with pleasure and humor the rodeo activity that led up to Bob becoming a champion. Deward and Melvin Gill have provided stock for many years for the rodeos in the Snake River country after buying an interest in Ralph Stephens bucking stock. "Clayton Butcher could ride any old horse and George Gill helped pick out many of the bucking stock," Bob said.

They remembered a rodeo in White Bird and Bob said, "It was down in the hollow and one afternoon we just bucked some pretty good horses down there and rodeo was born in that area." They laugh as they tell of Mark Rook finishing up a session of bulldogging by riding the horse into a bar at Grangeville. Both horse and rider were order to "Get out!" from the first saloon, but were invited to "Come on in," by Geary at Matt's Place. They accepted the invitation and were a considerable attraction.

The Sewells retain memories of events in many communities in the area. Cottonwood held rodeos in the mid 1940s with stock owned by Guy Cash of Grangeville. Cash advertised the rodeo and riders paid an entry fee which was used for the winners. Rodeo at Slate Creek was held in Jack Merrick's field just above the Robie Ranch. At Nez Perce, Cecil Hill and his son Wayne, put on a rodeo with Guy Cash's unbroken stock that would "fight you to a stand still," Bob said.

The Riggins area first rodeo was held across the swinging bridge about 1941 and garnered several cars of people who drove across the cable bridge and onlookers from the other side. "But I can remember the 1941 Chevy that just barely held a couple of people, but we managed to wedge mother and dad in and we parked alongside the field to watch the riders."

Jack Percifield (whose son Doug still rodeos) put on the first Riggins rodeo.

Kathryn and Bob think that the first rodeo in McCall was held in about 1952 out amongst some jack pine trees beyond the "Chicken Roost" restaurant. Guy Cash, the saddle bronc champ from the Northwest, went on to Madison Square Gardens to perform. In the Riggins Rodeo their son Darrel qualified for the National finals and followed rodeo for several years. He bought Mexican Corriante steers, a different full-blood breed than ordinarily performed in events and believed to be better rodeo cattle. Darrel Sewell became a champion steer wrestler at the Lewiston Rodeo in September 14, 1981. He put the stop on his steer for a time of 6.3 seconds in the championship wrestling, but still finished out of the money. He did better in the team roping as he and Tim Fuller, Clarkston, finished first to win over six hundred dollars a piece. Darrel became a team roper, wherein one of the team ropes the steer by the horns or around the neck and the other ropes both hind feet.

Bob and Dean Oliver vied at a matched roping at the Council Rodeo where both put up twenty-five dollars and roped three calves each. Dean had become such a champ at roping that the few misses that he made were well remembered. Bob recalled that Dean missed his last calf at that roping.

Bob and Kathryn celebrated their sixtieth wedding anniversary on July 22, 2000.

Rodeo Named for a Blow Fly

Years ago in Idaho
Long rides we'd often make
Close on the tails of wild fantails
In those high and rugged breaks.

A high rolling divide
About twenty miles wide,
Between the Salmon and the Snake
Timber on top grew a rank heavy crop
Surrounded by rough rolling breaks.

A large expanse of virgin land
That nesters had not found
In this wild land were many bands
Of ponies roving 'round.

Some wore brands of other lands
But a lot of them were "slicks."
Others, no doubt, belonged about
To settlers along the cricks.

But most of them belonged to him
Who could ride like the autumn wind,
Down steep hillsides and loose rock slides
And corral them in the end.

In this narrative poem, cowboy and poet W.H. Bill Eller
described the area of the Joseph Plains where the annual Flyblow
Rodeo was held. At Joseph, Idaho, between the Snake and the
Salmon rivers and below the mouth of Getta Creek, and general
vicinity there were fifty or sixty families raising cattle on small
ranches. Phebe and James Aram, with fifteen thousand acres, had
the largest ranch.

Their son James wrote a detailed story of life in the area named for the historical Nez Perce Chief Joseph. His brother, John, and sister, Narcie, contributed. After Jim's death the others contracted with Kristi Youngdahl of California to do further detailed research and put their memories into book form. They dedicated it to Jim and his widow, Ruth. All of the children learned to ride and the boys tamed the wild ones, rounded cattle and branded. They wore the gear of the working cowboy: jeans, boots with spurs, gloves and chaps. Their roundups were the real thing, driving herds of up to two hundred cattle, fording rivers, up and down mountains until reaching Cottonwood and the stockyards. There the sorting took place and the next day and the cattle were herded into train boxcars for shipping to Portland. John remembered the hard work in all kinds of weather and decided that ranching was not for him. He rose through the ranks in the timber industry and became the president of the gigantic Weyerhauser Company. Jim came to a similar decision and became successful in the real estate business.

Either by design or necessity the men and boys who lived on the Joseph Plains were bona fide cowboys. Most of the women and girls were capable of helping with herding, driving, and the roundups. They all worked hard for days, and sometimes months on end, without diversion. Before the lid blew off, eventually someone who knew the cattle business and its workers became the creator and organizer of local entertainment.

At Flyblow, west of Boles and between Yellow Pine and Spring Camp, was a suitable site for an arena with chutes to handle the bucking horses and calves. It secured its unusual name from the heavy population of blow flies, which liked to nuzzle themselves into the damp wool of the sheep during the springtime showers. From such warm, damp and soft comfort, the flies settled down to laying eggs. The eggs soon became maggots which sought out and crept into any moist skin or open sores they could find. When the hot sun came out and dried out the

wool and evaporated the moisture, the ranchers rescued the suffering animals with turpentine and sheep dip.

Into this inimicable community came W.I. Bill Rook. Along
with being a cattleman, he was a creator and organizer for entertainment, who decided a rodeo on the home stomping grounds
was a dandy idea. He was described by neighbor cattleman and
poet Bill Eller in his poem *The Calico Band* with:

Old Bill Rook knew the range like a book
And commanded a rough riding crew.
No steer was born, nor ever wore horns,
That could dodge the big loop he threw.
And he was willing to bet there never was yet,
Either up or down a hill.
Any son of a gun who could get more run
Out of a pony than could old Bill.

Bill not only could ride the rough ranges, but was bright
enough to know that people hungry for entertainment would be
willing to pay fees from which he could recoup his expenses and
make a bit of money to boot. The time was late in the 1920s or
early 30s. Ranchers and cattlemen and families living between
the Salmon and Snake Rivers were numerous for that time and
place. Bill's three sons, Mark, Vance and Jack, along with several
of the ranchers, gathered horses, mules, scrapers, shovels and
other equipment and carved out a rodeo corral which doubled as
a racetrack. It was located near the Jack Pine school and rodeo
was a part of the annual July Fourth celebration for residents of
the Joseph Plains.

Posters were printed and placed in windows in the nearest
towns of Cottonwood, Craigmont, Lewiston, Winchester, and
White Bird along with advertisements published in the nearby
newspapers.

Hundreds of people came in wagons, carrying feed for their
own horses, and living in tents for several days. Among others,

the Soltman family lived in the Joseph area, and Dr. Jack Soltman of Grangeville, the son of pioneers, remembers stories of those rodeos and celebrations.

An Idaho Appaloosa holds a tight tether for the cowboy intent on tying
the small calf. A distraught mother cow gazes at the action. The
Appaloosa is the horse of choice for many Idaho rodeo and trail riders.

Cut 'em Loose!
It's Rodeo Time

GRANGEVILLE

The slogan "Cut 'em Loose!" suggested by Salmon River cattleman George Behean back in 1912 was so successful in bringing from five to seven thousand eager fans on each of four days to the little town of Grangeville's first rodeo. It "was on every tongue" for days before and after. It is still used in advertising and promotion and a patent is registered in the U.S. Patent Office.

"No fancy rewards (for the cowboys), just a lot of fun," is how Beatrice Sloane Wright described the first celebration . The rodeo was held in an open field between South Meadow and Crook streets. No grandstands, no seating except that provided by the viewers if they brought along boxes or chairs, no high fences and no refreshments were available in those days.

The cowboys were local youngsters and men whose daily work was to ride and break wild broncos. Carnival type sideshows and concessions lined downtown's Main Street and the women of the town and countryside provided food for a big picnic. "New potatoes and peas as the first treat of the garden season, and if we had good luck, there would be fried chicken and homemade ice cream."

The *Idaho County Free Press* of September 26, 1912 devoted the entire front page and much of the rest of the newspaper to heralding the triumph in a banner headline as "the Greatest Show Ever Held in the Northwest."

Later the rodeo was joined to the county fair, but unpredictable weather in early fall brought about a change to the weekend nearest the Fourth of July. However, that first annual event set the goal for success for the future.

By the 1920s, rodeo had become an even bigger event and

professional stock was furnished by Ben Zehner, who arrived on Camas Prairie in August 1887. Ben had an Idahoan's love of rodeo and would travel miles to attend any auction where he might purchase good bucking horses. Among the rodeo stock he provided was the famous bucker called "Widow Maker."

An immortal to the Nez Perce, Jackson Sundown, the popular Culdesac cowboy who was the nephew of an even greater Nez Perce immortal, Chief Joseph, was a star whenever he appeared. Sundown rode in Grangeville's Border Days Rodeo a number of times.

Guy Cash Jr. remembers stock contractors for the early rodeos included Everett Colburn and J.C. "Doc" Sorenson, Slim Riley, and George Hannah. Colburn and Sorenson were among

Jackson Sundown with friends Elizabeth Wilson, left, and Nancy Johns. Both young women were students at Carlisle Indian School in the early 1900s. This picture in Nez Perce country may have been taken during a session of Talmaks, Presbyterian Encampment. Sundown (who was named Baptiste) raised and trained buffalo-chasing and racing horses about 1890, after his return from exile in Oklahoma with Chief Joseph and his company. *Courtesy of Eugene Wilson, son of Elizabeth.*

Guy Cash of Grangeville bulldogs at Pendleton.

the premier contractors from the 1920s to the 1940s. They sold out their operation to Gene Autry. Colburn became the managing partner of the Autry Rodeo Company. Both Autry and Roy Rogers, two of the country's best known rodeo stars, died in 1998. Guy Jr. remembers that the Maynard brothers from Slate Creek, Jack, Ken and Don were all rodeo performers with Jack riding bareback and Ken and Don rode bulls. Also competing on a state level was Paul Luffman of Peck.

Grangeville proudly claimed a number of star performers. They included Jack Percifield, Earl Hibbs, Jack and Don Maynard, Muggs Bentley, Clayton Butcher, Bob Sewell, Mark Rook and the five Clay brothers: Eddie, Tommy, Frank, Larry, and Dick; and the four Cash brothers: Guy, Walter, Manford, and Eddie. The Cash boys all participated in rodeo and the youngest, Guy, went on to become a world class bronc rider and bulldogger. *(See Chapter 16.)* Among the other great riders at Grangeville was Pete Wilson in the early twentieth century; Bob A. Robinson and Darrel Sewell, who were both National Finals contestants. Guy Cash went on to become a world class rodeo cowboy and made rodeo his professional career. For his winning ways, one writer tagged him with the nickname "Cash and Carry," because, he wrote, "his name is Cash and he always carried off the money."

Guy Jr. has become an expert on rodeo and could write an Encyclopedia of Rodeo. He may do so.

Muggs Bentley

The year of 1912 was noted not only for holding the first rodeo in Grangeville, but as the first which a future rodeo champion, Muggs Bentley, then barely a year old, rode in the parade. His uncle carried him in front of him on horseback. It was as though he had been inoculated. Rodeo became a big part of his life.

He was born near Grangeville at the end of the road on Gill Point, west of Tolo Lake. When he was about nine, his family moved to an area amongst a number of others settlers, adjacent to the forks of the Snake River, and situated between Doumecq Plain and Joseph, Idaho. Where today there are no schools, at that time there were five on the Joseph side and two near Doumecq, one with thirty-two pupils and the other with thirteen. Life wasn't easy for those settlers and everyone worked to get by.

As Grand Marshal, Muggs Bentley proudly leads the parade in Grangeville, where he lives and has always been an admired rodeo champion.

Bentley's father operated a stageline from White Bird to Bolles, a drive of thirty-two miles which required two drivers for the round trip. Wagons until it snowed and then sleds were used. The thirty horses he owned were shod with sharpened shoes for a better grip when they tramped on ice. The road traveled was a Star mail route. He knew horses well from the Spanish American War when he worked breaking them for the U.S. Cavalry.

At sixteen, young Bentley took the job of driving a six-horse freight wagon from White Bird to Bolles. It was a natural that he would take to rodeo. When only seventeen he entered the 1928 Genesee Rodeo and won the bronc riding event. He competed in the Lewiston Roundup. He preferred saddle bronc riding, the event in which he made the most money, but he also liked bull-dogging and was good at it. He didn't care for bareback nor bull riding. "I enjoy watching the bulls if someone else is riding them," he smilingly said.

A lifetime membership in the Professional Rodeo Cowboys Association, which comes when a rodeoer goes for ten paid-up years with no "black marks," has been his for many years. As such, he is entitled to attend any PRCA event without cost. He is now eighty-nine years old and hasn't competed in a rodeo since the 1964 one in Hamilton, Montana, when, he said, "I just decided I wouldn't beat this youth."

There was another time when he thought his career was in danger. At the Susanville, California rodeo in 1946, he was bucked from a horse with such a jolt that a neck vertebrae was cracked and the collar and other bones were broken. He recovered enough to keep on bulldogging but lost his sense of balance for saddle bronc riding.

Rodeo was never far from his life. He worked with horses during the seven years he packed in the St. Joe National forest in the 1930s; ranched four years at Spring Camp, twelve miles beyond Bolles; and the eleven years he logged at Elk City after running a shovel and dragline.

In 1982, Grangeville honored the beloved cowboy as

Marshal of the Day for the Border Days parade and rodeo. So, the year-old baby who had ridden in the saddle with his uncle at the 1912 parade had come full circle, with many of those in-between years as a competitor in Border Days Rodeo.

Those Early Days

Grangeville residents, merchants and rodeo lovers by the hundreds have supported the annual Border Days celebration since the beginning. The late much-loved John Olmsted, co-owner of the *Idaho County Free Press* and one of the more "rabid" rodeo supporters wrote a short history in 1976. He called it simply *About Grangeville Border Days.*

Writing that rodeo was held every year since 1912 except during World War II. It was first held in open pastures near the town and was strictly for the local working men who made their living cowboying. Saddling was done in the open and there were no seats for spectators and no corral. It was for the enjoyment of the Idaho County residents. It is always on the weekend nearest the Fourth of July and has become a popular Homecoming for high school reunions and former residents.

The Main Street parade on each of the three days always jams the sidewalks and the person selected for the Grand Marshal honor is a well-known, hard-working citizen or cowboy. The honor is coveted. Special attractions for the parade and rodeo have included thirty youths riding bareback with no bridles, a twenty-one dog hitch a half-block long, bagpipers, four-horse hitch of matched Belgians, Kooskia Saddliers, and the queen and her princesses.

Originally the Grangeville Cowboy Band, directed by Jack Running was widely known and made appearances at other towns to promote the rodeo. The thirty members were outfitted in wooly chaps and ten-gallon hats. Editor Olmsted wrote, "It is said that before a man could get a job in Grangeville he had to be able to play a musical instrument." The band was unique and received invitations to horse shows in Chicago, the Elks convention in Los Angeles, and traveled to Wyoming. In later years, the band is made up of elementary and high school and local musicians.

The Wild Horse Ride is one of the most popular events. From five to seven wild horses with ropes attached were turned out of the chutes to be met by cowboy teams. One cowboy handled the rope and his teammate carried the saddle. They attempted to saddle the mustang out in the open and one tried to jump on and ride to a designated spot. The same shows were presented all three days.

Winners of the opening day events at the first rodeo in 1912 included: Wild Horse Race, Bert Rhoades of Salmon River, first; Arthur Seale, eastern Oregon, second; and Ed Nelson, Forest, third. Steer Tieing: Del Blanchett in 47.5 seconds, first, and Art Accord, 80 seconds, second. Stake Race: Clark Gill, Salmon River, first, and Walter Jarrett, Tolo, second. Mrs. Frank Ferris of Harpster was named the most graceful lady rider and on the second day, she won the Women's Stake Race.

Other winners on the second day include: Wild Horse Race, Marion Tipton, Salmon River, first; William Minert, Snake River, second; Jess Kitchen, Kamiah, third; Albert Johnson, Salmon River, fourth; and Len Wringer, fifth. Joe Dixon of Salmon River with a time of 64 seconds, won the steer tieing contest, and Del Eagle of Wyoming with 74 seconds was second. Roy Irwin of Salmon River won the stake race and Arthur McFadden, Salmon River, won the barrel race.

The famous bucker "Cyclone" was drawn by Elmer Mitchell of Pendleton. The horse made a few powerful jumps and the rider bit the dust. Lonnie Collins did a bit better on the Brockman sorrel bucker but was forced to pull leather.

Just hearing of the Friday "Lewiston Day" parade brings deep wishing to have been in Grangeville to see Del Blanchett and Doc Denny lead 517 saddle horses and riders down the main street twice, crowding the people back onto the curbs to use the entire width of the street. Grangeville's streets are noted for their roomy width.

John Olmsted's writings assure readers that this was a genuine Idaho rodeo, with, "There were strains from the Grangeville band, the Lewiston fife and drum corps, intermingled with cowboy yells and the discharge of six-shooters. At the conclusion of the parade there was a cowboy stampede, the streets presenting the scene of a mad race of more than five hundred spirited cowmen."

Events and winners that day were: Wild Horse Race: Arthur McFadden, Salmon River, first; R. Seale, eastern Oregon, second; A.W. Williams, Grangeville, third; Jim Kennedy, Grangeville, fourth; and W.E. Seale, eastern Oregon, fifth. Slim Bunnell of Cottonwood won the mule race, and Bob Gill, Salmon River, won the stake race.

Saturday was closing day and was "turned over to the Salmon River people, the men from the cow country south of us, who did so much to make the show a success." A big parade of horsemen from the river country was followed by a drove of two hundred wild steers from both the Snake and Salmon ranges. "The afternoon program was a real hummer, with Jackson Sundown declaring he would ride the bucker 'Cyclone' for any amount of money, with all the riders taking part in the celebration swearing vengeance on the horse. It was decided by the management to bar the horse from the rodeo and probably save a life." A parade of Indians in full costume was made at the grounds and a war dance performed.

Final days winners were Walter Brockman, Salmon River, first in the stake race; Joe Dixon with 87 seconds, first, and W.I. Rook, 89 seconds, second in steer tieing. Both from Salmon River. Rooke won the barrel race and Lew Miner, forest ranger from the Salmon River country was declared champion bronco buster.

Salmon River, Let 'er Buck!

RIGGINS

En route to the Riggins Rodeo, less than fifty miles from Grangeville, one travels south on U.S. Highway 95 over one of America's most spectacular mountain drives (in Idaho we call it a "hill") is the White Bird Hill. From the summit of 4,245 feet one can glimpse, to the west, the rugged Seven Devils mountains guarding the Idaho side of Hells Canyon, deepest gorge in North America. Through it surges the mighty Snake River.

Thousands of owners, trainers, and managers of rodeo stock, cowboys and girls and fans of the sport have enjoyed that

Riggins is one of Idaho's best hometown rodeos and widely attended. Pickup men and judges are shown here with a bronc buster and his horse. *Courtesy of James H. Teall.*

bit of scenic wonder over the years, as they converge upon the little town nestled in the Salmon River canyon at the confluence of the Main Salmon and the Little Salmon rivers. Residents call it "the heartland of Idaho." They also say it is "The narrowest town in the USA." It is at Riggins where the well-known "River of No Return" flows out of the wilderness and curves north to parallel Highway 95 for about thirty miles before rejoining the wild country to the west of White Bird Hill.

The year 2001 is the fifty-third anniversary of the Salmon River Cowboys Association Rodeo events were held at least seven years before the association was formed. It is always set for the first full weekend in May. The eighteen hundred feet elevation brings balmy weather at that time of year.

Because Riggins is, indeed, a narrow town, rodeo riders and supporters met a number of definite challenges in building an arena 'way back in 1942. Along with much history of the area, we heard the rodeo story at the dining table in the home of the Ace Bartons (located on Ace Barton Street, naturally) one hot July evening in 1999. The townspeople think so highly of Ace and to express gratitude for all he has done for the area, that the street was named for him when he retired as mayor.

Ace remembers that the first rodeo was held at the home place of brothers Jim and Ben Large, on the bench east of Riggins. Directions given were, "Large's Bar on the Salmon, halfway between 'It' and Peace Creek." Clyde Grider had a cabin on the flat with the sign, "This is It."

The rodeo was moved up to the airstrip across the Little Salmon. The ground also doubled as a football field. It was reached by a swinging bridge, which all participants and the stock had to cross. Numerous and huge boulders were picked up and cactus dug and removed before the rocky land could be leveled.. "Then, Clark Hill and his son, George, put a springtooth harrow to the ground." Among the youngsters who helped clear and clean the land were Ace, Frankie Heath, Jack Rice, Warren Colton, Dan and Don Wilson, and others. "All the people up and

George Russell of Riggins, Idaho, takes his turn in the arena as the cowboys in the background await their turns for bull-busting.

down the river were excited about the rodeo and two-to-three hundred showed up," Ace said.

In 1942, the arena was built by Jack Percifield, Dick Crooks and Padgett Berry, the latter a Canadian cowboy. George Stevens of John Day Ranch provided the cattle. The bucking horses were furnished by McKenzie Creek, Frank and Everett "Tim" Taylor. Percifield moved the arena the next year across the Little Salmon to the previous site of the Civilian Conservation Corps camp. Harley Tucker of Joseph, Oregon, furnished cows and calves, some of which he had bought from Clay and Emma Davis, who ranched on the Snake River side of the divide. They were trailed down Cow Creek to Riggins.

In 1944–45, Idaho's World Champion saddle bronc rider Guy Cash, who ran cattle on range beyond the Pollock bridge, provided stock for a Professional Rodeo Cowboy Association event. The Riggins Chamber of Commerce was a sponsor.

In 1946, the arena was again moved, this time to a penin-
sula between the Little and Main Salmon rivers, where the lumber mill had been located. Ace Barton remembers that at one
time a "Suicide Race" down the steep hill was held. "But lots of
horses were crippled up, so that race didn't last long."

The Summervilles, Jim and Velma, arrived in Riggins in
1945 and became staunch promoters. They opened the
Summerville cafe, club and dance hall, a popular stopping spot
for many north-south highway travelers. Their hall was also used
as the school gym. They were not performers, but there were no
stronger builders of Riggins Rodeo, donating the hall, public
address system, selling tickets and driving the queens and
princesses to other rodeos promoting the one in Riggins. Warren
Brown, McCall lumberman, was always generous in his help and
donated lumber from his Salmon River Lumber Company to
build and repair the arena.

The Summervilles, joined by Josh Alkire, Ed Clay, and cowboys in the area, sponsored rodeos in 1946–47. Ralph Stephens
and Kermit Stippich took a gamble and brought their bucking
string from Midvale. It paid off. They or partners and successors
continued to be contractors at Riggins. In 1979, Stephens and the
Gill brothers, Deward and Melvin, became partners. Two years
later, Melvin sold his interest to the other two and in 1989,
Stephens sold to Deward. And Gill Rodeos have provided bucking stock since.

Rodeo was progressing so well that the Salmon River
Cowboys Association was formed in 1948 and continuously
sponsored the rodeo. Of the original signers Larry Clay and Bob
Sewell remain active. Other early members included Stewart
Aiken, Tommy Clay, Shorty Derrick, Clark and George Gill, Pink
Hayes, Bill Howerton, Bill Lassiter, Max Newman, Hubert Sewell,
Gene Toothman, and Ken Twilegar. Rodeo participants were Rich
Anderson, Dick Clay, Deward and Melvin Gill, Darrel and Bow
Sewell, and Larry and Claud Smith.

Success is measured by the 903 tickets sold in 1944 to

more than 3,000 in 1999. There has been an increase from one hundred to about two hundred and fifty contestants during the same years. The bleachers always filled early, but hundreds found sitting room on the hillsides with a great view.

Many beloved citizens and community workers have served as Grand Marshals. They include Clark Gill of Lucile, several times and the last when he was ninety-nine years old; Gene Tooman, Stewart Aitken, Tommy, Larry and Hazel Clay, Warren Brown, Firman Gotszinger, Ralph Stephens, Bob and Kathryn Sewell. Avo Hardin, Vera Schleicher, Velma Summerville, Ace Barton, Kenny Heath, and Bob Spickelmire.

All-Around Cowboys include (some of them named several years): Buck Abbott, Larry and Dick Clay, Wayne O'Neil, Buck Godby, Deward Gill, Red Abel, Jim Lightfoot, Tom Eddy, Billy Stevens, Lonnie Wright, Bob Sewell, Dee Pickett, Dave Morrison, Wayne Thawley, Lee Woodberry, Casey Cox, Bob and Barry Johnson, Larry Smith, Ron Currin, Rich Anderson, Kelsey Felton, Darrel Watson, Margret Smith, and Jim McGinn. *(See Chapter 17.)*

* * *

James H. "Jim" Teall was born and spent part of his childhood in the little town of Abasorake, Montana, before moving with his family to the Dalton Gardens area, now grown to the point of adjoining Coeur d'Alene. Johnny Flanagan, a favorite

Two leaps and a stop with the cowboy still in the saddle as seen at the May 1, 1954 Riggins Rodeo. *Courtesy of James H. Teall.*

family friend in Abasorake, was a genuine cowboy and whetted
the appetite of young Jim for any and everything pertaining to
roundup and rodeo.

Over the years, Jim attended rodeos throughout Idaho and
other states. His poem, "The Bronc Stomper," has its setting in a
Riggins bar where a defeated cowboy ponders the ups and
downs of a bronc rider's life.

> The rider sits in a Riggins bar
> Alone with his empty glass.
> His money is gone, his credit cut off,
> The moment of truth has passed.
> The roar of the crowd has faded away,
> The women have come and went,
> The chutegate swings on a rusty hinge
> And the money is long since spent.
>
> The riders come from the Joseph Plains,
> And the canyons down on the Snake;
> From the bleak Canadian prairies
> And off the Missouri breaks.
> They're young and they're tough and reckless,
> With their spurs strapped high on their heels.
> They know that a bronc is spooky,
> And they know how that first jump feels.
>
> They've been breaking the colts on the ranches,
> And all of them think they can ride.
> 'Til that first big iron jawed outlaw
> Strips them of all their pride.
> There's a helluva great big difference
> In a colt and a little luck,
> And a grizzled old pro of the bronc string
> That really knows how to buck

There's Cheyenne, Tucson and Las Vegas,
Calgary, Pocatello and Santa Fe,
Lewiston, Ellensburg, Caldwell,
And only the good ones stay.
There's Spokane, Pendleton, Nampa,
And the years go tumbling past.
"Til, at last, we comes to Riggins,
The bar and the empty glass.

For the big roan stumbled and balked today
And barely got out of the chute.
The day-money went to a rough, raw kid
From up by Cottonwood Butte.
The saddle will hang on a hockshop wall,
With a ticket that's long overdue.
The spurs that have hung in a horse's neck,
Will be hanging there, too.

Someone will buy the saddle and spurs,
In time for the next big show.
As long as there're horses, saddles and spurs,
The riders will come and go.

McCALL

For many years the rodeos in Valley County were the home-grown type when riders from the little towns would gather in a field to compete against one another. They started sometime during the early 1920s with local ranches providing the stock. Frank Elds is likely the oldest rancher in the McCall-Donnelly area and the Campbells of the famed Circle C Ranch in New Meadows had cowboys working for them on the ranches and the range. About 1990, the first official Idaho Cowboy Association Rodeo was held at McCall.

Now called the Frontier Days Rodeo and the arena is about three miles south of the town on Idaho Highway 55. Even the

**Two attractive visitors to the 1996 Riggins Rodeo from McCall were
Sammy Allen, left, Frontier Days Junior Queen and Margaux Edwards,
McCall Frontier Days Senior Queen. They have decorated their saddles
with large bouquets of flowers and have draped McCall Frontier Days
serapes over the backs of the horses. Riggins holds the first rodeo of
the season on the first Saturday in May.**

highest ranked of Idaho cowboys still like to participate in rodeos
in the region and McCall is a favorite. Bareback and saddle bronc
riding, calf and team roping, bull riding, and bulldogging, are the
traditional events. Scoring in the bucking competition, saddle and
bull riding is based equally upon the performance of the cowboy
and animal in an eight second time. Scores above 80 are bound
to bring in money; in the 70s, likely to place and in the 60s is an
average spot to be. Calf roping is done from a speeding quarter
horse with the shortest time to rope and tie the calf bringing the
prize. A time near or on the ten-second mark should be a money
winner. Team ropers try to lasso the horns and heels of a speeding steer while staying on equally speedy horses. The champions
handle it in ten seconds or under. A team is also needed in bull-

dogging with the mounted "wrestler" working with the hazer who attempts to keep the steer on a straight path so the dogger can plunge from his horse directly on to the head and the horns of the steer, and wrestle it to the ground in the shortest possible time. It is actually possible to accomplish all this in less than five seconds.

Cowgirls compete in goat tying, breakaway roping, and barrel racing. In barrel racing, the girls and their horses race in a cloverleaf pattern around big barrels. The one who finishes in the shortest time (usually in the range of eighteen seconds) is the winner.

In breakaway roping the calf comes scrambling out of the chute and the cowgirl tries to get a loop over the calf's head. They then apply a tight rein, stopping the horse, and when the end of the rope which is lightly attached to the saddlehorn breaks away their time is determined.

Goat tying is timed from the second the girl leaves a timing chute at one end of the arena and races her horse to the other end where a goat is tied to a stake. Rules call for the cowgirl dismounting, throwing the goat, and tying three legs.

The little cowboys and girls vie in mutton busting, staying on a wild sheep for the required eight seconds.

The rodeo opens on a Saturday and is preceded by a colorful parade along the downtown streets of McCall.

CASCADE

Just twenty-six miles south of McCall is the town of Cascade, where a rodeo is held in conjunction with the Valley County Fair. It is usually held during the second week in August at an arena adjoining the fairgrounds on the south end of town. The arena is just west of the Boise Cascade Mill. Bleachers to accommodate several hundred fans are set up for the rodeo.

Cowboying at Council/Cambridge

RIDING FOR THE GLORY

On Idaho's far western border the rodeo season gets underway early in Adams and Washington counties. It happens in June every year when young riders from all walks of life converge to attend Rodeo Bible Camps of Idaho, Inc., in Cambridge and Council. About one hundred and fifty come from Montana, Washington, Oregon, and California and from Rupert to the Canadian border in Idaho.

"Those kids have been coming for some twenty years," says Cheryl Zeranski of Weiser, camp secretary. Her late husband, Bert, was the first president of the camp board. She emphasizes that Bible teaching is the focus of the camps with rodeo as the recreation.

Volunteerism makes the camps possible, according to Cheryl, with some seventy people helping to organize and work. "Donations from the stock contractors, belt buckle designers, help in the kitchen and other spots, make it all possible," she said.

Gary and Vonda Walker originated the event in LaGrange, Wyoming, it spread to other states. Gary owned the rodeo stock and Vonda was secretary. Churches in the various areas made the first contacts.

Rodeo Bible Camps became so popular that soon two groups were formed. Fifteen-to-nineteen-year-olds hunker down at the Adams County Fair and Rodeo grounds at Council. Those with Stetsons fitting twelve-to-fourteen-year-olds hang them on pegs at the Washington County Fair and Rodeo grounds at Cambridge. All the kids take their own sleeping bags, with the girls moving into the exhibit halls and the boys camping outside.

As the years passed, the camps turned to stock owner

Laci Holmes and Cody Judson pose proudly with the buckles they won.

Deward Gill, formerly of Lucile, Idaho, for the bucking and racing stock which he donated. In recent years, the board of directors borrowed stock from wherever available. Contestants bring
their own mounts and take responsibility for feeding and caring
for all livestock.

Long after they have outgrown participation, a number of
the young people return to camp to help with the newcomers.
One camper, Margaux Edwards of Donnelly, daughter of Idaho's
longtime treasurer, Lydia Justice Edwards, became Miss Rodeo
Idaho and went on to place fifth in the Miss Rodeo America
competition. *(See Chapter 5.)*

Tyler Crockett of Indian Valley, located thirty-five miles
north of Weiser and one of Idaho's most scenic areas, is the son
of Ron and Linda Crockett. His brother, Jeff, and Tyler learned
about cattle and rodeo being raised on the family cattle ranch.
The Crocketts ran three hundred head of cattle and when the
boys were little they learned to ride calves. By the time they were
ten, they were riding steers. When Tyler reached fourteen, he
attended Rodeo Bible Camp and rode his first bull.

He completed in High School Rodeo from 1988 through
1992 and won the District Three championship in 1992. That

year was a good one for the amateur, as he won at team and calf roping and bulldogging and the Reserve All-Around championship. Ranking fifth in the state, he went to the invitational at Fallon, Nevada, where he won fourth in bull riding. Other towns where he rode as an amateur included Cambridge, Weiser, Jerome, Shoshone, Hailey, and White Bird.

Tyler received a three-year rodeo scholarship at Treasure Valley College, where he placed third in the region two times, second once, and qualified for the College Nationals at Bozeman, Montana. He then received a rodeo scholarship at the University of Nevada Las Vegas. There he bulldogged and rode steers and won the Grand Canyon regional championship and qualified for the College National Finals. He received his Professional Rodeo Cowboys Association card in 1994, and turned to full-time professional in 1997. While bull riding in 1998, he placed in the PRCA top one hundred bull riders. He tore a hamstring while in a rodeo at Santa Maria, California.

Tyler has moved to a smaller cattle ranch near Buhl, Idaho.

SURE ENOUGH COW COUNTRY

Dick Parker confesses to becoming a "hopeless rodeo junkie" at age eight. The year was 1939 and from the opening action he was addicted. "Back then there was a race track at Cambridge where the Clay brothers, Ed, Frank, Tommy, Larry, and Dick of New Meadows, put on quite a show. They rode race horses, saddle broncs, and bareback," Dick said, "while I had to get by with only one rodeo fix a year, because the family finances could not include another trip of that distance just for fun." But the hook was set so deep that Dick remains a rodeo aficionado these sixty-plus years later.

Prior to the building of the Adams County Rodeo grounds in Council in 1948, when Dick was old enough to be a contestant, unofficial rodeos were sometimes held with the arena formed by a circle of Model T Fords and spectators. Victor Craig remembers that Hugh Beggs brought wild horses in from the

Brownlee range and was the first person to put on a rodeo in Cambridge. That arena is now Main Street.

The first rodeo board included Johnny Williams, Barr Jacobs, John Fraser, Roy Stewart, Bud Mink, and several other ranchers and working cowboys. A news item declared the first show a success and that two rodeos a year were being planned. April Petty (Kampeter) was chosen to ride a horse into the arena to be auctioned. She was the first rodeo queen. For the next several years the queen was the one of three contestants who sold the most raffle tickets. Eventually a contest was held where the contestants were judged upon appearance, horsemanship, and riding ability.

In 1976, as part of Idaho's Bicentennial celebration, all former Rodeo Royalty members were invited to attend and be introduced at the rodeo. The response was surprising with one former princess coming from Montana.

The first performance of the Adams County Rodeo came roaring out of the chute with a saddle bronc ridden by Johnny Ross of Vale, Oregon. He made a spectacular ride on a horse called "Yapi Pie Pete." Johnny and brother, Don, rode for a few years and later acted as pickup men. In early days there were thirty or forty contestants. Now there are several hundred. "There were a lot more all-around cowboys in those days, with some contesting in all five events," Dick Parker wrote.

The rodeo board was concerned that although the grandstand was full, the treasury was empty. Workers took tickets as cars came into the arena area, but those in the announcer stand could observe crowds of people coming in from the east after the rodeo was underway. The board called upon the willing Lions Club to join the rodeo volunteers and solidly fenced the entire arena, with ticket booths on each side. There were only about half as many in the stands at the next rodeo, but the board was happy to note they had taken in twice as much money. Dick Parker explains, "A lot of folks didn't feel like they should have to buy a ticket to their own hometown rodeo!"

As in other towns, when the arena was originally built there was a race track around it. A problem soon cropped up, because the track grounds sloped up, toward the east, and the races were run counter-clockwise. A well-founded cause for concern was the very fast downhill home stretch which with a right smart, sharp and dangerous turn at the bottom where the track diverted between the bleachers and the arena. It was such a dangerous situation that after a couple of years, racing was stopped. Dick Parker, considered one of the best rodeo announcers in the state, remembers some of the excitement of watching those races and the aftermath of close calls. "There was never a really big crash, but there were a lot of heated arguments about crowding on that last turn. After one such incident, I remember a lady beating Frank Clay over the head with her quirt."

Since the beginning there have been lights around the arena. Early they were on short poles. Dick remembers night rodeos in the late 1950s. The first several years of rodeo in Adams County, there was a one or two day spring rodeo and the same format in autumn. If it was a two day program, the riders had two head of stock to ride in each event. "We just rode bareback and saddle broncs at first and bulls were brought into the string in the late fifties," according to Dick.

There has never been a different rodeo string in that arena. Ralph Stephens and Kermit Stippich furnished the stock and that has never changed. Stephens was born and raised in the Crane Creek area just out of Midvale. He and his wife Mary raised cattle and hay on their ranch. He and Stippich went into the bucking stock business and they supplied rodeo animals in many towns in Idaho and Oregon. Stephens bought out Stippich. In 1979 he sold to Deward and Tami Gill. The name is now Gill Rodeos but the stock furnished is from the original herd. Stephens and Stippich wintered stock south of Midvale where Crane Creek drains into the Weiser River, south of Midvale.

"Sometimes our spring rodeo was the first one for which the

cattle would be rounded up and they'd really be wild. The splinters would just fly as they came bounding out of the chutes. They had been tied down for what must have seemed like an hour to cattle, so they were more than be ready when the rider called for them. They had some really great horses and Deward Gill still has some spectacular horses and bulls in the string."

Dick went on to say that Gill leases much of his stock to the Professional Rodeo Cowboys Association (formerly RCA-Rodeo Cowboys Association). Good entertainment was a hallmark of the Adams County event. The Brogan brothers, both of whom went on to be pro riders with the RCA, presented a fine roping act. The nationally-known Jay Sisler of Emmett performed with his Australian Shepherd trained herd dogs. There were trained horse, mule, and dog acts.

Prices now exacted for genuine clown acts have become too high for many small rodeos. Some of the good ones of former years included Super Stevens, who clowned and fought bulls; Curly Heath, a great clown and bullfighter, whose grandson, Matt, is following in his footsteps.

One of Dick's rodeo sidelights was from Mary Stephens who said she had to buy milk one year because her milk cow had a calf by one of the rodeo bulls, and the calf was so mean that he wouldn't let her near enough to milk the cow.

Council riders who went on to high rankings include the late Jim Roeser of Caldwell/Owyhee, who took part several times in National bareback riding; Harry Charters, world champion steer wrestler; Enoch Walker had already been world saddle bronc champ when he rode at Council; national champion in the Women's Rodeo Association Jan Alley rode in the lady bareback section featured for several years. A local rider, Charley Stovner, became so good as a pro saddle bronc rider that he made his living at it. The bareback riding champ in 1997 was a graduate of Junior Rodeo and Rodeo Bible Camp.

As years have moved on more semi-professional cowboys who hold various jobs during the week ride rodeo on weekends.

One of the 1997 winners sells vacuum cleaners. There are still enough area contestants to retain a local flavor to the rodeo. In 1984, the chutes and pens were in poor shape. All were bull-dozed into a pile and burned. New metal chutes and pens were built. Dave Wilson brought a dozen members of his Naval Reserve unit to help. Replacing bleachers was next in having a topnotch facility.

All the facilities and arena are kept in use. The Council Riding Club's more than one hundred members in the 1970s held many practice sessions and two play days a year. For several years the Idaho Girls Rodeo Association held their rodeo there. Pulling contests, horse shows, a bullarama, Little Britches and Junior rodeos and the Bible camp make extensive use of the facility.

A bonus of having an arena and bleachers took place when there was a between-cities breakdown of one of the trucks carrying a performance group of the famed Austrian Lippizaner horses. While the truck was being repaired the troupe put on a show at the arena. The Lippizaner is known worldwide and has powerful muscles which permit them to perform intricate and difficult drills and movements. It was a treat for Council to have such a performance.

In 1949, Dick, along with a number of other local riders, rode bareback and saddle broncs at Cambridge and Council. The two events were much alike with the corresponding stock and most of the same cowboys. Among them were the four Clay brothers, the Brogan brothers, Everett Harrington, Leo Mink, Dick Armacost, John Williams, and Dick Fisk. Stock furnished by Stephens and Stippich now have descendants bucking and running at Council. There has never been a different rodeo string in that arena.

Dick recalls that some of the great old horses with colorful names were Indian Mountain (from the mountain so dear to the hearts of the oldtimers and locals), Geronimo, Double Ought (Ralph Longfellow's saddle horse), Sally Rand, The Mop, Idaho

Punkin, Eagle Bronc and the saddle horse that bucked until he was thirty-two, Wild Red.

A big decision for Dick back in 1948 took only a fear-filled six seconds riding an exhibition bareback horse called "Devil's Dream." He was bucked off, but made up his mind before he hit the ground that he was going to become a full-fledged cowboy.

Nearly fifty years later in 1997, the rodeo was featured on Public Television as a model of small town rodeos. Dick Parker summed up Adams County Rodeo well, when he said, "Rodeo has been a great source of entertainment for our community over the last fifty years, and I hope it lasts another fifty."

CAMBRIDGE RODEO

Gretchen Clelland of Cambridge remembers that the early rodeos in September were not held until the crops were in and the harvest completed. They were so popular that schools were let out on a Thursday, so the children could attend. "It was called Kids Day and people came from miles around to attend and to visit." The rodeo from 2 until 5:30 in the afternoon was followed by dances each night.

"The stock was gathered from local ranchers, with all of them donating the use of stock, as well as time to help put on the rodeo," Gretchen said. She remembers that there were no true rodeo bucking bulls, but mainly two-year-old steers. "I know my Dad took our bucket calves (milk cow calves we raised on the bucket) for roping calves. And some young kids tried to ride some of them.

"The bucking horses were mostly work animals, with maybe a spoiled saddle horse thrown in. I only remember the local riders that I knew well. Albert Freymeyer was pickup man a lot of times. Lee Langer was killed by a one-eyed horse. Lee fell on the horse's blind side and so the horse couldn't see him and stepped on him."

Gretchen went on to say that the races were good ones and

"Tracy" shows his high leaping style to rider Dennis Holmes of Midvale at the Cambridge Night Rodeo. *Photo by F. Lyle.*

the relays the most exciting. The riders changed horses each time they circled the track. There were three circles made with two riders with six horses. Orville Perkins and a Mr. Saling provided teams from Indian Valley and Manns Creek for the chariot races.

Called the "Upper County Fair and Rodeo," the 1946 Washington County event at Cambridge holds a special place in the memory of Gib Keithly, now of Spokane. "The sights and sounds and smells," he writes, "were very real to me then, and they are not hard to recall now." The Keithlys lived at Midvale, eight miles south of Cambridge and the Weiser, the largest town and county seat, was twenty-three miles south of Midvale. The only time they drove to the Weiser Rodeo was in 1945 when Gib's cousin, Claudia June Keithley was the queen. Gib has memories of her in a beautiful white western outfit on a handsome pinto (Claudia remembers it as her bay horse "Bonnie"). To Gib, the Weiser event was big and he was small and young and a long way from home.

Not so with the Cambridge show, which was smaller and close and familiar. He and his faithful friend, Harold Hood, observed the posters on telephone poles and in store windows announcing the coming of the Upper County Fair and Rodeo in mid-August along with a big parade down Main Street. The boys could see themselves in the parade and even winning the prize money for "best in class." Hood's dad loaned his stocky little

Gilbert "Gib" Keithly, now of Spokane, vividly remembers the Upper County Fair and Rodeo at Cambridge, eight miles from his family's ranch. This picture with the pony was taken when he was about twelve. Gib and good friend Harold Hood dressed as old prospectors, down to the corncob pipes, and were hailed as a bright part of the parade. He also remembers the Weiser Roundup where his cousin, Claudia, the Rodeo Queen, was cheered as she galloped around the arena. Slim Pickens was the clown distracting the charging bulls. The boys ate their first "thin" hamburgers and thought they'd taste nothing better during the rest of their lives.

horse and the boys dressed as prospectors. From the packsaddle, on both sides of the horse, hung cast iron skillets, picks, shovels, a couple of old guns, and canvas bedrolls, and a sign lettered "Cambridge or Bust." The boys each had a corncob pipe which they loaded with coffee grounds.

The crowd along the sidewalks applauded when the boys stopped briefly in the street to re-load and re-light their pipes. They received the two dollars and fifty cents second prize in the historical category. Even more satisfying was getting their names in the newspaper.

The gates opened to spectators a little after two in the afternoon. The fair and rodeo chairman led the mounted procession with the American flag on a standard, placed in a cylinder on his saddle. As Gib relates it: "He charged through the gates and paused. The crowd in the grandstand came to its feet at the sight of the flag, and everyone quit talking. The silence was awesome. He then raised his right hand, and motioned forward. The grand entrance began in dignified cadence. Behind the chairman followed almost anyone who had a horse and wanted to be a part of the event.

"There wasn't any music at Cambridge. We didn't have the capability of recorded sound. So there wasn't any grand flourish of marching bands which typically opens a rodeo. Our was done in silence. Sometimes we don't appreciate silence, and feel that something must be said or some noise made to mark the event. Not so at Cambridge then. The burden was on us to keep silent, and we did."

With understanding and sympathy, Keithly wrote of the one Indian family on horseback in the arena parade: "The Indian man rode alone. The woman carried a small child on a papoose board. They were not brightly dressed, and one would only know their heritage by skin tone and the long, black braids. They did not glance around as they rode by the grandstand. They looked straight ahead, and slightly downward. There was no applause.

"It had only been about seventy years since my family had

come to the fertile lands along the Weiser River and staked out
their homesteads on what had been the hunting grounds of these
native Americans. My grandfather, J.L. Keithly, traded with the
Indians about the turn of the century. My great-grandfather
Griffin fought them and once fled from them, retreating from the
homestead near Midvale to the settlement at Salubria. I don't
count among my relatives people who were killed by the Indians.
On the other hand, I do not know how many Indians my people
killed. Even in 1946, there were strong memories of altercations
with the Indians, and while people in the grandstands didn't
shout deprecating remarks, they did not proffer respect. We
viewed the Indians in silence, just as they viewed us."

Keithly told of the clown with the bright red nose, a black
cowboy from Oregon or California, whose name he didn't know
(he could have been George Fletcher or Slim Pickens, both of
whom rode in Idaho rodeos). The show of amazing feats by
Australian shepherd dogs were likely those trained by Jay Sisler
of Emmett. He remembers there were other attractions, and of
eating four thin and delicious hamburgers.

"By the end of the rodeo that hot August afternoon my
mouth was dry and my head was full of new notions. I wanted to
be a traveling cowboy who rolled his own cigarettes. I wanted to
be an Indian who lived along the river. I wanted to be the only
black cowboy in the rodeo. I wanted to be a clown, and wear a
bright red nose and ride a unicycle. I wanted to be a local boy
who won a prize against the skill of professionals. I wanted to be
the announcer at the rodeo, who kept it all going. And I wanted
to be Doc Whiteman, who was always called when someone was
injured and needed medical attention. I never wanted to eat anything again except thin hamburgers."

River Country Rodeo

WEISER

There have been numerous plays on the word "Weiser." At one time a Hollywood songwriter actually composed a little ditty called, "People are Wiser in Weiser." In some cases they are. That certainly applies to rodeo. From the amateur events held in the early 1900s to professional rodeo today, thousands gather in Weiser to watch the great western American sport. Early amateurs bucked horses, held stagecoach and relay races, did trick riding and fancy roping in a field near the old high school. Little money was involved, but a hat was passed and the collection divided among the winners.

The three day event was eagerly awaited and excitement mounted as the street carnival was set up. There was dancing every night. Schools closed, permitting pupils to attend. Special trains ran to and from the upper country and to Nampa and Boise, bringing fans to Weiser. All the hotels were booked well in advance, so homeowners provided room and board for renters. Local riders who took part in the first four roundups included Eldon Cooper, saddle bronc; Jim Fleetwood, steer roping; and Jerry Watson, racing.

With the exception of a few years during the Great Depression, rodeo has been an ever-growing event in Weiser, county seat of Washington, where pioneers started settling in the 1860s. It was about seventy years later when the little settlement at Mann's Creek, northeast of the village of Weiser, saw lots of rodeo action. In the early 1930s, Cecil and Walt Bruce trailed their bucking string to Cambridge and Weiser and onto Halfway, Oregon, for rodeos. Cecil's son, Claude, remembers they trailed them to Caldwell for a private rodeo.

There were no chutes. They simply snubbed the animals until riders were settled in the saddles and then turned them loose, jumped back out of the way and watched the fun. Cecil and Walt also rode horses Roman style and took part in chariot races.

Claude was about five years old when the Sunday rodeos were taking place, but he remembers hearing how his mother, Kathleen, met his dad. In saner moments she served as rodeo secretary, but on a dare she rode a bucking horse at the Cambridge event. Cecil was participating and admired both her beauty and courage.

Some years ago, when Cecil died his sons performed a touching tribute to a genuine old-timer. His body was taken to the cemetery by team and an old box-wagon which had a small platform extension in back of the driver on either side of the box. His sons accompanied him, standing ramrod straight on the platform sides of the wagon.

In 1993, a Youth Rodeo Club was organized, according to member Niki Knudson. "We have a queen and princesses and a lot of high school kids take part. We have an adult leader and members of the Weiser Valley Roundup are always there to help."

The Youth Rodeo Club and Weiser Valley Roundup joined to organize a Ranchers Rodeo in October 1993. Contestants came from Washington, Payette and Adams counties in Idaho and nearby areas in Oregon. All ages, from grandparents to kids, took part. Farmers provided stock, including goats, sheep, and steers. Youngsters scrambled for a variety of small animals.

* * *

"He's a shuffler on a bull," said the bull riding Jim Shoulders. He was talking about Kenny Stanton, former Mann Creek resident, who qualified nine times for the National Finals Rodeo, according to the 1981 *Weiser Signal American* story written by Eydie Huston.

Kenny first entered a kids' rodeo in Redmond, Washington,

A beautiful shot long before the Roloflex and Rolodex shows Smoky Branch waving his Stetson and remaining seated while smiling on wildly bucking "Glass Eye" at the 1923 Weiser Roundup. *Courtesy of Weiser Museum.*

Lloyd Coleman waves to the judge to signal "steer down."

when he was nine. When he graduated from Redmond High school in 1959 he was the only one wearing Wrangler jeans with a slit up the side of one leg to make room for a cast. He was released from the hospital to accept his diploma only upon agreeing to return for further treatment.

He came in eleventh among pro rodeo's award winners in 1963. In later years he and his wife, Ginger, ran a bull riding school on Mann's Creek Amateur rodeos were held in Weiser as early as 1906 or 1907, years before Kenny Stanton became a legend in his own time. According to Beth Mack in her *History of the Weiser Roundup* amateur events were in an open field east of the old high school. Old-timer Lester Applegate said "We didn't charge, but the hat was passed for donations." Nor were there grandstand, bleachers, corrals, or fences. Applegate recalled a heart-pumping sight when a bucking horse jumped over a high-set baby buggy and baby without touching it. "However," he said, "the mother and baby left the field immediately."

Note the silk blouse and fringed skirt worn by Mildred Douglas as she rides a wild steer at an early-day Weiser Roundup.

Fred Harding sticks
with "Calamity
Jane" at the 1917
Weiser Roundup.

Guy Schults lands
prone upon the back
of the steer with one
hand on the horn.
His horse gallops
onward, but the
pickup will soon
rein him down. All
this action before a
huge crowd at the
Weiser Roundup.
*Courtesy of Weiser
Museum.*

This is the bucking style
of Dave White which
took second in the
money at the Weiser
Roundup in 1917.

East Court Street was ungraded in 1915, and races were held in conjunction with the first annual Harvest Carnival. There was a purse with riders competing for awards as low as three dollars on up to seven dollars for first place. The first professional event was held the following year on the athletic field in back of the old high school. Rodeo champions came from many states and Canada. In those early days the Weiser Roundup was runnerup to Pendleton and on a matching rating with Cheyenne, two of the largest rodeos in the country.

Dates for the event have changed several times and is now held the second weekend in June. It was called the Hells Canyon Rodeo for thirty years until the mid eighties when it became the Weiser Valley Roundup. For many years it was known as the oldest professional rodeo in Idaho. Exciting contests marked the show from the early days. Featured were roping, bronc riding, bulldogging, trick riding and fancy roping, men and women bronc riders, relay races from one-fourth to one-half miles, Roman, chap and maverick races. To complete the colorful and exciting show the Umatilla Indians performed dances after the contests. Contestants chose their own saddles and women riders used both reins and sometimes hobbled stirrups.

Many well-known men and women and those who later became so appeared at Weiser. The woman champion of 1916, Katherine Wilkes, and John Spain, 1912 champ, appeared at the first roundup and came back several years for the annual rodeo.

An early-day Weiser Rodeo Parade going down Main Street passes the Washington Hotel (tall building).

Exciting as the rodeo was, all eyes turned skyward during the 1919 Roundup to watch Lieutenant Warren R. Bruce perform stunts twice daily in his ninety horsepower Curtis flying machine. Internationally known Hugh Strickland, who became the world champion bronc buster that year, and his wife, Mabel, one of the foremost saddle bronc riders, appeared in 1919. Other famed Idahoans Frank and Bonnie McCarroll appeared at Weiser many times. Frank was a champion bulldogger and Bonnie rode broncs. Yakima Canutt, 1919 saddle bronc champion of the Pendleton Roundup, attended many Weiser rodeos over the years. James Galloway was the first director and Jim Harris the announcer. George Pence was the official starter, a position he held until 1936.

One of the first acts of the new Weiser Roundup Association in 1920 was to buy twenty acres of land on West Ninth Street and build new rodeo grounds, which are still being used. In the meantime, deed for the land was turned over to the Idaho Cavalry Association which held ownership until 1964. It was then deeded to the Weiser Valley Fair and Rodeo Association.

The new facilities inspired Roundup workers to put together an amazing show for October 6–8, 1920. Two carloads of fifty-two longhorn steers, some carrying horns six feet across, were shipped in from Texas. Arriving at the same time were one hundred bucking broncs and one hundred and fifty racing horses. Later in the 20s, Ed McCarthy and Ed Moody, both former riders, furnished race and bucking horses for the Roundup.

In 1922, two locals riders "Shorty" Kelso and Louie Blevins started their rodeo careers. Other cowboys and cowgirls who rode during the 1920s include: Ray Bell, Norman Cowan, Oklahoma Curley, Donnie Glover, Bonnie Gray, Jack Kirscher, John Glover, John and Frank Spain, and Ed Wright.

Idaho's Bonnie Gray brought her ten thousand dollar high jumping horse King Solomon to the 1924 Roundup and they made a hit. In front of the grandstand each day, she jumped him over a car filled with courageous viewers. The crowd roared its approval.

Jack Henson of Weiser seems to be perfectly at home with his saddle riding the neck of this bucking bronc at an early-day rodeo before an audience of the home folks. He was the first Weiser cowboy to ride the circuit.

A favorite son, Jack Henson, entertained and thrilled the homefolks from the time of the 1919 roundup on through many successes. He was the first Weiser cowboy to ride the professional circuit. the *Weiser American* lauded him for "one of the hardest and showiest rides ever witnessed (1926) at the Roundup grounds."

Here's how the reporter saw it: "Jack Henson astride 'Broken Box' rode his way into the championship. Bringing his mount out of the second chute in high pitch, Henson raked the bronc from bow to stern and into every contortion known to a bucking animal. With the gun announcing the end of the ride for the judges, Henson sailed his sombrero high over the bucking chutes and 'rode it out' until picked up. A crowd of five thousand all behind him, rose in a deafening roar of applause and yells. They knew he had won. After years of hard riding, one of their own had fulfilled a hope."

Frank Kennedy won second in calf roping and Jim Fleetwood won the cowboy's quarter mile and the Snake River Pony Express races. Years later Kennedy would go to Washington, D.C., as a staff member to U.S. Senator Herman Welker of Payette.

For the next four years Jack Henson placed in the money, often first, in saddle bronc competition in Cheyenne, Calgary, Salem, Pendleton, various states in the Southern circuit, and Madison Square Gardens, where he gained another first. He quit the circuit about 1930 and competed only in local rodeos. Jack and Wilda Henson bought property and became ranchers up Little Rock Creek.

Roundup activity slowed considerably during the Depression, but some of the locals who continued to contest in the thirties included the Bruce brothers, Jim Fleetwood, Jack Henson, Russ Jackson, Frank Kennedy, Clair Kirk, Chet and Lee Thorson, Jerry Watson, and Frank VanMeter. Rodeo was discon-

These men were named directors when the Weiser Rodeo was reactivated in 1944. Left to right are Claude Wade, Eldon Cooper, Jim Fleetwood, Gene Pringle, Wallace Laird, Fitz Mink, Chet Thorson, and Verne Chamberlin.

tinued from 1937 until 1944. The seven-year hiatus was too lengthy for a group of men who liked rodeo and felt it was good for the entire area. So, Del Barton, Verne Chamberlin, Eldon Cooper, Sam Lund, Gene Sprinkle, Doug McGinnis, Chet Thorson, Claude Wade, and Jerry Watson set up a legal Rodeo Board and announced that the Roundup would be open to both amateur and professional contestants. Residents of the entire area applauded their efforts.

Chet Thorson is pictured with a favorite Quarter Horse and an appreciation trophy from the Weiser Roundup Association. He led the movement to reactivate the rodeo in 1944.

Vivacious Karna Thorson of the Bar 7X cattle ranch near Weiser was Miss Northwest Cowgirl of 1957 and National Intercollegiate Rodeo Queen. Karna started trick riding at the age of twelve under the guidance of her father and received many rodeo honors. In 1955, she rode as Princess of the Snake River Stampede and was selected Queen of the National Intercollegiate rodeo held in Weiser; in 1956, she was Princess of the Weiser Roundup, Miss Rodeo Idaho, Miss Rodeo Pacific Northwest, and a finalist in the Miss Rodeo America contest.

They were called the "unsung heroes" and told they were as important as the cowboys and cowgirls and that without their untiring efforts, the rodeo would never be held. New chutes and pens, four corrals and a bandstand were built and a parade and two dances were held each day. Locals responded and many took part in the events. Others filled the grandstand and bleachers.

It was in Weiser in 1948 that Wilbur Plaugher, who became one of the best, first performed a rodeo clown. The scheduled clown was injured and Plaugher volunteered and stepped into the slot. He returned many times with his clown acts.

In 1951, Weiserites Frank VanMeter, one time holder of the world bulldogging title, and Dwight Maddox, bronc and bull riding money winner in most of the rodeos in the northwest, led the top entries. VanMeter had appeared in every home Roundup since 1933. Many Weiserites remember that he performed outstanding bulldogging acts without removing his eyeglasses.

Dwight Maddox was raised on Mann Creek and started early to ride saddle broncs and bulls, and compete in bulldogging. He was most successful in bull riding. He placed second in the saddle bronc event in Pendleton in 1944. In 1949 and 1954, he competed in Madison Square and Boston gardens. Dwight and his wife Marge have lived on their ranch on Lower Crane Creek for more than forty years.

Karna Thorson was celebrated for trick riding on her trained horse. The queen and her court were chosen by the Indianhead Saddle Club on the basis of riding ability. *(See Chapter 17.)*

Indicative of the importance attached to the queen contests, is the large turnout of townspeople for the pageant in 1945 when Claudia Keithley, daughter of Mr. and Mrs. Claude Keithley of Midvale was Weiser Rodeo Queen. Her court of honor included Hazel Woodland and Christy Ann Sargent. They and the twelve other contestants paraded for an hour, riding their horses the full length of the track and a program of several events showing the

riding ability and showmanship of each girl. Claudia led the
parade during the three nights of the rodeo and represented
Weiser at public functions throughout the year.

At the 1960 Hells Canyon Rodeo, highly respected Bill
Carson was honored for all he had done for the entire area. A
special feature in 1961 was Mrs. Corrine Williams of Fort Worth,
Texas, as the only woman saddle bronc rider and bulldogger. In
1965, Lou Farber and Claude Wade were honored for consistent
support of Weiser Rodeo. Among the hundreds who served in
various capacities to keep the sport continuing, by holding office,
judging events, working the rodeo, helping Youth Rodeo Club,
some standouts are Bill and Nona Nauman, Bob Hogg, Pat and
Lavina Palmer, Larry and Nancy Barnum, Paul and Jeri Striker,
Victor Craig, Bob Eisenbarth, Don and Pat Mitchell, Art and
Mary Correia, and Paul Ellwood.

The last RCA approved rodeo was held in 1967 and since
then the Weiser Valley Roundup has been Idaho Cowboy
Association approved. The Weiser Valley Roundup Association
and other friends of popular saddle bronc rider Buck Tiffin sponsored a trophy in his honor in 1967. Some of the successors to
have their names engraved on the trophy are Rance Morgan,
Charley Stovner (twice), and Mike McLean.

Harley Tucker of Joseph, Oregon often supplied stock con-
sisting of fifty bucking broncs, Brahma bulls, and dogging steers.
Townspeople dressed in rodeo gear days in advance and merchants flew flags and pennants. Downtown sidewalks were covered with slogans: "Ride 'em Cowboy," "Powder River, Let 'er
Buck," "Widow Maker on the Loose," and "Go Rodeo."

Three of the well-known Grand Marshals are Dwight
Maddox, formerly an outstanding contestant; Hugh Mack, who
worked for years on the stripping chutes and furnished calves for
the dressing event; and Fred Hust, unofficial caretaker of the
rodeo grounds and a worker in the stripping pens for a quarter
century.

EMMETT

The Payette River Valley in which much of Gem County is located has a rich and romantic western history starting in the mid-1800s. Desperadoes and vigilantes, cowboys and Indians, horse and cattle thieves, and the famed Pickett Corral Fort providing protection for the stock owned by early day settlers make up that history. Mountains where cattle and sheep have grazed for years are situated above the little community of Ola.

Because genuine cowboys were living the life without the organization, a rodeo was not held until about 1933. It took place in the county seat of Emmett at the ballpark, then located at the site of the present municipal swimming pool. The rodeo was held on a Friday and Saturday and the producers were local residents. David Little, well-known Gem County sheep and cattleman and former state legislator, who rode a horse from the time he could toddle, took part in many of the rodeos and remained a supporter for years. He did much research for this recounting. Among those providing him information are Sterling Alley, Orville Harris, and Eddie Heath. David's father, Andy, the largest sheepman in the United States in the 1920s, hired as many as six hundred men at one time and had nearly as many horses. It was only natural that members of his family were interested in cattle and horses and all things relating to them.

For the first rodeo, Fred Hale brought along his bucking horse "Cecil," and "Cecil" came with a reputation for landing cowboys on their padded spots. A cowboy was attempting to ride him when Cecil decided to get away, jumped the pole fence and seriously injured one of viewers. The injured person sued and successfully collected from the city of Emmett. The action soured many of the local citizens on rodeo. Jack Macomb furnished most of the bucking horses from his ranch, fifteen miles north of Emmett. Several area horse ranchers had animals tough to stay on, and were willing to furnish them.

The rodeo was not a financial success and there was not

enough money to pay the city for renting the grounds, so it was extended to the third day to pay off the debt.

In the earlier days, smaller and more personal rodeos were a pastime at family and community gatherings such as the Fourth of July and Labor Day. Usually someone had a horse difficult to ride and another would take up the challenge, often after a fortifying shot of home brew or moonshine. Others would corral cattle, tie a length of rope around the middle and over the back and issue a dare to anyone to take a ride. There were always takers and sometimes bruised-up cowboys. These homespun fun times were the beginning for many rodeo cowboys. They weren't compensated for the entertainment, but usually a collection was taken and given the successful rider. In case of an injury, the hat was always passed and the contributors generous.

Most of the early rodeos also had horse racing. A makeshift track was established. Little remembered one rodeo at which a hopeful jockey was riding his neighbor's race horse. He rode through a gate onto the track and took the lead in the race. Just a few yards before the finish line, the horse spied the place where he came onto the track, and, like an arrow, sped for that spot. He saw the gate was closed, slammed the brakes on all fours and stopped, but the rider sailed on over the fence and right into the crowd. No real damage was done, except for one well-shaken would-be jockey

There were still hundreds of horses in Gem County in the 1940s. They were used on the farms and ranches and riding clubs flourished. Emmett had both a senior and junior riding club. Local riding and racing events took place. In the potato races, the rider carried a sharpened stick to spear a potato at one location and ride like the wind to another. The races continued until all but one rider was eliminated. Others included stakes races, with riders dodging through stakes driven into the ground; pole bending, where riders weaved between a line of poles; egg race, where the rider carried an egg in a spoon between the place of pickup to the original starting line.

As the clubs developed, more sophisticated events ensued. In one drill, the riders circled and crossed an arena with precision. The precision teams were soon entertaining at the rodeos. With the renewed interest in horse events, members became involved in building a racetrack and rodeo grounds at Tom's Cabin, a cafe and watering hole five miles west of Emmett. The facility was used to entertain members and their families, friends and neighbors at informal horse racing and drill events.

With a good facility and much interest, it was decided to sponsor a full time rodeo with contestants restricted to residents of Gem County. Tom Gribble, owner of Tom's Cabin, and David Little agreed to sponsor the event. Gribble had several bucking horses and Little, who was changing his horse-breeding program, agreed to supply brood mares which had not been broken to ride, and might be good bucking horses. Little also rounded up some of his cows and calves for the wild cow milking and calf roping. The cattle were fresh off the range and gave the cow muggers (those who hold the wild cow while his partner does the milking) a rough time. Little said, "I found that out from experience, as I was trying to mug the cow and she got me down. The only injury was to my pride."

Rodeo sidelights make for great memories. There was a relay race where the riders raced around the track, jumped off the first horse and mounted a second, around the track again and finished the race on a third horse. On the final day there were not many teams entered and Jay and Gene Sisler, local cowboy brothers, had only two horses they wanted to run. Little had extra horses and suggested they use one of his on the final lap, as he wanted to run two others together to find which was the faster. Jay Sisler, who was riding the other team, and Little agreed that whoever was ahead at the last lap would hold up so they could race his two horses.

Little was well in the lead and waited quite some time until his uncle, George Cruikshank, showed up riding his other horse. As they were racing, Little yelled to ask Cruikshank what had happened to Jay. The answer was that Jay had injured an ankle, hence Cruikshank took the spot. It was discovered that Jay's ankle was broken when he jumped to the ground from one horse and was unable to run to the second.

He and brother Gene went to a cow camp ten miles northwest of Emmett and were confined there while his ankle healed. While recuperating, and walking on crutches, Jay and Gene trained a litter of Australian puppies. The pups showed a lot of promise in becoming rodeo performers. Jay trained them to walk between his legs as he propelled himself around the camp on crutches. Other tricks were added and one show-stopper was when the dogs balanced themselves at each end of a pole while Jay lifted them shoulder high. From the cow camp, he and Gene developed dog acts that appeared in most of the major rodeos in the United States and Canada.

Jay Sisler of Emmett and his trained rodeo dogs were a crowd pleaser at many rodeos throughout the entire country. Here, Jay poses with two of his Australian sheep dogs "Stub" and "Shorty" balancing on a slim rod. *Photo by McCall, Denver.*

After the two-day racing and rodeo events, Little and Gribble settled up their sponsor account. They advertised, set up purses for the horse races, and bought silver buckles for prizes. In addition to Little furnishing most of the horses, the cattle for cow mugging and calf roping, he served as one of the pickup men and asked some employees to work the chutes, saddle horses, and ready the cows and calves for events. When they toted up profits and losses they had four dollars to divide. Little said, "Let's spend my share on beer." At that point, he had received all the experience in producing rodeos that he wanted.

But it was not the end of rodeos for Gem County. Horse trader Orval Roeser attended the rodeo and loaned his top horse to Little to use as a pick up horse. After the rodeo, Little told him that he was going to dispose of the brood mares they had used. Little remembers, "With some stick whittling while sitting on the running board of my pickup, we made a deal and the horses were his."

The Roeser name is a distinguished one in rodeo circles, and Little recalled that he had known three generations of the family. Years before, Little had sold slaughter horses to Orval's dad, Bert Roeser, for as little as three quarters of a cent per pound. A thousand pound horse brought seven dollars and fifty cents. When the rodeo took place Orval had two of his sons, Terry and Jim, with him. Jim drew one of the bigger, wilder cows and took quite a ribbing from his father when he was thrown "off a farmer's cow."

Jim hung in there and became so good that he joined the Rodeo Cowboys Association when only seventeen. Following high school graduation in 1953, he joined the pro rodeo circuit, winning go-rounds at Madison Square and Boston gardens.

For more than thirty years, Madison Square Garden in the center of what was considered America's most sophisticated city, New York, was the high spot for which cowboys and cowgirls from across the nation reached. To achieve a place in the annual October championship rodeo in "the Garden" was simply the

greatest. The purse was the largest, trophies the finest, entry fees
the highest and competition was the best that each circuit could
provide. All performed before millions of New Yorkers in a glit-
tery setting. It ended in 1960 when there was no agreement on
a contract to bring the cowboys to the "Big Apple" and the contest was moved to Dallas and its new indoor arena. Las Vegas
now holds the championship event.

In Emmett, riding clubs remained active. Some of the wiser
heads had Gem County purchase land for a combination fair and
rodeo grounds. Bonds were sold and property south of Emmett
was purchased. The enthusiastic riding club members cut and
hauled poles from the forest and constructed a set of rodeo corrals and railing for the racetrack. Both junior and senior riding
clubs used the facility for many fun events on weekends. Gem
County formed a fair board and with the help from the county
has produced county fairs and rodeos for many years. At the
beginning, rodeos were held during the day. Later, lights were
installed and the rodeo became a nighttime event.

David Little believes that the first rodeo producer was Jake
Pope of Twin Falls. Pope had a complete rodeo string of bucking
horses, calves for roping, and Brahma bulls. The bulls were the
crowd pleasers and Emmett produced a team of rodeo clowns.
The first team was made up of Harold (Curly) Heath and Orville
Harris. After a few years, Curly's son, Eddie, joined him in the
clown act. They played Emmett and other local rodeos in southwest Idaho. Curly and David Little attended high school in
Emmett at the same time. If Little was competing when Curly
announced events, he "roasted" Little about his activity in politics.
Heath is now in the real estate business and an auctioneer.

After Jake Pope, Sterling Alley of Garden Valley was hired
to produce the Gem County Rodeo. Alley says that the Emmett
rodeos were not very lucrative. He remembers that he was to get
a percentage of the gate receipts, and during his first production
there were about fifteen people in the grandstand.

Women's bronc riding was part of the program when the

National Finals Rodeo was held for the first time in Las Vegas. Sterling Alley's daughter, Jan, and her two daughters were the only contestants. Jan competed in her first rodeo at the age of twelve. She has been a contestant for forty-five years and still competes.

"Even after the disaster with the rodeo at Tom's Cabin," Dave Little says, "I still have the bug. I competed in McCall, Cascade, Horseshoe, Bend, and New Plymouth. I tried my skill at calf roping about the time Idaho's World Champion Dean Oliver was first starting to compete. One time at Horseshoe Bend, I tied him in calf roping. We both missed! I recall one of our calf ropers, Buck Knight, good-naturedly hanging the name 'Empty Loop Oliver' on him. Rodeoing was lots of fun but time consuming."

Competitors included Buck Knight, Eggs Beckley, a bronc rider; along with Wally McConnel, who appeared in Madison Square Garden; Buck Buchanan, Al Book, Marvin Hornbeck, Don Bentley, Emmett Newell, Delbert Branch, Elmer Bowman, Don Shoemaker, Clarence Bowman, Kid Combs, Larry Hill, and Red Leavitt, who broke his jaw in the Emmett Rodeo in the early 1930s; Jay and Gene Sisler, Don Skippen and Mary Skippen, Parker Woodall and Sylvan Williamson. Also taking part were Walt Love, Chuck Tyson, John Wright, Bill Willburn, Tom Pulley, Dow Meek, Smiley Wilcox, Wayne O'Neil, Gordon Fullerton, Ron Hyde, Harold Woodland, Dwight Maddox, Art Hale, and Glenn and Mary Stillwell. Most of them have long since become inactive, but rodeos continue in Gem County.

HORSESHOE BEND

Rodeo started in Horseshoe Bend in the 1930s and as with all the good ones, volunteers working with enthusiastic gusto made it a success. Right from the start there were good crowds of two hundred or more residents and visitors from the area. There had always been horses on the farms and ranches and some raised to supply the U.S. Cavalry, which, provided protection for the early-day settlers. Horse owners were generous in loaning the animals for the rodeo and there was an abundance of riders.

Mary Jane Dobson, whose family members are old-timers of the area, told of the prize stallion "Old Planter," owned by Garner Miner, who regularly entered horses in the fall races sponsored by Boise Cascade Timber Company. Many of the local residents had race horses as well as rodeo stock. Hank Clark had a horse he named "Tim Brainard," in honor of the great-grandfather of Mary Jane Dobson. George Cartwright prized the horse "Rival," which was a gift to him from Bob Brainard, Mary Jane's great uncle. Another well-known horse was "Gallant Man," said to be an ancestor of "Gallant Fox," a later Kentucky Derby winner. Tim Brainard came to Idaho from California in 1863, the year Idaho Territory was established under President Lincoln. It contained all of what is now Montana, most of Wyoming, parts of North and South Dakota and Nebraska. The Idaho Territory was the largest land mass ever officially established and named by the United States. And it was all "horse country." Brainard originally went to California from Maine. When he arrived in Placerville, Idaho, he established a general store to supply the gold miners thronging the area.

In the 1920s and '30s the government loaned stallions from the Cavalry to the local ranchers to breed their mares and they were all thoroughbreds and retired race horses. The loans were made to improve the stock from which the Cavalry chose the best animals. Harold Grabner, a horse trader, was hired to inspect and select mares to meet the Cavalry's standards, and later sell the offspring back to the government. "There were lots of horses in the Horseshoe Bend area," Mary Jane said, "with draft and work horses also in demand. The miners needed them and it wasn't easy to meet the demand of the Cavalry."

John Lemp of Boise once had a government contract to furnish one hundred and fifty saddle geldings. The government rejected one hundred of them saying they were "somewhat" trained, but not enough. To satisfy the buyer, he had to purchase one hundred from other sources. Lemp owned a thousand with another thousand at Shafer Creek, which served as headquarters for his ranching operations. This land was left to his sons and was purchased from George Cartwright by Ben Dobson and his father Len in 1926. Len made a cattle ranch of it with Ben helping. They raised beef for the military and Ben took over when Len became ill in 1947. Ben's siblings were John, Melvin, Ruth, and Ethel.

This land, called "The Lemp Field," had a large amount of timber on it, but plenty of space for rodeo. Harold and Mike "Slim" Young leased it for a year and held weekly rodeos, which were said to be full of "great fun and wild rides." Warren "Buck" Buchanan rode saddle and bareback and from wins at the local rodeos went on to Cheyenne, Wyoming to a regional. He lived on Dry Creek and has two sons, Dennie and Buckie, who were known as "Sons of Buck's." Asa Black held rodeos at his place in Bruneau. He and Ben's uncle, Frank Dobson of Star entered a roping contest in Boise and Frank won. Ed Moody furnished the bucking stock at the Bend when rodeos were held on the old company ranch owned by DeChambeau and Hannifan.

Other rodeo contestants included Parker and Kay Davis Woodall. Later, their son, Parker Glen joined them. Kay was the daughter of Chuck Davis and her brother Glen rode Roman races in Nampa. The Roman racer rides two horses at the same time, with one foot on the back of each horse. Kay contested in the women's stake races.

Parker Jr. and his sister, Marian, were riding horses when many youngsters were still toddling. They rode from the family ranch near Ola four miles to the spot where Shirt Creek ran into Porter Creek. That is where the school was located and it was four miles back home after school. Parker Glen continued his interest in riding and was an active member of the University of Idaho Rodeo Club. He received a Bachelor, Masters and Ph.D. degrees in education from the U. of I. His career, far from the horseback hills of Jerusalem, Horseshoe Bend, and Ola, took him

as science instructor and coach to Pilot Rock, Oregon, where his
football team won the state championship; assistant superintendent at Rigby, Idaho and Las Vegas, Nevada; six years as state
and federal director of education; superintendent at Coeur
d'Alene until he resigned to organize Northern Idaho Bank,
became its president until the bank was sold and he remained to
help the new owners until he retired.

Parents of Mary Jane and Robert were John and Jean Quinn,
longtime residents of the area, and John was the postmaster of
Horseshoe Bend. Mary Jane learned all about horses and rodeo
from babyhood. She said her father "couldn't carry a tune in a
bucket, but he would put me on his knee and sing, 'Come a ti yi
yippee, yippee yi, yippee yo, Come a ti yi yippee, yippee yo.'"
Perhaps Mary Jane and Ben Dobson sang the same cowboy song
to their boys, Joe, who was then five, and Steve, four, to induce
them to be crown-bearers in 1949 when Josephine Dean was the
queen. Betty Rynearson was also a Horsehoe Bend Rodeo
Queen. A tragedy occurred at the 1950 rodeo when Lucille
Marsters and Ruby Mabe took part in the women's race. Ruby
died within minutes after the race.

John Quinn was one of twelve children and one brother,
Harold, bought a store at Horseshoe Bend. He was founding partner in the well-known Quinn Robbins Company in Boise. The full
dozen of Quinns were raised in the Jerusalem area.

Canyon Blazes Cowboy Trail

CALDWELL NIGHT RODEO

Reminders of how and why the western cowboy became an American hero are abundant with each showing of the Caldwell Night Rodeo, as today's riders prove worthy beneficiaries of that renown. That two cities in one county, Caldwell and Nampa, less than twenty miles from the capital city of Boise rank so high in the rodeo world when all put on splendid events annually, attests to the strength, the character and the volunteer assistance of those involved.

The Caldwell Night Rodeo celebrated its sixty-fifth year from August 17-21, 2000 at the grounds with thousands attending. Bobbie Farish, spokesperson, said that the atmosphere is the reason for the popularity. "The spectators are so close to the action they feel a part of it. The nation's top cowboys and bulls are featured."

The *1998 Professional Rodeo Cowboys Association Media Guide* and its listing of the "Top 50 PRCA Rodeos of 1997" show the Caldwell Rodeo in the number eighteen slot with total prize money of $171,411. The Snake River Stampede is twenty-first at $166,215. Pocatello has been in the top five for several years and listed as third one year. In 1997 Pocatello was fifth with a purse of $425,000.

Back in 1924, a United States Army officer arrived in Caldwell to inspect the 116th Cavalry and its facilities there. Based upon his report to headquarters, the Army warned that a National Guard unit would be established other than in Caldwell if new facilities were not built. Caldwell's Guard officers were quick to meet with members of the Commercial Club to plan a fundraiser to meet the challenge. A rodeo and gymkhana with racing was held October 2-4. Along with a bucking contest, there were stake, potato, egg and spoon, polo ball, and pony express races. It was a big success and members of the cavalry and business people met to form the Caldwell Amusement Association. Work began when the association took out a loan. A covered grandstand with an arena and race track took shape.

Ed Moody, whose name was linked with the Snake River Stampede from the get-go, was named the first arena director. Ed not only helped Nampa, but other communities sought his advice on their rodeos. Mustangs from the ranges and other horses rounded up in Jordan Valley, the Owyhee breaks, and the Weiser area were brought in for the events. There were no chutes, so the horses were snubbed behind the grandstand and the animals were pulled and tugged into the arena. If the horses bucked the men who brought them in were paid two dollars each. If not, no money. The best cowhands of the day and area took part and included Chet Keltner and Red Parker, Boise; John Davis of Homedale; Joe Dunn, Cy Johnson, Ed Moody, and Val Wiseman, Caldwell.

Danger is always present as an element of the excitement of rodeo and Bill Spencer and Charlotte Davis suffered injuries. Spencer, riding the bronc "Tar Baby" was thrown and suffered a broken leg and internal injuries. When it was learned that he had no money for medical expenses the fans donated one hundred dollars to help. Davis, unofficial queen, fell from her horse during the quarter-mile dash and was struck in the head by another horse. Both riders survived the first rodeo.

The July 18, 1979 *News-Tribune* had quoted a reprint of from an area newspaper of 1924: "All in all, it was an orderly crowd. Moonshine was not particularly in evidence, nor were there many of the underworld types who follow such shows. Occasionally a girl shocked the folks by smoking a cigarette openly and brazenly while treading her way around the jam on the street."

Success brought another rodeo in 1925, and on up the line.

Harry Charters, Dennis Sharp, and Jim Roeser compete in the "Wild Horse Race" at the 1952 Caldwell Night Rodeo.

No rodeos were held from 1926–1935. It was an immediate success when restored in 1936. The next year lights were installed and was the first rodeo in southern Idaho to have a night rodeo. During World War II rodeos were halted, but the crowds returned with the first show after the war, The largest crowd recorded was in 1949 when eighty-five hundred filled the grandstands. In the 1960s, the rodeo began losing money despite the crowds and the featuring of movie and television stars. The board adopted a new stance of featuring the rodeo riders and ropers with the slogan, "Where the Cowboys are the Stars." It grows more popular each year.

With great pride Caldwell claims record-setting Dee Pickett as one of its own. The *1998 ProRodeo Cowboys Association Media Guide* lists him as one of the Nation's top cowboys with the abbreviated description: Hometown: Caldwell, Idaho; Height: 6-1; Weight: 185; Born: Sept. 8, 1955, San Diego, CA; Family: wife, Brenda Lee; daughter, Sara; son, Cody [now a rodeo contestant

and football quarterback for the University of Washington];
College: Boise State University and Walla Walla Junior College;
Other Occupation: raising horses; Special Interests: All sports;
NFR qualifications: Calf roping 1979–85; Team Roping:
1978–87, 89, 93–94 (invited 1988, '90–92); PRCA member-
ship since 1978; 1997 earnings and finish: $23,337;
Achievements: World champion All-Around and Team Roping
(with Mike Beers), 1984; Original Coors Rodeo Showdown Team
Roping co-champion (with Martin Lucero), 1992; Wilderness
Circuit All Around champion, 1980, '82, '85–86, Calf Roping
champion 1980–81, Team Roping champion, 1978, '80–82,

This group of white-hatted cowboy businessmen from Caldwell are
having fun as they present Idaho Governor Len Jordan with a leather
bag in which to pack his rodeo gear and appear at the Caldwell Night
Rodeo in the early 1950s. Left to right: Fran Blomquist, Eddie Cole,
Clair Hull, Governor Jordan, Coley Smith, and Ellis White.
The photo is furnished by Beth and Dennis Smith, widow and son of
Coley. Brothers Dennis and Randy Smith laughingly remembered that
the committee hired the singing rage, Miss Patty Page, to entertain for
five nights. The weather was terrible and financially, the 1964 rodeo
was a disaster of massive proportions. The Smith brothers emceed
programs on ESPN and at benefits to pay part of the bills.
Future rodeos did well and a rodeo caravan ran through the towns in
Boise Valley. Dennis Smith and Phil Reberger dressed western and fired
blanks at one another in the streets. They organized a shootout in
downtown Caldwell with an audience of ten thousand.
Courtesy of Beth and Dennis Smith.

'84–87, '90, '94; PRCA Team Roping Rookie of the Year, 1978; Career Earnings: $1,388,983. *(See Chapter 16.)*

SNAKE RIVER STAMPEDE

With people, events and rodeo, great things often arise from small beginnings. The nationally known Snake River Stampede at Nampa, a rodeo ranked twenty-first among the hundreds held in the nation in 1998, began in a modest way. The year was 1915 and a group of cowboys were holding a bragging contest on who was best on a bucking horse. Two listeners decided to call the bluffs. Vic Elver and Lawrence Delp tied some ropes on posts around a vacant lot in downtown Nampa and invited the cowboys to contend. Only two of the fellows qualified for the finals and even the winning horse was so startled that it jumped into the middle of the crowd. Prize money was one hundred dollars, a huge purse for that day. The purse grew along with the contest then given the moniker "The Buck Show."

The next year, Nampa businessmen knew they had a good thing going and incorporated the Harvest Festival with "The Buck Show" as the main attraction. In 1919, they elected officers and hired Ed Moody as rodeo producer and stock supplier. This he did for seventeen years. Friendly and outgoing Leo Cremer became the producer in 1937 when the Nampa Harvest Festival and Rodeo became a night show. For the next twenty years Cramer provided the stock until the Beutler Brothers became producers.

Shows continued to be held at the recreation park north of town, and it became so successful that the board, along with changing its name to Snake River Stampede, "The Wildest, Fastest Show on Earth," purchased ground and built a stadium with a grandstand seating more than ten thousand. Because the shows sold out in advance, a fourth day was added to accommodate the crowds. Many traveled from faraway places and the event grew by word of mouth.

Nampa was excited with the success. Rodeo board president

Billie Warner
squares the
lariat loop as
he ropes this
calf at the
Snake River
Stampede,
Nampa.

Steve Dollorhide rides the hide of "Bill Blue Ski" at the Snake River Stampede.

A.T. Bullock said as early as 1924, "If the businessmen will get behind this show in the manner it deserves, there is no reason why Nampa cannot have, in a few years, an event that will be as well-known as the Pendleton Roundup or Cheyenne Frontier Days." The businessmen took him seriously and other communities in the area were encouraged to participate. A festival princess was chosen from each nearby community and from them, one was elected queen. She reigned over the rodeo, bicycle race, parade and fiddlers' contest.

During the Depression, the rodeo was one of the few affordable entertainments and crowds continued to increase. A remodel in 1934 added five horse, steer and calf chutes, and three hundred and fifty seats. In 1935 Nampa's Gold and Silver Jubilee was celebrated by adding another fifteen hundred grandstand seats. More significant changes came in 1936 when it was determined the next year's rodeo would be held in July, rather than during the festival in September and it became a nighttime event. In a naming contest, after much debate and many brainstorming sessions, Snake River Stampede won over other suggestions, such as Thunder Mountain Rodeo and Ski Hi. It was a growing time with added lights, eight bucking chutes, and twenty-five hundred more seats in the grandstand.

Certain names surface repeatedly when discussion turns to the leaders who were there from the beginning: Ed Moody, Marge Greenough, Leo Cremer, Bill Showalter, and Wick Peth. They and an increasing number of volunteers kept the event a continuing success. Some of the reasons are extracted from issues of the *Idaho Free Press* and the *News Tribune* in the 1920s and early 1930s: "Ed Moody was both a widely-respected bronc rider and stock contractor"; Marge Greenough thrilled audiences with her famous saddle bronc busting exhibitions and "became so popular at Nampa that she was invited back several times"; Leo Cremer dazzled Nampans for years with his rodeo producing abilities and unbeatable riding stock; Wick Peth gained fame as one of the best rodeo clowns in the nation. He first captured the

laughs and affections of Nampa Rodeo goers in 1960 when he
displayed courage on home turf.

President of the rodeo board from 1947 to 1951, Bill
Showalter became a hero to the homefolks when he oversaw the
building of a new grandstand in 1950. Gene Autry, the first
movie and television star to appear, had agreed to headline the
show if ten thousand seats were provided. A twenty-year loan
was taken and the Gene Autry Stadium was instituted. The
stands were jammed every night and hundreds more stood outside to listen to his singing over the loudspeakers. Gene Autry,
who made so many lifetime friends in Nampa, died in 1998.

Other show celebrities who followed included Rex Allen,
Roy Rogers and Dale Evans, Doc and Festus of television's
Gunsmoke and the Sons of the Pioneers. When the days of
singing cowboys waned, the rodeo board brought in famed western singers and it was in Nampa that Reba McEntire made her
debut as a headline entertainer.

Rex Allen, popular
Hollywood western
movie star, was a
great favorite of
Idaho rodeo fans
and appeared at a
number of the
shows across the
state. This shot was
taken at Coeur
d'Alene by Kyle
Walker.

The extra entertainment aided greatly in filling the stands, but, after all is said and sung, it is the cowboy and cowgirl who are the stars. During the late 1980s, the western singing celebrities were traded for more rodeo events. Women's barrel racing, team roping, the Wrangler bullfight were added and within a few years "mutton busting," the event popular with the kids, was included. The Miss Rodeo Idaho contest also takes place in Nampa during Stampede week.

In any list of outstanding world and national professional cowboys, close to the top will be found the names of Dean Oliver and Dee Pickett. *(See Chapter 16.)* Nampa claims both of them, saying that Oliver won his first calf roping championship at Nampa, and that Pickett learned roping from his Nampan uncle. Caldwell also makes claim to the duo, and who can blame other places in the state for only referring to them as "belonging to Idaho?"

Also listed among the 1950s rodeo famous who added to thrills at the Snake River Stampede are: Harry Charters of Melba, Deb Copenhaver, Pete Crump, Willard Combs, Sonny Davis, Tater Decker, Zeano Farris, Bill Linderman, Gerald Roberts, Jim Shoulders, Casey Tibbs, Harry Tompkins, Tom Tescher, Guy Weeks, and Marty Wood.

The new breed of rodeo contestant arrived along with the 1960s. Many of the young men and women were graduates of colleges and universities, some of which had added rodeo to the curriculum. A few even flew their own planes, permitting them to compete in as many as one-hundred rodeos a year. Riding, roping and steer wrestling were being taught at schools headed by people who had studied horses and other animals for years. Those teachers include more than a few retired from the arena.

Rodeo in the Owyhees

OWYHEE COUNTY

Wild and rugged Owyhee County is enormous and holds within its borders small deserts, great sand dunes, flat sagebrush land, rolling hills and ragged rock formations leading to mountain ranges reaching as high as six thousand feet. It covers almost five-million acres and is second only to Idaho County in the north central section of the state with its five-million, four thousand acres. It carries the original spelling of the then-territory of Hawaii, from which trappers were brought in 1818 to work in the Boise Basin. Several of them went on an exploratory trek into the Owyhee area that winter. They never returned. By spring they were presumed dead. The region was given the name of their birthplace and it was retained when the county was established in 1863.

Bruneau Canyon is the steepest in the nation; a chasm so narrow that a rock can easily be thrown across it at the top, with walls so sheer as to be nearly perpendicular. The geography and topography are as untamed as the wild horse herds for which it has been home for ages. The remaining herd of hundreds once numbered into the thousands. The first stampede in the Owyhees was in search of gold in 1863 when a group of prospectors heard of a gold discovery on Jordan's Creek. Stampedes or rodeos of the horsey kind have followed on Owyhee ranches throughout the county. It was into this wondrous country we drove on a hot August day to talk to the family of the late Jim Roeser, a born and bred cowboy still admired for the high standards he brought to life in and out of the arena.

Kathy Gaudry of Kuna loaded her big pickup with daughter
Claire, son Matt and the author along with a bountiful lunch and
cold drinks. We headed southwest with the sun and spirits high
as we drove through the green farmland of Canyon County on
Highway 95. The terrain abruptly changed to one of rugged
rocky pinnacles and dry gulch indentations as we left the main
highway and approached the Owyhee Hill entry of the road to
the Roeser Ranch on Squaw Creek. The creek has its headwaters
on Squaw Mountain, south of the ranch where the family members often see small bands of wild horses.

To the traveling visitor, Owyhee history could start at the
top of the hill about three miles from the Roeser's attractive and
utterly-western home. There is placed a sign: "Charles Brown—
Victim of Violence." Charles Brown was a notable sporting man
who frequented a neighboring gambling hall in the evenings. On
this particular evening he won a good sized pot of money. When
other players caught him cheating and charged him with it, he
snatched the poke, dashed out the door, grabbed the reins and
sprung onto his horse. The cheated players were right behind
him as he headed toward Marsing. When they came within
shooting distance, his lifespan was shortened. They buried him in
a shallow grave in a nearby gully located about one-quarter mile
southeast of the shooting. The grave was covered with huge boulders. On one of the largest is carved a simple message: Charles
Brown—1885.

With that bit of Idaho lore lodged in the mind it is easy to
imagine the thousands of mustangs running wild throughout the
colorful land. The Roeser Ranch is the place to hear about it.
Jim's son Tim and his wife, Rita, and their children have occupied
the home since the death of his father in 1997. They are both
rodeo-wise and carry on the family tradition. An outdoor arena
is available for their children and other young riders. They practice roping, barrel racing, pole bending, goat tying, calf and team
roping. To practice for the flag race, the American flag on a standard is placed in a bucket of sand. The kids ride up to and pick

Horses and roping are favorite pastimes of Tim and Rita Roeser and their children, Jeff, Kallie, and Scott.

up the flag, dash across the arena in an event timed for eight or nine seconds. Jim Roeser's covered arena is a sixty foot wide and ninety six foot long area used in cuttings, riding and roping during the winter months. It is also used for mechanical-cow cuttings and Four-H Club meetings.

Jim was born May 29, 1933 to Orval and Florence Quinn Roeser of Caldwell and graduated from Caldwell High School in 1952. The following year he joined the Rodeo Cowboys Association and competed in bareback and saddle bronc riding. He qualified for the NFR in saddle bronc in 1959–60–62 and qualified for the finals in bareback riding in 1961 and finished the season ranked thirteenth. His best season was 1960 when he earned money at thirty-five of the thirty-seven rodeos he entered to qualify for the Finals. His cowboy traveling companions were Bob A. Robinson of Jerome, Frank Davis of Bruneau, Larry Davis of Homedale, Kenny McLean of Okanogan Falls, British Columbia, and Jackie Wright of Dayville, Oregon.

Jim and Lola Layher were married in 1955 and lived in

Proud father Jim Roeser (center) is seated with his sons (left to right) Mark, John, Dan, and Tim, on a log cut especially for that purpose.

Caldwell. They became the parents of four sons; Dan, Tim, John, and Mark. Lola died of cancer in 1970, and Jim's second wife, Carlene Solomon, an accomplished rider, had been a well-known child singing star. They were married in 1977. She died in August, 1996.

Rita moved to Idaho from Livermore, California, and participated in the Idaho Cowboys Rodeo Association's rodeos. She tied goats and did breakaway and team roping. In the Idaho Girls Rodeo on July 25, 1999 at Garden Valley, Rita won fourth in the breakaway in 2.34 seconds.

Long before Rita and Tim and their children were involved in rodeo, his father was making a living at the sport. This was during the days when his boys and rodeo prize monies were both small. Much of the story of Jim Roeser's success is told in the trophies, paintings and photos which grace the walls and end tables in the living room. A silver

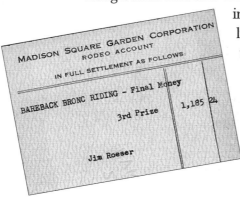

MADISON SQUARE GARDEN CORPORATION
RODEO ACCOUNT

IN FULL SETTLEMENT AS FOLLOWS:

BAREBACK BRONC RIDING - Final Money

3rd Prize   1,185 24

Jim Roeser

statue of a horse and cowboy carries the message: "Snake River Stampede Champion Bareback, Nampa, Idaho, 1956." There are many other awards leading up to World Champion bareback rider in 1953 at Madison Square Garden in New York City.

Five years after the New York win, Jim received wider acclaim when he rode "War Paint" in the July rodeo at Weiser. The horse was called "the toughest horse in the circuit" by the top ten bronc riders and had thrown some of the best, including Casey Tibbs, George McInmire, and Arvin Nelson. He was the first rider to draw and fellow riders razzed him as it was his second time to come up against War Paint. He had managed to stay with him for a full second before being thrown at the Roseburg, Oregon rodeo. This time was different because he knew what was coming. War Paint bucked so high out of the chute that the

Jim Roeser rode "War Paint" thirteen times in his rodeo career, winning eleven of the rides. This photo is taken in 1963 at the Oakdale, California Rodeo.

audience could see under his legs and feet. Jim felt he was four feet in the air and lowering his head. "He kept on going in a succession of leaps with all four feet off the ground. But this time I gave him a little more rein and kept my weight back. He's the toughest horse I ever rode," Jim said. When asked if he would ever ride him again, he said, "It's okay with me, if War Paint doesn't object too much." The prize money was $275. Behind the champ in the Weiser finals were Les Johnson, Jack Wright, and Bob Bailey.

Riding was a natural for Jim. He and his brother, Terry, and sister, Barbara, were born to the ranching parents. Their father, Orval, had a bucking string and with his friend Ed Moody, produced rodeos at Burns, Ten Mile, Vale, Star, Marsing, and Homedale and places in southeastern Idaho.

Prominent among the trophies in the living rooms at the homeplace is a golden horse atop the thirty-eight inch Clara Boag Memorial Trophy with the name and date; Jim Roeser 1961, heading a listing through 1975. Other winners and years are: Harry Charters 1962; Mark Schricker 1963 and 1964; Dean Oliver 1965; Ken Stanton 1966; Harry Charters 1968; Ken Stanton 1969; Bob Ragsdale 1970; Donnie Yaudell 1971; Clay Finley 1972; Bob Ragsdale 1973; Bob Johnson 1974; and Wayne Thawley 1975.

Jim came home from the Madison Square Garden Rodeo of September 23 through October 18, 1953, with the Championship and first prize award for bareback riding and the then-munificent sum of eight hundred and forty dollars. He won the bareback awards at the Calgary Stampede in 1952, 1962, and 1963. He was the All Around Cowboy in 1963. In 1959 in Dallas he placed at the National Finals Rodeo. Jim made front-page news in the February 8, 1960 Fort Worth (Texas) *Star Telegram* when, "After ten days of fierce competition Jim Roeser of Wilder, Idaho won first place among the saddle bronc riders." He was also the saddle bronc champion at the Southwestern Exposition and Fat Stock Show. Rex Allen, the popular cowboy singer and entertainer, performed at many events at which Jim rode and they became fast friends.

Jim expressed his philosophy at a June 18, 1987 meeting of the Caldwell Night Rodeo board of directors. The *ProRodeo Sports News* item of that date reported: "All directors of the Caldwell Night Rodeo were wearing rodeo gear at a meeting for young rodeo fans and participants meeting in the First Presbyterian Church. The PRCA gold card holder (Roeser) told the children, 'You don't need to tell people what you can do—just show them. If you feel like crying when you get hurt in the arena don't cry. Wait until you get back behind the chutes. Then you can cry.' "

During his growing-up years, Jim worked on various ranches, including the Albert Black Ranch at Bruneau and the UC Ranch out of Wells, Nevada. He began his bareback and saddle bronc riding then. He was a tall and lanky six-foot blonde, with twinkling blue eyes and a wide smile. He was described as, "Always having a smile for everyone."

Wilford Brimley

One of his best friends was Wilford Brimley, formerly of Caldwell and now living on a ranch in the neighboring state of Utah, the state where he was born on September 7, 1934. Years ago, he and Jim became such good friends they bought adjoining ranches in the Owyhee hills in 1986. Long before he became a television and movie celebrity, Wilford was a horseshoer. With all his shoeing gear in the back, Wilford traveled in his pickup from ranch to ranch. By the 1960s, Wilford was getting into stunt riding in movie westerns.

He and Jim were about the same age and Wilford has three sons near the ages of the Roeser children. Both liked the Owyhee country and the way of life it offered them and their families. When the opportunity presented they bought adjoining property. They then formed a partnership and purchased three hundred head of whiteface cattle and Black Angus bulls. Wilford also rode cutting horses and trained racehorses. The Roesers built both of their houses and barns in 1986. On the ranch, the two friends could combine their love of ranching, horses, and rodeo.

As with others who began movie careers as stunt riders and extras, Wilford soon became an actor. After making the decision to make acting a career, he located in Los Angeles and became known as one of the most dependable of the character actors. He has more than fifty movies to his credit and then added television acting in numerous films. Many of them classed as westerns, but he also was in Tom Clancy's *Op Center* and John Grisham's *The Firm*.

To millions of television watchers, he is most thought of as the kindly grandfather who urges the eating of hot oatmeal—"It's the right thing to do." Sometime ago a cartoon strip had a wife telling her husband they were having oatmeal for breakfast. He responded by saying he didn't like oatmeal. She replied, "What do you have against Wilford Brimley?" The final drawing showed him scratching his head and saying something to the effect, "This country is going crazy!"

Another of Roeser's cowboy close friends turned rodeo clown and then actor was Slim Pickens.

At ages eighteen and nineteen, Jim Roeser won the all-around cowboy championship. He won for the first time on July 5, 1952 at Caldwell and for the second time at the Ten Mile Rodeo. The following week he joined the Rodeo Cowboys Association (later called the Professional Rodeo Cowboys Association) and began to enter competitions throughout the country.

On a warm April 8, 1997 when spring was bustin' out all over the Owyhee country, Jim drove his pickup and trailer about five miles from the ranch and into the hills where some of his cattle had strayed into an adjoining field. He was expected by Vern Cobb, former employee and a longtime friend. When he didn't show up, Vern went to the home of Jim's oldest son, Dan, on down the road about seven miles. Vern said, "He isn't back yet, I'm going to look for him." Vern was joined by Dan, and Wade

Reany and left immediately in search. Vern waited at the highway with his pickup while Dan and Wade went further up the hill. They soon found Jim's horse alone where he had walked down to the fence line. Dan reached his Dad first and Jim's dog "Ike," a fine border collie, was beside him. Dan called back to Wade to get to a phone and call 911. Before help arrived they realized that Jim was dead. Ribs on both sides of his body were broken and they believed his horse stumbled and fell upon him.

A large group of very sad friends and family gathered at the Marsing-Homedale cemetery a few days later to attend the burial of one of Idaho's top rodeo champions—Jim Roeser.

Lonnie Wright, Honored

A cowboy would be hard put to garner more awards than has Lonnie Wright, who won his first award as a bull rider when he was thirteen. He is now sixty-one and such a strong supporter of the Idaho Cowboys Association that the association has named for him a rough stock All-Around category to Idaho Cowboy Association sponsored rodeos. The announcement was made in July 1999 in his hometown of Murphy and he is the Owyhee County appraiser. He came by his interest in riding and rodeo by watching his father ride bucking horses.

Some of his many wins include the team roping, bull riding and calf roping twice in each category; winning the All-Around Cowboy each year from 1966 to 1971; and at the Homedale Rodeo winning the All-Around ten or more times. He won the team roping championship awarded by the International Rodeo Association and has more belt buckles than he can ever wear and enough prize saddles to outfit a rodeo of his own.

When he thanked the ICA for the honor, he said, "When Harry Charters and Bob A. Robinson and others put the ICA together it was a good association. Right now they have a good board of directors and some good kids coming up. It takes people who aren't too radical or have too much special interest. We have to keep it going."

He concentrates his own participation in the ICA and the

Intermountain (Eastern Idaho) Professional Rodeo Association rodeos.

The Joyce Ranch

The Joyce Ranch received its name from Matt Joyce whose homestead was located on Sinker Creek about twenty three miles from Silver City and six miles from the county seat at Murphy. With the one lone parking meter on Main Street in Murphy, it is plain to see that more cowboys ride horses than drive cars. That parking meter has been the subject of many news items, magazine articles and a favorite subject of photographers and travel writers from all parts of the country.

Joyce was one of the thousands who came to the United States during the Irish immigration that followed the potato famine in 1845–1850. The "Great Famine" caused the deaths of over a million people from starvation and disease. Another million were forced to emigrate and sooner or later most of them located in the United States. He was born in Ireland's enchanting Galway Bay and was a sturdy young man who wanted to work. Once in America, he started a barge service freighting cargo up and down the Mississippi River.

When the Civil War broke out in 1861, young Joyce struck for the West. In Nevada he heard of the rich gold strike in the Silver City area high in the mountains. It was not his plan to become a miner. Always interested in food and fiber, he wanted to work at something to feed the miners pouring into the area.

In 1865 he homesteaded the one hundred and sixty acre ranch on Sinker Creek which still bears the Joyce name, but is commonly called the Nettleton Ranch. From that original acreage, upon which he stocked a herd of dairy cattle and planted a garden, grew the gigantic spread that is now 10,840 acres larger than the original.

Matt Joyce married and fathered nine children, each of whom filed on an additional one hundred and sixty acres as a homestead when he or she reached twenty-one. One daughter, Maggie, married Villo Nettleton. His British ancestors were pas-

Owyhee County wild horse roundup, coming into the Nettleton family's famous Joyce Ranch. *Photo by Harold Rhodenbough.*

sengers on the Mayflower and gradually worked their way west. Villo's son Hubert, known as Hugh to friends, married Helen Zaehringer. They had two children, Paul and Mary. All lived on the ranch and much of the land was and is roamed by the Owyhee's famed wild horses, although slowly diminished from thousands to hundreds. The Nettletons gradually purchased additional acreage as it became available and today the Paul Nettletons own eleven thousand acres. Most of it is sagebrush land, but they raise cattle along with a herd of twenty-five horses on six hundred and fifty acres.

Roaming of the Wild

Some stick with the belief that wild horses of Idaho are descendants of those brought to the country in the sixteenth century by the Spaniards. Others, including Paul Nettleton of the Joyce Ranch, think that the majority of them were fugitives of the Old Oregon Trail pioneer wagon trains and wandered away in the decade from 1830 to 1840 when loosed from the harness during overnight camping.

Many believe they are the descendants of the mustangs of the early days, small, wiry and tough. They were preferred by the Indians and cowboys. The word mustang comes from the Mexican word *mesteno,* meaning an animal with native characteristics, wild and unmanageable. It applied to wild cattle as well as the horses. Eventually it was applied to the horses alone. Some cowboys refer to them as "Broomtails." Fierce and fighting stallions fought off inferior breeds, keeping the standard at a high level. Settlers bringing the law with them cut down on the original mustangs because the law ruled that all mustangs belonged to the ranch where their grazing land lay. Many mustangs were killed off to preserve the grass because a band of mustangs required about fifty square miles to graze.

Old timers say that today's wild horses are an inferior breed that have become wild a second time and do not have the wiry toughness nor the fighting heart of the original mustang. Inferior or not, there is nothing quite so entrancing as to look up from the

At the late Hugh and Helen Nettleton's Sinker Creek Ranch in
Owyhee County two wild horses show primitive fury at being
confined to the corral after a life of freedom on the range. The word
"horsepower" comes alive as they battle it out. The Nettleton's son,
Paul, and his family now own the Joyce Ranch and have watched
many mustang roundups. The author was perched on the opposite
top corral rail beside the late Harold Rhodenbaugh, nationally
recognized photographer, when he snapped his new Roloflex at the
perfect moment. Earlier they watched Joyce Ranch cowboys roundup
and bring in about twenty-five spirited animals.
Photo by Harold Rhodenbaugh.

creekside in which the Joyce Ranch is located and see a string of
wild horses silhouetted against the setting sun as they are herded
along the rim of the hillside into the valley below.

From the early 1800s, the Owyhee has been considered
good country for all kinds of livestock. Its high lush grass, sagebrush land with a plentiful supply of water in the high country
make it a horse heaven. They winter in the low country and
Nettleton says, "There were probably up to twenty thousand
horses, most of which were wild in those days. After the
roundups seventy-five to eighty percent of the horses were
imprinted with the brand J for Joyce or MJ for Murphy Joyce."

Today the U.S. Bureau of Land Management is in charge of
the wild horses and yearly roundups are held to adopt off the animals and keep the numbers down.

GRAND VIEW
Walt Yarborough

A cowboy with a flair for western dress is Idaho State
Senator Walt Yarborough of Grand View. Always well-polished
cowboy boots were worn with western-cut jackets and trousers.
Walt's tie of choice was a bolo, usually a polished gemstone from
the Idaho hills. He told of the rodeos held in Grand View up until
1951. Cattleman Lyle Brace of the Brace Ranch furnished all the
stock. Walt said Lyle got the stock from the Paiute and Shoshone
tribes, whose members organized roundups of wild horses in the
desert and on the mesas. "Those were some rodeos!" Walt
exclaimed.

He told of Ace Black, son of the well-known Albert Blacks,
starting rodeo again in the late 1980s. As a young man Walt left
his home state of Missouri during the Depression years and
headed west. "Missouri had gone through two droughts, one right
after the other and the corn only reached two feet tall. We had
no grain and so we slaughtered the hogs and buried them in big
trenches. I knew I had to move and so I started out west and
landed in Hamilton, Montana. There I worked for the J.C. Penney

Company during the Christmas rush. Jobs were scarce and I helped out my uncle on his dairy. I moved further west and south and Owyhee County was the best thing to happen to me." Walt became involved in cattle and rodeo and eventually served as president of the Idaho State Fair and Rodeo Board.

Lyle Brace of whom Walt spoke as providing rodeo stock, arrived in the Owyhee country as a boy along with his younger brother, Neil, and their parents, Earl and Winnie Brace, about 1910. They bought the Lambert place on Juniper mountain and stocked the nearly two thousand acres with four hundred head of Hereford white face beef cattle. Lyle's daughter, Belva McCullough, now of Prineville, Oregon, remembers her parents telling of the family traveling by covered wagon from the White Bird area to Owyhee. Part of the route was on the Old Oregon Trail near Baker City, Oregon. The boys were seven and ten and it was a true adventure for them as they camped along the way. It was in a bar in Jordan Valley that Earl heard the Lambert place was for sale and bought it.

During the early 1950s, they purchased "the old Ray Brooks Ranch on the south side of the Snake River," Belva said and remembers that her father had two cherished Russian wolfhounds along with the beef cattle and horses. The three hundred horses on the ranch were primarily thoroughbreds and sold to the U.S. Army.

Frankie Dougal of Jordan Valley and her late husband, Chuck, worked for the Braces for many years and recalled that "ranch rodeos" were often held throughout the county. The Brace boys, Frank and Charlie Maher, Tex Payne, Don Dennie, Jack Staples, and Chuck Dougal participated in rodeos on the ranches, riding rough stock and practicing team roping and bronc busting. Rodeos were held in Murphy, Grand View, Bruneau, and Jordan Valley. Frankie remembers that several of the cowboys won saddles and silver buckles in competition. As Walt Yarborough said, "Those were some rodeos!"

Rodeo in Ada County

Built in a valley with a river called the "Boise" running through it, Boise City was established as a military post in 1868. It was only four years later that indication of the town becoming a rodeo mecca made its appearance in the form of horse races.

Western Idaho Fair

It is a short ride from the arenas of Caldwell and Nampa to that of the capital city and every August hundreds of rodeo fans from both cities drive to Boise for the Western Idaho State Fair and Rodeo. According to Don Bich, former manager and board member of the Western Idaho Fair and Rodeo Association, a forerunner of the rodeo took place more than a hundred years ago when the Boise City Jockey Club sponsored a horse race at the Ada County Fair and cattle show in October 1872. It was a success and by 1897, was such a biggie that other western states were eager to participate. Carpenters worked overtime building stalls to accommodate the hundreds of horses arriving by railroad. Newspapers gave the races as much coverage as the fair proper.

Cowboy contests gained equal attention. Authentic cowboys from southern Idaho ranches rode their working horses in half-mile running races, twenty mile relay, and steer roping. Top cowhands included Fred Bennett of Soda Springs who won over well-known cowboys Joe Black of Owyhee County and Jack Dolan of Cassia County.

In 1897, a new grandstand was erected for the fair. Locals loved it. Arthur A. Hart authored a booklet, *A Centennial History 1897–1997,* for the Western Idaho Fair in which he quotes the *Statesman* newspaper, "Probably nowhere else in the world is there a grandstand from which such a view can be secured as that which is spread out before those who attend the races here on a fall afternoon. The structure is at a point where the full sweep of the mountains is in the field of vision . . .."

Several towns in Idaho nominated a local girl for fair and rodeo queen, and winner was twenty year old, six feet tall and blonde Bessie Vollmer, daughter of a Lewiston merchant. Maude Horrie and Theresa O'Farrell, both of Boise, were runners-up. Fifteen hundred parade participants included a hundred cowboys sporting shiny revolvers, and the royal carriage was pulled by four white horses. Among the others were volunteer fireman dressed in red, white, and blue, businessmen, reporters, doctors, grocers, butchers, and the Gate City Oregon Short Line Band from Pocatello.

From its founding, in 1849, volunteers directed the Idaho Intermountain Fair Association's operation. In 1902, John McMillan was named president. McMillan emigrated from Scotland and, with others of his family, had a definite influence upon the growth and development of southwestern Idaho. Descendants of the family are still involved in rodeo. Three hundred racehorses called "The biggest string of thoroughbreds ever seen in the West" came to Boise.

In 1899, a bucking bronco contest was added to horse racing and steer roping. While those contests were shaping contemporary rodeo, the skill of the cowboys and the danger of the sport brought out large crowds. On August 18, 1902, William S. "Buffalo Bill" Cody arrived in Boise a week before the fair with his Wild West Show. Among his performers were Sioux Chief Sitting Bull and gun-toting Annie Oakley. In the early 1900s, Boise held a twenty-mile relay race and polo was popular with large crowds attending the matches.

By 1913, the rodeo had come into its own and was named the Boise Stampede. Riders, doggers, and stock arrived after participation in the Cheyenne Frontier Days and the Pendleton Roundup. Western movies had become popular. Hoot Gibson, who had a run of many years, beginning with the "silents" and successfully made the transition to the "talkies," was only eighteen when he appeared in Boise. The previous year he won the "Cowboy Champion of the World" title at Pendleton. In Boise, Gibson won the relay and pony express races and was a finalist in bronc bucking event.

Rodeo celebrities and western singing groups attending the fair and rodeo, included the great Yakima Canutt in 1920 and Slim Pickens in 1946. Both were genuine cowboys before they became movie stars and, over the years, appeared many times at various Idaho rodeos. Pickens built an enviable record as rodeo clown. He was a great favorite with Idaho audiences and made many lasting friends in the state. Years after his rodeo appearances, in July 1966, he visited both Lewiston and Winchester. As the driver in the popular film *Stagecoach,* he appeared for the premier of the film and attended the celebration of the seventy-fifth anniversary of the Winchester rifle in the little Idaho town of the same name.

Canutt was a repeat winner as all-around world champion in 1917, 1919, 1920, and 1923. Much of his Hollywood acting career was during the days of silent films and, after 1930,

From neighboring Washington, Yakima Canutt performed at so many Idaho rodeos, he is often said to be an Idahoan. The State would have happily adopted him. This picture displays the charm which won many friends. The steer has been "dogged" and Yakima gives a big smile and raises his hand in victory. *Courtesy of Weiser Museum..*

involved appearing in stunt scenes. He later directed hazardous scenes and continued to do so until over seventy.

Among the best known rodeoers were Frank and Bonnie McCarroll who lived in Boise. *(See Chapter 17.)* Both appeared at Pendleton, Cheyenne, Chicago and Madison Square Garden, as well as performing in before crowned heads in England.

In 1938, the fair and rodeo board contracted with Moomaw and Bernard of Washington state to handle the rodeo. Nineteen riders and doggers from Idaho were among the hundred entrants.

Boise Rodeo has continued to grow along with the Western Idaho Fair. On August 25 and 26, 2000, the Idaho Cowboys Association (ICA) celebrated forty-four years of offering rodeo competition levels to all ages. Audrey Eldridge of Nampa and Boise, promotions director, said "The ICA offers an opportunity for young athletes just starting out, as well as past Pro Rodeo Cowboy Association champions, to experience the thrill of the sport while staying near home and traveling as a family." She added that in many cases more than one member of the family competes against another.

ICA president is Andy Bowden of Fruitland and Brad Carpenter of Nampa is vice president. Orla Knight of Glenns Ferry is secretary.

Only the top fifteen in each event competed for more than forty thousand dollars in cash and prizes. The top fifteen money winners compete in rodeos during the entire summer. Contestants from all over the Northwest join local cowboys and cowgirls. To add a bit of zest to the program, Bull Fighter Tim McNeery rode a bull backwards.

The ICA Edmark GM Superstore 2000 Championship finals resulted in the following winners: Mark Gage, Jordan Valley, saddle bronc; Toby Miller, Nampa, bareback rider; Joel Scrivner, Nampa, calf roper; Cherie Scrivner, Nampa, barrel racing; Jeff Bowden, Meridian, steer wrestling; Marlow Eldridge, Nampa, team roping; Kyle Joslin, Eagle, bull riding; and his sister,

*Action is
king
at the*

*Idaho Cowboy
Rodeo Finals*

*at the
Western
Idaho
Fair.*

Lori Joslin, breakaway roping. The stock contractor was Bill Stephens of Caldwell. Committee member is Mick Hessler of Weiser.

Many Idaho communities hold smaller rodeos and often in conjunction with fairs. Twinkie Stafford of American Falls, which sponsors an annual rodeo, is president of the Intermountain Pro-Rodeo Association. Meridian holds an open rodeo for youthful participants but is not ICA sponsored. ICA rodeos include Apple Blossom Days at Payette and Gold Dust Days at Idaho City, both held in May; Weiser Valley Roundup, Nyssa Night Rodeo, White Bird Days, all in June; a second Gold Dust Days, Idaho City, Rupert Rodeo, Elmore County Fair and Rodeo at Glenns Ferry, Adams County Fair and Rodeo at Council, all in July; Minidoka County Fair and Rodeo at Rupert, Gem County Fair and Rodeo at Emmett, Cambridge Rodeo, Owyhee Fair and Rodeo at Homedale, and the Payette County Fair and Rodeo, New Plymouth, all during the month of August.

Meridian Lions Rodeo

The Meridian Lions Club has sponsored an amateur open rodeo for young riders and old timers for the last eleven years. It is held the last part of September on a Saturday and Sunday and there were one thousand paid admissions in 2000. It is completely local for western Idaho and eastern Oregon riders and one hundred and fifty contestants entered. Mutton Bustin' contests are held for the kids and adults compete in bareback and bull riding, calf and team roping, steer wrestling, saddle bronc riding, breakaway roping, and barrel racing.

"We borrow an arena, seats, and chutes but own the bleachers," explained Lion Club member Fred Beckman. "The money goes for good causes, primarily to the eye bank at Saint Alphonsus Hospital and to support the Eye Testing trailer," he added.

Mountains and Space

ELMORE COUNTY
Mountain Home

It had been many years since Mountain Home held a rodeo, so three balls of fire, Dena Ranft, Billy and Kristen Riley have led the effort to arrange the Mountain Home Optimist Junior Rodeo the second weekend in August since 1998. The Optimist Club decided that such a project for the kids would be of benefit to the area. The rodeo grounds was given to the city years ago when the former rodeo group disbanded and the event is held with a minimum budget. There is a modest six dollar entry fee for each event.

Donations are accepted and a raffle is held, but there is no entry charge. About one hundred youngsters participated and three hundred parents and grandparents generally make up the cheering gallery. From six to sixteen the boys and girls vie in steer and calf riding, roping, barrel racing, and pole bending. For the five-year olds and under who have their own stick horses the events include riding stick horses to race around the barrels, ride up to the goats and untie the tails, roping of animal dummies, and mutton bustin'.

Glenns Ferry

An Idaho State Park at Three Island Crossing along the Snake River now marks the spot where hundreds of horses, oxen and horse teams pulling covered wagons and immigrants along the Old Oregon Trail in the westward movement. "Betty thinks I'm crazy, but it is really something to do what those wagon train drivers did in the 1800s," Bud Allen said of his wife's reaction to his developing the exciting and somewhat hazardous Three Island Crossing Reenactment the second weekend in August each year.

In 1986, Bud was the first driver since wagon train days to take a team and wagon across the river. Previous to that for a couple of years he had taken just the horses. From 1986 through 1993, he took both the wagon and team. Two of his sons, Buddy and Jody, performed as leaders and a third son, Rick, kept the rope to steady the wagon. Since then a ferry was built and Bud continues to make the annual trek, but now drives the team and wagon onto the ferry.

Much rich history is lodged in Elmore County and most of it has to do with cattle and horses and rodeo. Bud Allen and many cowboy friends were holding rodeos long before official membership in a semi-pro association and later the Idaho Cowboys Association. Some of the cowboys remembered by Bud are twins Calvin and Alvin Gorrel, bronc riders, and a third

Elmore County Rodeo Royalty 2000: (clockwise, starting on the left) Claire Gaudry of Kuna, Senior Queen; JaDene Palmer of Mountain Home, Junior Princess; Courtney Mitchell of Mountain Home, Junior Queen; Amanda Fittje of Nampa, Senior Princess.
Courtesy of Studio 60, Nampa.

brother, Dan Gorrel, who was a good calf roper. Bud Godby and Ernie Stevens were calf ropers and all took part in riding the circuit in Idaho, Oregon, and Nevada and sometimes into Montana. "I guess you could have called us the 'Weekend Warriors', as we took off for some rodeo or another. We never made much money, but we had a great time," Bud said.

During the days before the Idaho Cowboy Association was formed, Bud often joined Dean Oliver, Bob Robinson, and Harry Charters, all of whom became world champion rodeo stars, as well as other outstanding riders in rodeos along the circuit. Bud was a bronc buster and bull rider, but "mainly it was bareback and calf roping." He has an interesting reason why he feels that the eight-time world champion calf roper Dean Oliver will never have his record broken. "Dean was so outstanding for that day when he was a champ, without all the training that today's young ropers receive. When Dean was calf roping, ten seconds was outstanding. Now it is eight to ten seconds with better horses and terrific athletes who have trained hard. This high school rodeo training is a great thing and roping, on the average, is a lot faster. So, some of these youngsters will do better, timewise, than Dean did and may even win two or three years in a row. Then along will come another youngster, who is even better trained and best the record. But it is not likely that another calf roper will remain champion for eight go-rounds.' "

The Allens have lived on a cattle and horse ranch at King Hill forty years and hacked the ranch out of the sagebrush. Betty may chide Bud about his bravado in driving a team and wagon through the Snake River at Three Island Crossing, but they proudly stood together in 1995 to be inducted into the Livestock Hall of Fame. "Betty has always been a great helpmate on the ranch and we are proud of our three boys and two girls," he adds. Their youngest son, Buddy, is now running the family farm. On the ranch they have two hundred and fifty "mother" cross Hereford-Angus cows which are bred to Simmental bulls to produce an outstanding animal.

That area and specifically the Butler family ranch was the first to bring Black Angus cattle into Idaho.

The rodeo grounds at Glenns Ferry are located at the east edge of town. The Allens have their own arena built by the family and now used by grandsons and a granddaughter to practice for rodeo.

When the Fair and Rodeo committees were choosing the person to be honored as the first Grand Marshal of the annual parade, they quickly decided upon Alice Trail, who has been involved in or a supporter of all the good programs, particularly for the young people, since she and her husband Lee moved to Elmore County from Payette in 1937.

She helped start 4-H clubs and became a leader over thirty years ago; was a leader of Girl and Cub Scouts, Job's Daughters, and a Sunday School teacher. She has seventeen grandchildren, sixteen great-grandchildren, and one great-great grandson. One grandson, Dennis Pruett, rode bulls in rodeo and a granddaughter, Holly Brooks, has done so well in barrel racing at home and Southern Idaho College in Twin Falls that she is attending the University of Idaho for 2001 winter-spring semester where she will be a member of the Vandals Rodeo Team.

TWIN FALLS COUNTY

Rodeo fans and boosters think it symbolic that Twin Falls County history began with the 1863 establishment of Ben Holladay's Stage Line. Aptly called the "stage king," Holladay named it the Overland Stage Line, but those who admired and appreciated him continued to dub it as his Stage Line. The first station was constructed at Rock Creek and the first store built in 1865 at the site of the Stricker Ranch. Cattle raising was an important industry until the late 1870s when a drought eliminated the cattle, but today in the mountainous areas, there are still thousands of cattle and sheep on the range.

As with many other Idaho rodeos, the Twin Falls County Fair preceded arena action. The fair began in 1907 with a

Halloween Festival and from then until 1915, due to weather conditions, the activities were spasmodic. A group of Filer residents made plans for a permanent county fair and funds were solicited to buy the present fairgrounds location. The purchase was completed in 1916 and some livestock sheds were built, the dining hall and buildings for the antique show and other displays were finished. In the first section of the grandstand the racetrack was graded. During the Depression years 1932–1934, the fair was discontinued, but the Pomona Grange sponsored a junior fair for 4-H and Future Farmers. There had been horse racing on the fast track prior to 1932. Actually, it was due to a waning interest in horse racing that the first rodeo was produced in 1935. The attendance was so good that additional grandstand room was needed.

The rodeo grew in attendance and a third addition was built in 1938. In 1950 new grandstand bleachers were added, making room for thirty-six hundred. In November of 1969 the rodeo grandstands burned and rebuilding began in 1970. That year Miss Rodeo Idaho, Lana Brackenbury (Parker), of Jerome was crowned Miss Rodeo America.

In 1971, Twin Falls had the honor of hosting the first and only national high school rodeo finals to be held in Idaho. In 1991, the County Fair's seventy-fifth anniversary was observed and the rodeo had a new PRCA producer, Ike Sankey from Cody, Wyoming. There were three nights of rodeo. Members of the Fair board were: Gary Grindstaff, Buhl, president; Jack Ramsey, Filer, vice president; Gene Schiffler and David Wood, Twin Falls; Jerri Cox, Castleford; Terry Cummins, Murtaugh; and Carl Feldhusen, Kimberly.

In 1996, a new manager, John Pitz of Worland, Wyoming, arrived as producer of events. A large video screen and wild horse races were added to the rodeo. The name was changed to the Magic Valley Stampede. Miss Rodeo Idaho was crowned for the last time at the Twin Falls County Rodeo. The queen pageant which had been held there for thirty years was moved to the

Snake River Stampede at Nampa, which could provide a larger audience. *(See Chapter 17.)*

Announcer from Hansen

Zeb Bell of Hansen is the only Idaho announcer ever to qualify for the National Finals Rodeo. He was so accomplished that he qualified five times.

Comments from newspapers around the country explaining the type of behind-the-microphone work Zeb Bell did for rodeo included: "As much a part of the rodeo as the bulls, clowns, and cowboys is the rodeo announcer. He (Bell) calls each of the events adding little anecdotes about the cowboys and stock, trades insults with the clowns and helps the fans enjoy the rodeo just a little bit more.

"They are the key and the link to the action. Announcers are the pacesetters, scorekeepers, and teachers. They acquaint the crowd with the cowboys, the stock, and the sport."

Zeb joined the PRCA after three years in amateur ranks. He was the "Man behind the Mike" at major rodeos from Washington to Wisconsin, and was invited back to every rodeo he announced.

For years, a microphone was part of his wardrobe. In the early seventies, Zeb was one of southern Idaho's best-known radio and sports personalities.

Despite the fact that Zeb walked with crutches, as a result of a polio bout, he was an active PRCA team roper and NCHA cutter when not informing rodeo fans about the arena action.

CASSIA COUNTY

Rodeo history in Cassia and Minidoka counties dates back to the early years of the century, according to historian Ralph W. Maughan, longtime columnist for the *South Idaho Press*. Cowboys organized roundups of wild horses from the rangelands to the south, and when they triumphed in climbing onto the backs of the snorting, bucking, whirling animals they did their best to ride for at least a few seconds. More often than not, the wild horse dumped the cowboy into the dust. Being a cowboy, he kept coming back for more and enjoyed the ride. Many wild horses were broken to ride and became part of the ranch stock as a result of these genuine roundups.

The first Cassia County Rodeo is said to have been held in 1911. Dean Draper, secretary of the county fair board, says it was in 1909. The site was Albion, then the county seat, and in connection with the fair. The old building in which it was held stood just outside the town in the direction of Mount Harrison. Horse races and various other events took place in an adjacent racetrack.

The Cassia County Fair moved to the present location in Burley in 1915, but rodeo did not become an integral part of the event until about 1931.

Old-timer Kelly Poulton remembers the first rodeos in Oakley were on the Al Nelson farm northwest of present Oakley High School. Later the Light Air Park was built near the site where the Latter Day Saints Church is now. Rodeos, horse racing, and other activities were well attended.

This first fair exhibit building in Cassia County was located in the hills above Albion, which was the county seat when that fair was held in 1911. A hometown rodeo occurred nearby. Lauri Harpster was the photographer and won first prize in the picture contest with this shot. The fairgrounds are now located in Burley and have modern exhibit buildings.

Early rodeos gradually included steer wrestling or bulldogging, calf roping, Brahma bull and wild bronc riding. Typical of the stringent rules limiting the participants were those for bareback bronc riding. The cowboy must ride without bridle or halter. A rope was looped around the animal's neck for handhold. The other hand was held aloft and could not touch the horse at anytime.

Horse pulling contests sorted out the team capable of pulling the heaviest load and often the Sheriff's Mounted Posse was a prominent part of the celebration.

About 1943, the popular riding club known as the Oakley Vigilantes established the current rodeo grounds, where annual contests are held.

Likely the first Cassia County Rodeo Queen was Jeanna Hitt, who was named in 1915. It is not known if others were chosen each year thereafter, but queens have been named continuously since 1937.

That year Ruby Parke of Declo was chosen by the fair board members and from that start, the present system was established on selecting queen candidates, based on riding ability, appearance, poise, and personality.

Now Mrs. Kalensky, the 1937 Rodeo Queen, still remembers that for the three days of the fair, she wore a white gabar-

Cassia County Fair and Rodeo Royalty in 1951 were Barbara Fairchild, Queen (center); Faye Adams (left) and Pat Jones (right), Princesses.

dine suit, red silk blouse, and white tie, with a matching white topcoat to protect against heavy rains. Burley merchants contributed the wardrobe.

Those directing Cassia's 41st Annual Fair and Rodeo in 1951 were Joe Carlson, Wes Sizemore, George McGonigal, I. H. Harris, Bob Wake, Clarence Matthews, Saul Clark, Glenn Bodily, and Roy Ehlers.

MINIDOKA COUNTY

Rodeo started at Rupert in Minidoka County in the late 1920s and the fairgrounds were located where Memorial School now stands. John Trevino, Don Dickson, and Lester Culley all remember the rodeos there, but not the precise date for the earliest event.

In the late 1940s, the Minidoka County Sheriff's Posse, headed by Ron Hawkes, purchased land for the Minidoka fairgrounds and rodeo. The grandstand was moved from the site in town and the Posse staged the first rodeo in 1948. Ron Hawkes' wife Verna, still an expert cowgirl at eighty-one, was named "Grandma Queen" of the rodeo in 1987.

After World War II the Wild West entertainment outfits began to specialize in rodeo and organized events began in the Cassia-Minidoka wide-open spaces.

Oakley cattleman Bruce Bedke says that the early day cowboys were entertaining themselves, rather than a doting public, and would round up some of the abundant wild horses out on the range, herd them into a makeshift corral or arena which was formed by driving cars and pickups into a circle. There were no fences, no grandstand nor any bleachers—just limitless fun and entertainment.

Leo Ellibee

Leo Ellibee was one Rupert cowboy who received much of his training in handling horses from the habit of his father of putting him on a skittish or half-broken horse and telling him, "Ride." During the years that he and his wife, the former Virginia

"Peg" Paulsen of Parma, owned and operated the little store at Pinehurst, Leo put together the story of his life. Nearly all of it had some connection to horses: working on ranches, driving a thirty-six head hitch during grain harvest, wrangling Idaho's wild ones, and later helped organize the Parma Saddle Club and drill teams, and outfitted and guided in the Big Creek area. A few of his well-known guests were Bing Crosby and the *Gunsmoke* cast stars Amanda Blake, James Arness, Doc, and Festus.

It was in 1924 when Leo was eleven that he moved with his family from Salt Lake City to Rupert and his uncle, Ira Whitney, remembered the trip as plagued with problems and Leo as a "wild, tobacco-chewing, cussing, hard-riding cowboy." While in high school, he spent the summers working on the Meadows family ranch near American Falls. He was soon entering the rodeos in Rupert and remembered a highlight of his life as going to the Madison Square Garden Rodeo with Bannock-Shoshone rider Willie Knight who enjoyed, along with Leo, wrangling wild horses out on the range. In later years, he wrangled in the Owyhee breaks, Jordan Valley, and in the Ola area. During the time he was hazing, his friend Lonnie Shurtliff flew the plane to guide the horses into the enclosures.

When the days arrived for Leo to hang up his saddle and tend to work at the Pinehurst store and the repair shop next door, he never lacked for old friends stopping by enroute to either north or south Idaho to reminisce of the great days cowboying.

Gaylord Phillips

Eighty-four years old on December 29, 2000, Gaylord Phillips of Heyburn still rode saddle bronc in the Old Timers Rodeo at Idaho Falls during the previous July. He also was honored as Grand Marshal of the parade. The National Senior Pro Rodeo Association sponsored both events.

Gaylord Phillips spent a good portion of his eighty-four years riding horses, sometimes bareback and others in the saddle. During his heyday, he entered forty or fifty rodeos a year, including Calgary and Madison Square Gardens, along with many in Idaho and Utah, Colorado, Montana, and Wyoming.

Born in Kentucky to the Luther Manley Phillips, he came west in a covered wagon and settled at Buhl when he was about eight. His father was a horse trader, buying, selling, and trading horses. When his mother contracted tuberculosis the doctor recommended a warmer climate. So the father built a covered wagon and the family traveled to Salina and Cedar City in Utah and other neighboring states. When Gaylord was about sixteen, the family moved to Rupert and he started rodeoing by riding bareback. "I also made an attempt at bull riding. Rodeo wasn't all fun. There are a lot of heartaches, too," he said. He explained that every time he won anywhere from three to five hundred dollars he bought cattle to graze on a little ranch he had. "I guess I won at bareback for eight or nine years and the money went to the ranch."

His memory took him back to times of riding with Bob Burrows of Idaho Falls and with Slim Pickens, renowned rodeo clown who later appeared in a number of western movies. "Slim also rode saddle bronc and bareback and he was quite a bull-bleeper. For years after we had ridden together, Slim would drive three-or-four hundred miles to stay with us when he was on the clown circuit.

"One season when we were rodeoing together in the sixties, that tall and skinny Slim's horse fell on him and hurt his right leg. My horse did the same thing with me, but injured my left leg. The guys we traveled with insisted that we bunk together since we had hurt opposite legs and it would work out just fine."

Gaylord says he is "half-retired" now. For thirty-five years he was an auctioneer for farm and estates sales. He and longtime friend Jay Whittle bought and operated the Burley sale yard for many years. He and his wife live on thirty acres at Heyburn where they run about twenty-five head of cattle.

Albion Saddle Bronc Rider

South of Burley on State Highway 77 is Albion, the hometown of Kent Cooper, an outstanding saddle bronc rider. He is often listed as being from Declo a few miles north. Both towns are proud to claim. It is likely that Vernal, Utah would feel the same. Kent's best ride with a score of 93 is the second highest saddle bronc score ever recorded and it happened in Vernal in 1980. That was before he reached the National Finals Rodeo. But, when he made it in 1981, he was on a roll and repeated four years in a row.

With Kent Cooper, it was not the number of rodeos in which he appeared, but placing in more of the ones in which he rode. Most cowboys on their way to the Finals go to the maximum rodeos allowed, but he made it by riding in half that number. Nevertheless, he placed about sixty percent of the time. He had injuries which kept him from attending more. In a rodeo at Whitefish, Montana, a horse fell on him and wrenched his knee. A second flipping horse in Burley gave him compressed fractures in three vertebrae.

He loves to ride and said, "If I wasn't rodeoing for a living, I would be trying to get my saddle horse to buck." In the winter he traps in the mountains near his home. Among the coyotes he usually gets are a few mountain lion, bobcats, or raccoon. He made his wife a bobcat coat, but sells most of the skins.

GOODING COUNTY
Gooding

In the early 1860s, Ben Holladay's historic stageline of thirty-three hundred miles across the country ran smack-dab through what is now Gooding County. There are still relics of a stagecoach station at Uhrlaub's Crossing and the stage horses rested at what was appropriately named Horse Heaven. Horses were known to the area millions of years ago when the primitive three-toed pygmy horse roamed the Hagerman valley. The discovery of fossil remains of the little horse has made it a fertile field for scientific research.

Gooding's interest in horses is deep in its soil and surges

above the surface at rodeo time. Key to the fine stock provided is Pat and Juanita O'Maley's Slash-T Rodeo Ranch. The development of rodeo stock began in the early 1980s when poor beef prices and water shortages compelled them to move into other areas. The result places them among Idaho's top stock providers for at least thirty rodeos a year. Among the many rodeos to which they truck their animals are St. George, Utah college rodeos; high school rodeos in Oregon; Shoshone, Emmett, Homedale, Jerome, Hailey, the new rodeo in Idaho City, and on the Fourth of July at Parma. And always at Gooding. Juanita said, "There's no lessening of rodeo in Idaho. In fact, it is on the grow."

Among their thirty-five bulls are several that have already become tough-to-ride legends. They include "White Lightning," "Smokin' Joe" (Don Gill, Gooding Fair and Rodeo manager, says, "No one has been able to ride him yet"), "Hang 'em High," and "E.T." When asked why the name E.T., Don Gill said, "Because he was first called D.T., and that didn't sound right. E.T. seemed to fit his red hide and red eyes and he looks like he is from outside this world." He went on to say that if "E.T." wasn't ridden at the 2000 rodeo in Jordan Valley, the three thousand dollar bounty that has been on him for a few years would be taken off.

Along with the bulls and thirty steers, the O'Maleys keep about two hundred horses and one hundred calves. They know rodeo from the ground up, and Pat was Idaho state bull riding champion in the years 1976, 1977, and 1981, as well as placing often during his quarter-century in the arena. Juanita is a member of the well-known Leguineche family and her brothers, Joe, Louie, and John are all interested in the sport. Joe's son, Jerome, won second in bull riding at the Idaho Cowboy Association Rodeo, held along with the State Fair at Boise in late August, 2000.

The O'Maley's two daughters, Tammy and Patty, have excelled in the arena as high school and college riders. Tammy vied in high school rodeos from 1990 through 1994, suffering injury to her fingers and putting her out of the sport. Patty won the national in college competition at goat tying and breakaway. She "practically put herself through Idaho State University and its master's program with her rodeo winnings," a proud mother said. In breakaway (the rope is tied to the saddle horn with a small string which breaks when the calf is caught), Patty followed in her father's boot steps as he has entered breakaway contests in Idaho, Montana, Oregon, and Washington for a number of years.

Seventy-fifth Year

The beginning of the millennium is the seventy-fifth year for rodeo in Gooding. It was 1925 when Gooding's Rotary Club decided to produce a harvest festival in the old Calvary barn. Along with festival were contests with sabers, horseback and other riding contests. This was the beginning of rodeo in the town. Pete Grubb of Salmon, one of Idaho's greatest bronc riders rode away with the overall championship from the tenth anniversary show in 1935.

Just as Pat and Juanita O'Maley are outstanding in providing animals for the rodeos, Don and Denise Gill are of equal importance in planning and managing the Fair and Rodeo. Gooding is more than lucky, it is blessed to have the two couples involved in the major activity of the year. Don feels that the tenth event in 1935 created a backlog of fun and goodwill that still permeates the modern shows. Merchants arranged an "arrest and penalty" program to encourage western dress for all citizenry and visitors in advance of the rodeo. Those who did not wear jeans, shirt, boots and Stetson were apprehended and padlocked to telephone posts downtown. The mayor, a U.S. Senator, county legislators, and well-known figures about town were among those who learned to hug a telephone pole.

JEROME COUNTY

The Jerome Rodeo is held in late July along with the county fair and is produced by the Slash-T Rodeo Company. There is an added purse in the neighborhood of five thousand dollars. It is sanctioned by both the Idaho Cowboy Association and Idaho

Professional Rodeo Association. There is no gate charge and attendance is stretching toward twenty-five thousand. Rob Lundgren is the manager.

Many fine riders and wrestlers have come from the area. One of the best is Mike Smith, steer wrestler, who stood third in the National Finals Rodeo rating in 1993. His career earnings near the half-million mark.

Another Jerome cowboy to whom the area points with pride is Mickey Young, bareback rider. When he reached his thirties he said, "I still feel like I'm eighteen. I stay in good shape and work hard on the ranch and run a lot." He has reached the National Finals many times and finished with the runner-up spot three times. He runs a bareback riding school at his Jerome ranch. He is devoting more time to the roughstock he raises on the family ranch and provides stock for a number of rodeos. He tries out roughstock personally and takes only the good ones to rodeos. Many of his horses have placed.

His wife is his secretary and their two children enjoy rodeo. They run the roughstock on their own thirty acres and six hundred they lease.

BLAINE COUNTY
Sun Valley-Hailey

North of the Magic Valley one need only to follow Idaho Highway 75 to reach the awesomely beautiful verdant valley and the towering peaks of the Sawtooth mountains which has become a vacation mecca for thousands. Early settlers prospered in mining, raising cattle, sheep, and crops. The geographical shape of the county has been called "bizarre," but it contains the mountains, streams and Sun Valley, as well as the Craters of the Moon National Monument. Horses were in abundance from the early days and many residents ride and/or rodeo. Thelma Ramey well remembers the days when her parents would load their car with family, friends and food and take along blankets and quilts for sleeping and head for the rodeo in Sun Valley. They camped and picnicked along the way; the rodeos were exciting and made memories to last a lifetime.

According to Rupert House, one of the Blaine County directors, the first rodeo he attended there was held in Sun Valley in 1941 or 1942. Union Pacific Railroad, owners of the world class ski facility and year-round vacation resort, sponsored the event and spared no expense. During World War II, the rodeo was discontinued. The arena was demolished in 1947. Anna and Wayne Clark, ranchers in the area, created a riding club in Hailey.

A rodeo was arranged in 1948 and a new arena built and a stock producer hired. Subsequent rodeos were generally self-supporting, but one or two failed to break even. At such times the rodeo directors took out loans at the bank, and residents held potluck dinners and pie socials to cover additional costs. "It is a great community and we were a real social and friendly group that has lasted these past fifty years, in spite of the concerns that come with rapid growth and local politics."

Eastern Corridor Rich in Rodeo

BANNOCK COUNTY

To the old-time rodeo performer and to the spectators who like to watch, there is nothing to match the stories about the bronc busters and bulldoggers, the riders and the ropers. They may listen to chatter about the weather, politics, and the economy, but very soon some comment will remind them of another cow story and it's back to the topic they love above all others.

Pocatello has plenty to remember and relate. Champions at the national level or area circuit include Harry Hart, Bert Sibbett, Dave Arave, Bob Shields, Edward and Leonard Arimo, Tracy Thompson, and others. All of them became cowboy legends. The original herding profession is disappearing as homes and highways take over the range on all but the largest ranches. The legend and tradition grow stronger as the old-timers remember and talk. Cowboying is a remembrance.

As in other areas of Idaho in the early 1900s, cowboys and horses from Pocatello and surrounding towns met informally for bucking contests. It wasn't until 1942, the first full year of World War II in which Idaho and the other states joined the fighting, that the first official rodeo was held. Many military men and women were stationed at the army air base and the commander thought they deserved a rodeo. He asked local leaders T.B. LeBailly and Earl Hutcheson and Grange members if a rodeo could be produced for base personnel and the Marines at the Naval Ordnance plant. It could, and was named the Victory Rodeo. The old Bannock County fairgrounds on West Quinn Street was the site. The money received went to recreational funds at both installations.

In 1946, the Victory had been won and Pocatello Rodeo

and Indian Ceremonial was chosen for a new name. The people of Fort Hall were providing much of the program. In 1959, the location moved to the fairgrounds on the east side of the city.

Idaho State University's Minidome (now Holt Arena) became rodeo home in 1981. The first show was dedicated to the late champion Harry Hart, 1939 world champion bulldogger and nationally known calf roper. He died earlier that year. With that move, Pocatello had the first indoor rodeo and each March the Dome is changed from a football field to a rodeo arena. The tons of sand and soil required to make the change is costly and along with other expenses and a lagging attendance caused the committee to talk about abandoning rodeo. Dave "Doc" Jones, rodeo committee chairman for a number of years, said that in the mid-eighties they were so close to calling it off that "we knew we had to do something and do it quick." What they came up with was a plan to host a national circuit finals championship rodeo. Dodge Truck Rodeo is a major sponsor of professional rodeo and its executive director Jack Lowry said that a national championship rodeo with the best circuit cowboys vying against each other might be the way to go. It was a radical concept and despite worries that cowboys might not want to travel halfway across the country, the committee said, "Let's give it a go."

They were taking a gamble but the first DNCFR in 1987 had a purse of $100,000 and the attendance was more than 27,000. The idea worked. Pocatello Rodeo committee members convinced the PRCA and NCFR to return the next year. With lots of community support, they held the 1988 event in the Minidome. The next March the purse grew to $130,000 and attendance to 33,000. Again, the directors had to convince the PRCA that Pocatello should be a repeat host city. Despite bids rolling in from Rapid City, South Dakota, Ogden, Utah, New Mexico and Texas offering much more money, the gigantic effort and cooperation from the city and volunteers, it was voted to hold it again in Pocatello. In 1989 the purse reached $175,000 and attendance was over 37,500. "By that time we were getting national attention and Pocatello, Idaho, and its rodeo was the most talked about show in the country," Doc Jones said.

In 1990 the purse jumped to $200,000 and a record attendance of over 43,000 and moved into the No. 7 slot nationally. Once again, the PRCA was taking bids from other cities as well as Pocatello to host the 1992–1994 events. Doc Jones said, "This is our rodeo and we intend to keep it." Southeast Idaho friends of rodeo and Idaho state officials joined Pocatello in the invitation bid. The stiffest competition to date came from Houston, Detroit, Oklahoma City, and New Mexico. Again Pocatello won and continued to rise in the DNCFR charts until it ranked as high as third and remains among the top ten rodeos in North America.

1994 Top Ranking Rodeos:		1998 Top Ranking Rodeos:	
	total purse		*total purse*
1. National Finals Rodeo		1. National Finals Rodeo	
Las Vegas, Nevada	$2,573,675	Las Vegas, Nevada	$4,185,576
December		2. Houston Livestock Show	
2. Houston Livestock Show		& Rodeo	
Houston, Texas	$330,649	Houston, Texas	$536,555
February and March		3. Cheyenne Frontier Days	
3. Dodge National Circuit Finals		Cheyenne, Wyoming	$486,285
Pocatello, Idaho	$231,428	4. Reno Rodeo	
March		Reno, Nevada	$481,868
4. Reno Rodeo		5. Dodge National Circuit Finals	
Reno, Nevada	$124,500	Pocatello, Idaho	$435,000
June		6. National Western Stock	
5. Original Coors Rodeo Showdown		Show & Rodeo	
Phoenix, Arizona	$120,000	Denver, Colorado	$411,301
October		7. San Antonio Livestock	
6. Calgary Stampede		Exposition Rodeo	
Calgary, Alberta	$118,750	San Antonio, Texas	$403,437
July		8. Southwestern Exposition &	
7. Cheyenne Frontier Days		Livestock Show & Rodeo	
Cheyenne, Wyoming	$117,000	Fort Worth, Texas	$362,238
July		9. Greeley Independence	
8. Southwestern Exposition &		Day Stampede	
Livestock Show & Rodeo		Greeley, Colorado	$282,291
Fort Worth, Texas	$112,000	10. Calgary Stampede	
January and February		Calgary, Alberta	$278,565
9. National Western Rodeo			
Denver, Colorado	$109,000		
January		16. Snake River Stampede	
10. San Antonio Stock Show & Rodeo		Nampa, Idaho	$205,001
San Antonio, Texas	$100,020	22. Caldwell Nite Rodeo	
February		Caldwell, Idaho	$179,330

Rodeo organizers offer large purses and are able to draw the biggest stars.

BLACKFOOT

One of the most stalwart of Idaho rodeo aficionados is Bob Shields of Blackfoot. Bob is the key link between the past and the present of Idaho rodeo. With an enviable record of many awards and riding in at least seven-hundred rodeos during his career, he added a link when his son, Shawn, became a champion bareback rider. Another link is his five-year-old grandson, Dayton, who is even now referred to as "a bull rider."

Raised in the little community of Tyhee on the Fort Hall Reservation located between Pocatello and Blackfoot, Bob worked hard on the farms his father leased. The family had about twenty horses and described his riding as a youngster with, "Horses were our escape from working hard and all day. We could ride our horses and relax away from the farms." He was a strong youngster and learned how to handle horses.

He entered the University of Idaho at Moscow in 1949 and soon became a part of the nucleus of an unofficial university rodeo team. One afternoon a rodeo-oriented friend, Carl Yokum, asked Bob it he would like to go out to Riverside (along the Clearwater River) and watch the unofficial U of I rodeo team practice. Bob was eager. He remembers that the students had a bunch of green horses, so wild that none of the students wanted to get on them. Bob jumped on a bareback and was promptly bucked off. He remarked that if anyone had a saddle he could borrow, he'd like to try again. The saddle was applied and Bob rode to a standstill. He joined the club and soon began to ride at every opportunity.

"I had no money and was spending all my spare time at the end of a pitchfork, shoveling manure from the stalls at the Ag College. I was paid the pittance of sixty-five cents an hour. So, when I entered a contest I had to win. I even skipped meals so I could pay my entry fees. I needed the money." When an appeal was made to have an official rodeo club, the University officials strongly opposed it. Bob transferred to Colorado A and M, because the school sponsored a rodeo club. He was soon winning contests in bareback, bronc, and bull riding. In 1954, he won the national championship in bareback and saddle bronc riding. He was also runnerup for the best All-Around Cowboy. The winner was Howard Hess who was riding for the now-official University of Idaho team.

Bob talked of the days when he worked as many as five rodeos in a week: Lehi, Utah; Elko, Nevada; Lander, Wyoming; Red Lodge, Montana; and Cody, Wyoming. "I tried to work the rodeos close to home, because I could make more money and be at home more." He was bull-riding champ at Caldwell one year and also at Pocatello. At his last rodeo in 1969 (his first was in 1950) at St. George, Utah, he won first in both bareback and saddle and came in fourth in bull riding. He remembers winning $720.

By that time, the business he established in 1961, the B–B (B bar B) Leather Company in Blackfoot was rolling along. He and his late wife, the former Gay Zufelt of Shelley and Humphrey had three sons, Jeff, Shawn, and Kelly. Bob sold the business to them in 1994. Of the three sons, Shawn, became a winning bareback rider. While riding the circuit, he won the championship title and went on to ride at Pocatello. His rodeo career came to a halt as a result of a neck injury caused, not by a bronc, but by the pickup in which he was riding. It hit a slick spot in the road and rolled. A spur developed on the neck vertebra and he was advised to quit rodeo. "Horses jerk, and that could have been bad," his Dad said. But Shawn has continued to work with riders and to provide an excellent glove which he developed especially for rodeo riders. The gloves provided before were stiff and bulky. He developed one called "regular/standard B–B bareback glove" and now has a new one called "The Flexer." In the latter, the best of leather is used and a wedge sewn into the side where each of the knuckles fit on the palm side and the glove is curved to naturally fit the hand. Cowboys liked his gloves so much that soon Shawn and the B–B had a comer on the market. In 1999 and 2000, fourteen of the fifteen top riders at the National Rodeo

Finals in Las Vegas were wearing Shawn's pliable, double-tumbled (for a softer fit) gloves. Gary Zufelt, a valued employee at the leather company, said that hundreds of cowboys throughout the country order the gloves. The word has spread throughout cowboyland and orders now arrive from New Zealand, Australia, Brazil, and Canada. The company also builds custom saddles, rodeo chaps, tack, bridles, reins, bits, and spurs.

Genuine cowboys never brag about their awards nor how important they are. "And," Bob Shields said, "If they tell you they've had virtually every bone in their body broken in rodeo, you can mark it down that they're damn liars. And you can quote me."

* * *

The Eastern Idaho State Fair and Rodeo was originally only a fair with some horse racing. It was billed as a "five day fiesta" and held on forty acres in Blackfoot. Thousands were attracted to the fair and a mile-long parade was made up of individuals, floats, bands, posses, and members of the Bannock-Shoshone Indian tribe in colorful dress. The night shows featured dancing by the Indians from the Fort Hall Reservation in their native dress.

Horses have been at home in the entire area since 1805 when Lewis and Clark were the first white men to see what is now Idaho. Trappers and explorers on their horses followed and then the Overland Mail, which crossed Teton and South Passes. President Lincoln found it necessary to send a mounted posse to protect the mail stage. Freight trains pulled by horses and mules hauled supplies into the mining towns from Utah. A man by the name of Joe Warren needed many horses in operating the stagecoach runs and ranged large herds on the nearby hills.

Bernell Elison of Blackfoot worked as a professional horse trainer before buying a construction business there. In the 1950s, he was among the first to start chariot racing in eastern Idaho. He also taught his son, Kenny, to bulldog and ride saddle broncs as well as how to train and race horses.

Kenny and his wife Vicky operate their own KV Construction in Idaho Falls, a delivery system and a ranch, a rodeo bucking horse brood mare business, and train chariot and flat track race horses. They have many wins to their credit and are looking forward to the Olympic Games at Salt Lake City in 2002. The Olympic Committee contacted the chariot racing association about holding the World Championships during the games.

Kenny and Vicky have a cattle ranch at Mud Lake and bought a bucking stock business from neighbors Kevin and Butch Small, both Professional Rodeo Cowboys Association saddle bronc riders. The Small brothers were born in Rexburg and Butch lists his hometown as Dubois in Clark County. He is well over a half-million dollars in earnings as a saddle bronc rider.

Butch has made it to the National Finals several times and won the Wilderness Circuit saddle bronc title back in 1980. Younger brother Kevin also took the Wilderness Circuit championship in 1983.

Crystal and Rodeo

Some may know almost as much, but no one knows northeastern Idaho cattle and rodeo country better than Vearl C. Crystal, now of Grant-Rigby. He lived all over the area and followed the cattle circuit long before rodeo circuits were organized. It was for good reason that he was called upon to stage a rodeo for the movie actress Jane Russell. She was in the Island Park area with her co-star Jack Butell to promote *The Outlaw,* the first movie in which she starred. Along with tending his cattle herd, Vearl worked for Allcott's Slash E Dude Ranch at Henry's Lake to make extra money. When Vearl was introduced to the raven-haired actress, it was as a "rodeo cowboy." The actress, a fine rider in her own right, insisted upon holding a rodeo. Vearl became an instant producer and that was the first of many rodeos he staged. Imagine a young Idaho cowboy casting Jane Russell in the featured role for an Island Park rodeo!

Vearl said, "The only horse she would ride was my main

roping horse, 'Old Paint,' a piebald. An old horse wrangler,
Charlie Brosick, gave him to me when I was in the seventh grade
and he was just a colt." As an aside, Vearl said that many years
later, Brosick was charged with murder, but was exonerated.
Vearl broke the colt to rope, and eventually became one of the
top calf ropers in the western United States.

This is getting ahead of the story of Vearl Crystal, who,
along with one brother, Demont, and five sisters, became accomplished riders. Let him tell of his early life: "I was born in a two-
room shack which my parents built north of Roberts. It reminds
me of 'the little house on the prairie.' The property is now the
Market Lake Wildlife Refuge. My mother and dad were Bern and
Bessie Crystal who arrived in Idaho from Cottonwood, Utah, in
1900. They milked cows, separated the milk and cream and
hauled it the fifteen miles to Hamer to be processed into cheese.
Along the way, they had to cross a creek, so it wasn't an easy
life."

He still laughs when he recalls learning to rope on his dad's
dairy calves and by paying his sisters a nickel everytime his lariat missed them as they darted out of the barn. They were speedy
and, "They needed the nickels to buy ice cream when a vendor
and his wagon came around once a week." He learned well and

**Jane Russell and
Jack Beutel wisely
perch on a fence to
watch the cowboys'
impromptu rodeo.**

Twenty-year-old Jane Russell, glamorous Hollywood star, and her co-
star Jack Beutel, age twenty-four, flew to northeastern Idaho after
completion of the film *The Outlaw,* the epic of Billy the Kid. Beutel
played Billy. Vearl Crystal accepted the challenge to produce an on-the-
spot rodeo and Jane asked to borrow his horse. "She was a good rider,"
the Idaho cowboy said.

while still a lad joined the family in herding about four hundred
cattle on a twenty square mile of desert west of Roberts. In the
spring they team roped every one of the cattle and branded them
so they could be sorted in the fall and returned to their home
ranches. They were paid three dollars a head for the grazing
season.

As a precursor to his rodeo career, Vearl joined Glenn
Yearsley of Mud Lake and picked up horses to run the open
range. They gathered more than a hundred head from the farms
and ranches in the Rexburg, Rigby, and Ririe areas and checked
them during the summer. "We gathered and sorted them in the
fall and trailed them to their owners, and it was all done on
horseback," he said. He was riding bareback broncs and roping
calves at jackpot rodeos while still a teenager.

Property in Island Park was acquired in 1940 and they changed their operation from the desert to trailing the huge herd eight days to the Henry's Lake ranch. He still entered jackpot rodeos in Rexburg, St. Anthony, and other towns on the weekends.

From 1941–45, Vearl served in the US Air Force during World War II. When he returned home to Idaho, he took advantage of the GI Bill of Rights provision for on-the-job training. He went to work in the Jefferson County assessor's office. The assessor died two years later. Vearl, then twenty-six, was appointed to the position. He was perhaps the youngest assessor in the country and served for one of the longest terms, twenty-eight years.

He was home from the service but a few days when he had a call from the village of Island Park, asking him to produce another rodeo, "similar to the Jane Russell event." It was his start as a rodeo producer. The first show had team and calf roping, wild cow riding, cow cutting, and bulldogging. The following year, they added bareback and saddle bronc riding. In the mid-fifties, he teamed up with Doc Sorenson and added steer riding and other acts. There has been an Island Park rodeo every year since 1946.

Vearl Crystal holds such reverence for our country's flag that he feels honored when asked to carry it in opening ceremonies at any eastern Idaho rodeo.

At age sixty-two, when most cowboys have hung up the saddle and lariat, Vearl won the calf roping event at the Old Timers Rodeo in Pocatello. He served successfully in the Idaho State Senate for several years, was popular on "both sides of the aisle" and was known for his friendliness and fairness. He left the Senate in 1988 and went to work building a rodeo museum on the ranch west of Grant. The museum was built of lumber he salvaged from old fences and buildings. It is situated next to the corral for rodeo stock.

Displays of cavalry spurs and bridle bits, chaps, saddles, silver-plated halters, and much more fill the museum, and include a box full of polished rocks from which young rodeo fans are invited to select one as a reminder of the visit.

The Crystals' son, Randy, is described by a friend as a "magnificent rider, who is poetry in motion."

Brenda Merrill Crystal, his wife, says, "He stays busy with the museum and rodeo. Vearl loves people and rodeo. He simply has to be doing something around people." Lucky people. Lucky rodeo.

Nixon's Buffalo Ranch

During World War I, when Sam Nixon acquired the three thousand acre buffalo ranch on the northwest part of Henry's Lake, it was home to nine head of buffalo. In one of the most magnificent scenic areas of Idaho, the ranch is located midway between Reynolds Pass at 6,836 feet and Red Rock Pass at 7,120 feet, and stretches to the foothills of Sawtelle Peak. Sam and his family moved from Butte, Montana, to Pocatello in 1902. The ranch was acquired from a bank in Butte, Montana, the town where he owned retail stores. Sam Nixon knew about the early west and working cowboys because he lived it. When ten years old, he came north from Colorado with his family in a Conestoga wagon.

Several years later, when the Blackfoot-Shoshone Indian Reservation was opened to filing on mineral rights, he was the first in line of applicants.

Two sons, Earl and James, operated the ranch and their children attended a one-room school even when the wind chill factor dropped to sixty-five degrees below zero. The buffalo were cared for and nine hundred head of white-faced Hereford cattle were added. Mary "Nickey" Nixon Smith, now of Coeur d'Alene, remembers that the National Geographic Society sent an emissary to convince the Nixons that the buffalo herd should be increased and not permitted to die out. They built a buffalo corral, and Nickey said that while they didn't like the job, she and her sister, Betty, took sturdy sticks and chased the animals out of the willows on the river banks so that visitors could see them.

In 1930, the ranch house burned to the ground. During the Depression in 1934, the Union Pacific Railway took many private railway cars away from railway officials and put them up for sale in a money-saving action. Sam Nixon bought a luxurious one with mahogany walls, toilet and shower, living, dining and bedrooms, extra beds that folded down, and a kitchen with a floor to ceiling icebox. Union Pacific took the car as far as Big Springs, where it was taken from the tracks and put on moving rollers to take to the ranch. It took nearly a month for the journey, and during this time, Nickey and Dorothy rode the car and did the cooking for the moving crew. Stops were made so small bridges could be taken out and strengthened to hold the weight of the car.

Not only on the huge ranch, but at the big rodeo grounds at Henry's Lake, Earl and James Nixon were bulldogging and bronc riding. The land which is now an Idaho state park and the Harriman Ranch was the site of many rodeos as were West Yellowstone and Mack's Inn. The latter still has rodeos. Children were welcome and many families arrived by cars and wagons to spend a day or two. Dances were a part of the festivities.

Island Park Rodeo

The Island Park Rodeo is an old and historical one. Mitch Jacobs now holds a shotgun, non-alcoholic rodeo three times each week during the summer. It grew into a tourist attraction and because of the "no alcohol" rule, many children are in the audience.

It would be impossible to hold an outdoor rodeo in that area during the winter months. Clen and Emma Atchley, who live about twenty-seven miles south at Ashton, tell of the winter during the 1930s when they operated a dairy and it was freezing cold. The milk froze in the pans before they could pour it into containers, so they hauled huge stacks of frozen milk "in the rounds" to the nearby farms and sold them for a dollar apiece.

Eastern Idaho Rodeo Association

The sport of buckaroos was growing by jumps and twirls. Autumn of 1970 brought a group of devotees together in Idaho Falls to form what had been in the planning stages for months—the Eastern Idaho Rodeo Association. Gary Miller was elected president; Jim Kluesner, vice-president; Mardean Miller, secretary; and Marsha Anderson, editor. Blanch Angell became the publicity director. There were one hundred and fifty in attendance and all were in agreement that leadership of the ICA was based in Boise, making it difficult for cowboys from the eastside to participate.

Prior to the formal organization, Gary and Mardean Miller met with someone who represented every aspect of rodeo in

Tonya Holmes of Midvale ties goats at the Eastern Idaho finals.

Eastern Idaho. The goal was to develop a champion cowboy from the area for every standard rodeo event. Enthusiasm was high and the first membership card issued was purchased by the late Adrian Sutton, a tough and successful bronc rider.

Four district directors named were: Loy Pehrson, Darlington, District One; Curly Angell, St. Anthony, Two; Verlin Freeman, Georgetown, Three; and Fred Nye, Pocatello, Four. Kenny Hall, Pocatello, was named publicity director. Rules were decided upon and a booklet published for participants.

Some of the All-Around cowboys from 1971 through 1986 were Galen Brower, Cal Stoddard, Benny Stoddard, Wilson Pate, Walter Parker, Bob Schall, Russ Miller, Val Christensen (four time winner), Ray Shively, and Bryan Anderson. When the cowgirls began barrel racing, winners included Kathy Barney, Kathy Bell, Jackie Roeser, Deena Shiner, Lisa Butler, and Sue Smith. Later breakaway roping was added and the stars were Sandie Gregory and Sherre Sagers.

JEFFERSON COUNTY

It was unheard of and unimagined, that a two-day gate of eight thousand people would turn out at Lewisville for the 1934 rodeo. That was the year the rodeo reached its peak and everyone commented on the fact that a little community claiming two hundred residents including those in the outlying area, could attract such a crowd. A carnival-like atmosphere with a ferris wheel and a merry-go-round was a magnet to pull in passersby. The first day an audience of three thousand entered the gate and five thousand on the second. Neal Erickson said, "There had never been as many people in Lewisville before, and there will never be that many again." People came early from all over to catch the chuck-wagon race, a favorite entertainment.

How much did Joe Erickson of the little village of Lewisville in Jefferson County, Idaho, love rodeo? To coin a phrase, "Let us count the ways." His son, J. Neal says, "Dad became so crazy about rodeo, that he financially lost a good part of our farm." Joe

Erickson put on the first rodeo in the early 1920s at his own ranch. Wild horses were still roaming the flats and hillsides and that is where Joe rode to gather the necessary stock for bucking and riding. From the wild horses on the range, Joe was able to provide a bucking string of about fifty animals. He also furnished the stock for rodeos in Blackfoot, St. Anthony, Rexburg, and Tremonton, Utah. His son recalls trailing horses all the way from Lewisville to Aspen, Wyoming for the bucking horse contest.

Neal remembers that the family lived in Blackfoot during the fair and rodeo. They took the stock a week ahead of time and pitched a tent in a nearby orchard. "I was six years old when I started learning to rope," Neal said, "by practicing on the single-quart buttermilk calves. I have a very clear memory of riding a roping calf out of the chute. He not only threw me but ran over the top after I was on the ground. Dad rode back and forth to keep an eye on my safety. Our good friend Homer Holcomb (who became a nationally known rodeo clown) came over and dusted me off and leaned over and said into my ear, "Neal, be sure to remember one thing. Cowboys never cry."

Not only was Homer Holcomb a fine rider of bucking horses, he became such an outstanding clown in performing antics to protect lives of cowboys who had been thrown, that he eventually was named to an honor spot in the Cowboy Hall of Fame. He has been gone a long time, but is fondly remembered by Idahoans who knew him. Particularly those in Lewisville. It was there he got his start. In 1929 he was earning twenty-five dollars for two days of clowning at the rodeo.

Neal remembers some of the little ditties that Homer used to recite in a singsong voice:

Oh, the geese they fly high in Bombay
Oh, the geese they fly high in Bombay
Oh, the geese they fly high and bleep into your eye
Yes the geese fly high in Bombay.

Neal has keen memories of the beginning of rodeo in Lewisville, the fact that it started during the Depression years and provided entertainment, recreation, and activity for nearly two hundred people who lived in and near the little crossroads village. The rodeo was actually started to fund the Latter Day Saints (Mormon) Church and by 1940, the promoters had contributed the grand sum of eleven thousand dollars to the church.

The earliest settlers in Jefferson County were Mormons and built irrigation systems to farm the outlying areas. The bantam town of Roberts had earlier been called Market Lake and was one of the first settlements in northeastern Idaho. The nearby lake along the Snake River received its name through the abundant supply of wild game birds used by early residents to feed their families. Jefferson County is one of the most uniformly level counties in Idaho. It is partly composed of the Snake River Plain where the river forms nearly sixteen miles of the eastern boundary line before making a semi-circle turn and flows back out.

There are several fields which contain buttes called Antelope and Circular, and on the east are the Menan Buttes. The area has been known for large antelope herds and one of the world's largest irrigation canals. Rigby was the county seat of Jefferson, established in 1913. Lewisville came into being in 1880.

With a near-total recall of early rodeo, Neal Erickson laughed as he told of the excitement in the great crowds brought forth by the chuck-wagon races. "Ten miles south from Grant, a chuck-wagon came to compete with Lewisville at the opening event." There was a quarter mile track and the wagons circled it twice. "My uncle, Ted Goody, was the helper who used the whip. George Walker held the lines and I mean they were really flying," Neal chuckled. The five Blackfoot Indian brothers by the name Lamose were all considered outstanding bronc riders. The twins, Franky and Willy, also raced. Neal remembered Gene Lamose as being six feet and six inches tall, with unusually large hands. "He could ride anything and was challenged to ride the horse 'Broken

Bones', named because so many people suffered just that in being bucked from his back. At one rodeo, Lamose was challenged by someone having hit the dust and said, 'I will ride 'Broken Bones' for twenty-five dollars.' It was a qualified ride and the hat was passed to raise the twenty-five dollars. It came quickly and easily because so many people wanted to see him ride." The horse did his darndest, according to Neal, to buck him off but was unsuccessful. After the ride, Lamose reached into the passed hat, took the money, said, "Thanks, boys" and walked away.

Joe Erickson provided the stock for rodeos in Rexburg, Rupert, St. Anthony, and Afton, Wyoming. It was during World War II that he sold out his rodeo line to "Doc" Sorenson and one of his partners.

Dora was the felicitous helpmate for Joe. She was not only a fine homemaker, but became such an outstanding teacher that a school was named for her. Neal recalled his first activity in calf riding, when he received what could be described as "somewhat of a battering." The next day his mother hid him under the grandstands so he would not be urged to enter another contest. When his father remonstrated with her, Dora said, "One cowboy in the family is enough."

As can be imagined, Neal was soon back in the arena. John Erickson, son of Neal and Veda, is the third generation to compete in rodeo. He and his wife Coleen are the parents of Jason, Jake and Jed, all of whom enter team and calf roping in the national high school events as well as Idaho rodeos.

Jed has won the Idaho champion high school roper award and team roped with Cody Pickett, son of world champion Dee Pickett. Born January 2, 1941, John has the enthusiasm of a high school roper and is still an enthusiastic participant in various rodeos at fifty-nine. He is proud that his family now boasts fourth generation rodeors and is pleased that his grandfather started Jefferson County Rodeo.

John reminisced about his grandfather and Charley O'Toole. Joe and Charley were partners. Coming from Ireland to work at

the mines at Gilmore, O'Toole ran a freightline from Gilmore to
Salmon in the early 1900s. He secured tax land at Hamer, purchasing it for fifty cents on the dollar. He ran many cattle on land
which is now producing Idaho's famous potatoes. John said that
Charley O'Toole always rode gray horses and owned quarter
horses or thoroughbreds. He permitted John to ride his horses as
soon as he was big enough to hoist himself onto the back of one.

"I think I was four or five when I was able to lead an albino
white horse up alongside a truck bed, climb onto the truck and
onto him from there."

Joe Erickson and Charley O'Toole scouted for horses from
Hamer north to the Canadian border, where at one time there
were as many as ten thousand head.

Although Charley O'Toole was short at just five feet two
inches and weighed one hundred and thirty pounds, he took part
in many rodeos. It was his favorite recreation, but he never forgot his native Ireland. When he died, his request was met to ship
his body back to the old country for burial.

John said that his grandfather, Joe, was the first one to bring
Brahma bulls into the area. One year he spent all of his money
bringing twenty-five to thirty of the bulls and suffered a tragic
loss when the temperature dropped to thirty and forty degrees
below zero. All the animals were put into the barn for warmth
but still froze to death. Of the original eighty acres that Joe
Erickson owned, sixty were lost to pay off debts.

"Dad, get me a horse," was the first full sentence Jason said
to John. Jason was about two years old. All of the boys were
strongly supported in their desire to ride in rodeo. Jason as a tiny
youngster would walk out to do his chores, dragging a halter and
a little oat bucket. He carefully placed the rope on the ground
with the oat bucket in the middle.When the horse came to
munch on oats, Jason would try to shinny up his leg and reach
up to get ahold of the horse's mane in order to climb upon his
back. "Horses are good with children and a bucking horse will
seldom step on a rider he has just thrown. But a bull will look for

a place on your body to tromp once you are downed while wrestling with him," John said.

John and Coleen's son Jake could "ride anything with hair on it" and roped from a horse at age eight. Jed roped from a horse at only six and was also heeling steers. In more recent years he and Cody Pickett, son of Dee, were accumulating awards and top earnings at a number of events. Jason started rodeo when ten. Another son, Johnny, roped but became more interested in cars. John refused to let any of their daughters become active in rodeo because of the "wild bunch" holding drunken brawls at post-rodeo celebrations.

Nearly twenty-five saddles are among the many and various rodeo awards John and his three boys they have received. In 1997, John, Jake, and Jed roped in the USTRC nationals in Oklahoma City. There are more than nine hundred teams roping in the USTRC. In the finals, Jake and John placed third with a win of twenty-seven thousand dollars and Jed and John came in sixth in another contest, winning sixteen thousand dollars. Among the three of them, they won a total of forty-three thousand dollars in one roping contest.

FREMONT COUNTY

For one of the newest states with a small population, Idaho has organized strong counties made up of a spirited citizenry. Those who settled Fremont County and later arrivals have "always been known for their toughness of spirit, their community-mindedness, their willingness to work hard and help one another, and for their dedication to deity," Diana Richman stated. The people also organized a number of get-togethers such as rodeos, parades, ball games, picnics, and dances through which they renewed their spirits after days of hard work and drudgery. From the organized activities, traditions grew and the Pioneer Day celebrations, commemorating the arrival of woman pioneers in Salt Lake Valley on July 24, 1847, came about and spread throughout eastern Idaho.

The first such celebration in the Fremont communities took place in 1902. Events were held in Driggs, Rigby, and Teton. The coming years added Rexburg, Twin Groves, Sugar City, Parker, Newdale, and Chester. Diana Richman went on to say, "These celebrations have been successes because of the efforts of the Latter Day Saints members, the various Chambers of Commerce, and other civic clubs and organizations."

That the people were hungry for such get-togethers was evident when fifteen thousand attended the first recorded celebration in St. Anthony, July 24 and 25, 1914. Many of them arrived by train, with seven hundred arriving at noon on July 24. Along with the cowboys' relay race, hat and running races, bronco riding, trick roping and riding, and steer bull riding, a number of races, pie and bun eating contests, baseball, wagon races, and rope spinning were on the program. The theme, "Pioneer Jubilee for People From Everywhere," brought people from miles around. The Gray Opera House sold out performances both nights. In 1929, leaders from St. Anthony and Rexburg discussed the separate celebrations on July 4 and July 24 and it was decided that the main Fourth of July celebration would be held at Rexburg and the Pioneer Day observance at St. Anthony. Pioneer Day celebrations have been held every year since then with the exception of the World War II years of 1943, 1944, and 1945.

Night rodeo became possible in 1937 when lights were added. The *Teton Peak Chronicle* reported, "Flood lights were installed on sixty foot poles that will make the fairgrounds as brilliant as sunlight."

Stock for that rodeo was furnished by Joe Erickson of Lewisville, who became well-known throughout the circuit for fine animals. Usually, the stock had been brought in by local ranchers.

The first RCA approved rodeo sponsored by the Fremont Mounties Posse was in 1948 in along with the Pioneer Days celebration. Producer of the show was Hall Western Rodeo Company of Ogden, Utah. In 1949, the Posse brought in cowboy singer and actor Roy Rogers and his specialty acts which featured the Little Red Pony and Trigger Junior. Included were acts produced by the famous Hollywood horse trainer, Glenn Kendall and his eight highly trained palomino horses.

After 1952, rodeos were again locally produced with competition among the local riders. The Snake River Riding and Racing Association (Riding Club) was formed in 1960 and sponsored Pioneer Days Rodeo. Stock was furnished by Jake Pope's Spur Rowell Rodeo Company of Twin Falls. The Idaho Cowboy Association gave its approval and later rodeos were sanctioned by the Eastern Idaho Rodeo Association. Now the Intermountain Professional Rodeo Association sanctions the performances. The Riding Club continued to sponsor rodeos produced by Curly Angell Rodeo Company, Hoggan Rodeo Company, and P&P Rodeo for many years with Pioneer Days Inc., the current sponsors.

William M. Hansen of St. Anthony became involved in 1914 and deserves much credit for the successes of the early celebrations. He was Chairman and Marshal of the Day for many years and, in 1961, last rode in the parade as Honorary Marshal.

Old-time cowboys such as Steve Broadhurst, a popular performer, rode a saddle bronc carrying an old wash tub filled with flour tied to the saddle, and was loudly cheered. Richman says, "Needless to say, he made a floury ride." Several of the Rigby brothers, Millers, Allens, Moons, Dopps, Nedrows, and many others were popular. Later, the Angells, Millers, Allens, Mortons, Hills, Gouldings and others were credited with making the rodeos such successes.

Hayworth High School Hero

A snazzy saddle, two shiney belt buckles, a set of spurs and a $1,100 scholarship which brought about a full-ride rodeo scholarship at Montana State University in Bozeman, were among the awards received by Jake Hayworth of St. Anthony in 1994. He was the cowboy hero at District 7 high school rodeo and made all of Idaho's rodeo world proud.

He became the all-around cowboy champion at the National High School Rodeo Finals in Gillette, Wyoming. Jake lined up 735 points to win over his nearest competitor, Mike Outhier of Oklahoma, by 55 points at 680. His parents are Herb and Polly Hayworth. Other young Idahoans competing were Becky Woodcock and Jerry Angell of St. Anthony; Hugh Baldwin, Jake Erickson, Jayme Goddard, and Aaron Orr of Rexburg.

Cowboy Country

IDAHO FALLS WAR BONNET ROUNDUP

War Bonnet Roundup—a stirring name for the Idaho Falls roundup which was inspired by the 1908 showing of William S. Cody's Wild West Show. The name honors old Chief War Bonnet and his Bannock Indian tribe. It evokes memories of a handsomely dressed Indian chief wearing an eagle-feathered headpiece which trailed down his back and touched the ground.

In 1911, the Jackson Hole (Wyoming) Frontier Rodeo Association sent a few members to Idaho Falls searching for horses to be used in their rodeo that summer. Rancher and stockman Burt Empey provided a dozen horses. Interest aroused, two Idaho Falls businessmen, Dow Williams and Billy Luxton, accom-

In the days when flags flew high across the main street of Idaho Falls and sleek horses and white-suited men led the parade, the War Bonnet Roundup provided the largest crowds in the entire area. Trains, automobiles, and horse-drawn wagons and buggies brought loads of people to the city. *Courtesy of Idaho Falls Historical Museum.*

panied rodeo contestants Ray Ellis and Frank Gable to the Jackson Hole event. Gable was a world champion rider and trick roper.

When the War Bonnet was put together as a roundup to be held with the fair, Williams and Luxton recruited businessmen F.H. Churchill, W.J. Coltman, Burt Empey, J.J. Hayball, J.H. Heath, J.I. Hubbell, Jack Neve, Frank Reno, and M.B. Yeaman to help organize and collect five thousand dollars to finance the roundup the next year. It was held for five afternoons at Reno, now Tautphaus, Park in September. The downtown merchants cooperated and the War Bonnet was on its way.

The next year several Jackson Hole cowboys showed up for the War Bonnet, and the rodeo circuit for Idaho began to take shape. Some of the contestants were Roy Van Black, Keyes Blair, Tee Lloyd, Hugh McClaar, Smokey Moore, Billy Sherman, and Jimmy Spears.

Jackson Hole Frontier Association, with help from Ralph Dixie, well-known Fort Hall cattleman, furnished stock. From the beginning, the War Bonnet was popular and the daily attendance was estimated at seven thousand. So many people attended, in fact, that the railway company brought in Pullman cars to provide more sleeping rooms. The cowboys, as most did in the early days of rodeo, pitched tents in the park and slept on hay.

Lee Caldwell rides a white horse, not to Banbury Cross, but at the Idaho Falls War Bonnet Roundup-in the early 1900s. Lee is wearing leather chaps and appears to be "pulling leather." *Courtesy of Idaho Falls Historical Museum.*

From the beginning, the War Bonnet Roundup filled the grandstand to overflowing, as seen in this picture of H.A. Strong riding the reinless horse "Maud's Sister." *Courtesy of Idaho Falls Historical Museum.*

Four- to five-hundred Fort Hall Indians helped make War Bonnet such a success by participating in all events. They pitched tepees and entire families lived at Reno Park. Beautiful leather and beaded costumes and feathered headdresses were worn for the parades and their riders excelled in both men's and women's horse races, roping, and bronc riding. The audiences were brought to their feet when they came in for the relay races, wherein a rider leapt from the bare back of a racing horse and landed astride another, without the horses slowing pace.

The Nez Perce, Jackson Sundown, then and now considered the great Indian cowboy of all time, was wildly cheered. Others included Captain Willis, outstanding roper and pickup man, and his horse, "Warrior"; See-Saw Wheeler; Jim McKie; and Lewis LaClaire, who was known for riding the notorious bucking bronc "Sitting Bull."

Another big reason for War Bonnet popularity was the awards purse, larger than Cheyenne and Pendleton prize monies combined.

Among the cowboys in the first three roundups were Ben Jury, Silver Haare, Joe Williams, O.U. Brown (who was killed in a relay race), Skeeter Bill Robins, Tex White, "Dismal Dick" Thornton, and Rube Boam, who, in 1914, rode the wild bull "Old Spot" to a standstill. Boam was bull and bronc rider, roper, and pickup man. Bulldogger Charlie Tipton was a great steer "hoolier." Those who were given the name were not content with wrestling the steer to the ground but "hoolied" the animal, driving him around the track to make the tackle in front of the grandstand and bending the bull's head around until the horns stuck in the ground.

Before chutes were provided, stock was driven from a corral at the arena edge, caught and saddled. Bareback riding and calf roping didn't appear on the schedule for several years.

A five-mile relay race called for stopping every half mile to switch horses and saddles. That was for the cowboys. The cowgirls were not required to change saddles and the Indians rode bareback.

Mersi Day Nickerson well remembers the War Bonnet celebration and she took part the first time as a teenager. Sporting a black and gold uniform and playing a clarinet, she was a member of the rodeo band, organized by musician and composer A.L.

Harry Robbins has half the bull down on his knees in the dogging competition during the 1914 War Bonnet Roundup in Idaho Falls. *Courtesy of Idaho Falls Historical Museum.*

Gifford, who chose twenty of his best young musicians to play during the rodeo.

Mersi now living in Salt Lake City, recalls that despite the days of the Depression and World War II, rodeo was a fun time for the kids. "There was a great parade with handsome cowboys, Native Americans in full and colorful costumes and the laughing and antic clowns."

Idaho is still known for wild horse herds, now counted in the hundreds and in early days by the thousands. Wild horses were rounded up for a popular racing event at the earliest rodeos in Idaho Falls. The horses wore blindfolds and two men held them as steady as possible while the riders mounted and tried to race around the track.

Within four years new events added included a trained horse putting on a show without a rider and a twelve-horse and rider Indian relay race.

Ed Duren, Extension Animal Scientist for the University of Idaho in Soda Springs, whose son, Kyle, is a PRCA bull rider, noted that the War Bonnet had a rodeo saddle on display at the 1998 convention of the National Beef Cattle Association in Denver.

HISTORIC TETON

A name adopted from the nearby Teton Peaks in Wyoming, Tetonia lies in the beautiful valley called Pierre's Hole. From 1829 until 1849, it was home to the famed summer rendezvous held by trappers and Indians. Several moves have been put forward to change the name to Teton Valley, but they haven't "caught hold" with the old-timers. They are a rugged breed who now rendezvous for rodeo.

The first rodeo was held in 1967 or 1968 and locals were the participants. They included Floyd Rammell, Jerry Peacock, Joe Hill, Weston Ball, J.P. Olsen, Wendell Campbell, Terry Eck, and Larry Peacock. Stock was furnished by the local farmers and cattle ranchers. Owners and operators of the large cattle ranches are Vernice Douglass, Dean Wade, LaVell Johnson, Dick Egbert, Joe Peacock, Frank Hansen, and Al Kaufman.

Women performers are Jerelyn Hill, LaRae Rammell, Aloma Campbell, Judy Cook, Wilda Ball, Gay Peacock, Donna Rigby, and Sharon Olsen. Local sponsors of the rodeo are Little Max's, Rammell Merc, Tetonia Club, Farmers Grain and Sessions.

The Rammells say that rodeo has changed in several ways including the use of professional stock, Royalty Queens and Princesses, and while under Eastern Idaho Rodeo Association membership had professional shows.

LARIATS OVER LEMHI

"Rodeo is Idaho," Fred Ramey said. "It is a way of life and in one way or another, rodeo has been going on since Idaho was a Territory. Horses and their riders had a big part in building this state."

Though many miles from the Lemhi Valley in which he was born, grew, and lived until retirement, Fred Ramey is in Idaho. He and his wife Thelma (Pearson) moved northwest from Salmon to Coeur d'Alene, upon the urging of their son-in-law and daughter, Bart and Patsy Templeman, and live next door. While being interviewed, Fred and Thelma shared homemade cookies and coffee at the polished thick-slabbed and seven-foot long pine table in the Templeman home a few miles from town at the far west end of Cougar Gulch. In reminiscing of their child-and-adulthoods in the Lemhi country, a rich chronicle unfolds.

Fred's grandfather, John Ramey, was one of those pioneers who spent much of his life riding or driving a horse as Lemhi and Custer communities were being built. John Ramey held many "firsts" but never stopped to think about it. He considered the jobs to be done, needs to be met, and he helped to build a community and a state. In what is today's primitive area of Idaho, John Ramey rode a horse to reach many destinations. Forest Service maps of the Chamberlain Basin show Big Ramey Creek, Little Ramey Creek, Ramey Meadow and Upper Ramey Meadow,

Ramey Ridge, Ramey Horizontal Control Station (with a triangle dot indicating house, cabin, or other building), Ramey Hill, and on the Yankee Fork, Ramey Creek. John Carrey, well-known Idaho author of *Chamberlain Basin Country,* and other histories, wrote: "In regards to the John S. Ramey family, in my twenty-eight years of working on books, here is my true knowledge. John S. Ramey was very well-spoken of and the old-timers I interviewed sure spoke a good word. He was a hunter and a scout. Rube Robbins, scout for Bernard, had him hired because he knew the country. Also, he had been through the country as a tax collector prior to the outbreak of the Sheepeater War. We had five or six neighbors along the South Fork who were in the campaign."

Marjorie L. Ramey Nelson, great-niece of John and cousin of Fred Ramey, wrote much of her great-uncle in her history, *Footprints on Mountain Trails.*

John S. arrived from Kentucky in 1866 at the beginning of the mining stampede when placer gold was found in the Leesburg Basin. He became a miner and merchant and married Maggie DeMoss. He was Deputy U.S. Marshal for years and elected the first Sheriff of Lemhi County. Many thousands of fortune-seekers, including three hundred Chinese, poured into the area. Astride a horse, he carried gold dust from mining camps at Pierce, Elk City, Florence, and Warren to Lewiston. There was not a jail when he became sheriff, so he transported prisoners to another town, likely Idaho City. Not only did he ride horseback, but so did the shackled prisoner. He was hired as a scout along the Middle Fork of the Salmon during the 1879 Sheepeater War. The Yankee Fork *Herald* of July 24, 1879, reported that John S. Ramey was "one of the best (military) scouts on the frontier." He also brought the best in riding to the frontier. He was a man who made a life and a living riding a horse, a forerunner of the rodeo cowboy.

As Fred thought of the valley, the mountains and rodeo, he said, "It didn't take much to hold a rodeo in that country. Just call up a neighbor who had horses and say 'Let's get together and have a rodeo.' And you had one. They had rodeos at May, Mackay, Challis, and Gibbonsville, which was quite a mining town. But it had a rodeo." Thelma remembered the dancing. "If you've never been to a dance at Leek Creek, you haven't lived. They called it a Hoedown, and they danced all night. Even the little kids." Leadore was earlier called Junction and is the center of a cattle and sheep ranching area. It holds the Fourth of July Rodeo at the combined rodeo and camp grounds.

Fred cited world champion bronc rider Burrel Mulkey as the prime example of riders who made rodeo famous in northeast Idaho. "Burrel came from prominent people in the Pahsimeroi. They were early day pioneers with knowledge of land, livestock and that included horses. Burrel hit the rodeo circuit when he was in his teens and became a world champ. And that was in the days when rodeo was real rodeo." Thelma remembered her parents, Fred and Alice Pearson of Blackfoot, as great rodeo fans, saying, "Dad never missed the War Bonnet in Idaho Falls. He loaded the car with family and anyone else who wanted to go, packed the car with quilts so we could sleep out under the stars at night, a supply of food, and we drove from Leadore. I remember the first rodeo after Sun Valley was built by Union Pacific. We drove, taking bedding and food, and camped along the way." Those great, elaborate rodeos in the thirties at the world-class resort drew hundreds of people. The resort no longer holds rodeos, but there are enough of them in the area to satisfy the most rabid fan.

The Salmon Rodeo, largest in the area, draws hundreds of viewers. People in Salmon are strong supporters of rodeo because it is such good entertainment, Fred said. Deena Shiner of Salmon was described as a "blistering barrel racer" several years ago and much credit was given to her special Quarter Horse gelding "Toad." Chuck and Joyce Briggs of Rigby bought their daughter "Toady Britches" in 1976 from trainer Bill Moss.

When Toad was a three-year-old, Deena was a high school senior and they finished second in the High School Rodeo district

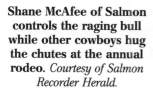

Shane McAfee of Salmon controls the raging bull while other cowboys hug the chutes at the annual rodeo. *Courtesy of Salmon Recorder Herald.*

and eighth in the state finals. She began team roping when Toad was five and started the barrel patterns. They entered many contests in different rodeos and Deena gave Toad credit for "always placing in the money." Deena and Steve Shiner of Salmon were married in 1980 and she and Toad celebrated by winning the Barrel Racing saddle. In 1983 they won another saddle in the EIRA competition. They decided to go pro.

In their first Wilderness Pro Rodeo Circuit finals at Las Vegas, they won the average. The next year at Billings they tied in the barrels with World Champion Charmayne James and her horse, Scamper, in the second go, and placed again in the average. They won Rookie of the Year in the Wilderness Circuit. After a year off for the birth of her first child, Deena and Toad took part in the EIRA and National Rodeo Association in 1986. Next they won the first Ladies All-Around Cowgirl Buckle in the EIRA.

Toad was seventeen in 1990 and Deena noticed he was having difficulty running on hard ground and was beginning to limp. A growth on his foot was removed but healing was slow. They took him to a specialist for surgery at Colorado State University Veterinary School in Fort Collins for the removal of a small tumor. Deena took him home to Salmon to recover at Dr.

Heckendorf's veterinary clinic. It soon was apparent he could not recover. He was euthanized and buried on the ranch. "No other horse can take his place," Deena said. She left the pro circuit and team ropes nearer home. She coaches her own children and nieces and nephews in Little Britches Rodeo and competes in jackpot and association rodeos and works on the ranch. Her career earnings are estimated at sixty-two thousand dollars.

CHALLIS CATTLE COUNTRY

Driving south from Salmon on U.S. Highway 93 for sixty miles along the eye-filling Salmon River, one reaches the little town of Challis, a center of Custer County cattle raising and mining. A group of citizens met in early July 1925, and decided to hold a fair and rodeo on September 17–19 and named a board of directors: M.A. Dillingham, chairman; Frank Cameron, secretary; N.C. Hovey, treasurer; John Kirk, Franklin Nickerson, George McGowan, Merle Drake, and Roy Chivers. County commissioners set aside ground on the old Woodson Ranch for a track, corrals, stables, pens, and a park. In August, a race course was built and work started on a covered grandstand, with seating for three hundred, and a judging stand. Many hours and days of volunteer labor kept the building project on schedule.

A big parade, led by the Salmon Municipal Band and the more than three hundred Challis school pupils, included Homer Holcomb (who was building a reputation as the country's funniest rodeo clown), a number of rodeo and race horses, and floats. Prizes of fifteen dollars and ten dollars were awarded to first and second place float winners. After lunch and a brief band concert on Main Street, the band led the crowd to the Fair and Rodeo grounds. A dance followed in the evening. The weather was cold and contributed to the deficit of five hundred dollars.

In true Idaho style, the committee announced another event for September 1926. Wild steers and horses were rounded up from grazing lands and the best rodeo hands from the area and adjacent states were invited. Bill Hamilton, a local rider who went into the clowning profession, was hired. Pony Express and Roman races were added. The rodeo was pronounced a success and the "deficit was only three hundred dollars."

The 1927 rodeo was held October 6 and 7 without the fair. Ben Hamilton and Alvin Ellis from the Pahsimeroi produced a two day event and brought along Hamilton's string of horses for racing, roping, and bucking. A good crowd showed and although "no money was realized a very successful time, socially, if not financially was staged."

The *Custer County Messenger* printed news of the plans for the September 20–21, 1928 Fair and Rodeo, news of its success and that Alvin Ellis was due thanks from the people for his time and labor. A young boy, Buzz Jones, was injured riding in the horse contest. Both legs were fractured below the knees and money was raised to cover his expenses. A benefit dance was held on October 5 and the funds given him. Apparently, it was the last big Fair and Rodeo for many years.

In 1976, a new rodeo grounds and grandstand were completed to welcome a new era for the sport. In 1977, a crowd of about nine hundred showed up to nearly fill the grandstand built to accommodate one thousand. That, too, will come to pass as the numbers increase each year. Challis is a member of the Eastern Idaho Rodeo Association and the rodeos are sanctioned by the group. Rodeos belonging to the association always have a goodly number from the EIRA, which is supportive of its members.

Rose Hamilton Johnson lived in Challis for a long time and now is eighteen miles south of Salmon. She remains enthusiastic and attends all Challis rodeos. Her grandfather came to the Pahsimeroi years ago and her father, Ben Hamilton, was born there. She was raised in the "land of many waters," the meaning of Pahsimeroi, and has no desire to live elsewhere. She ranches and trains high school rodeoers. She remembers rodeo riders at Challis were Galen Brower, bronc rider and bull roper; Dale and Neil Aravy; Jim Martiny, a bulldogger. He also team roped with

Rose's nephew, Ted O'Neal. Ted rode in amateur shows for sometime and then went to the Professional Rodeo Cowboy Association circuit which has top cowboys contesting.

Max Hogan was the producer of the 1977 event and was followed by the Crystal brothers, Demont and Vearl. All of them "charged us practically nothing," Rose said, "and that is one of the reasons we have been able to grow the rodeo." While Vearl still produces rodeos, Demont spends winters in Arizona and provides shows in the Mesa-Tucson area. Demont and Rose were among those inducted into the Eastern Idaho Horsemen Hall of Fame in 2000. Rose rode while in high school and was a charter member of Idaho State University's College rodeo team. She has high praise for her coach, Bob Shields, now of Blackfoot, who organized and taught the teams.

Rose's brother-in-law, Don O'Neal, in the Pahsimeroi, has highly trained his paint horses to do many tricks, such as standing on hind legs, bowing to the audience, step up onto pedestals and pose for the crowd. He has shown them in Salmon, southern Idaho, and California.

Blume Ranch

Ten miles downriver from Challis where Morgan Creek rushes into the Salmon River is a cattle ranch that was owned from the 1880s until 1939 by the J. Blume family. Blume's son Fred married Effie McKendrick from a well-known area family, and they remained on the ranch and ran two hundred and fifty head of cattle. Their son, Lloyd, was born in 1905 and was a bonafide cowboy. The Blumes annually held an informal ranch rodeo for the cowboys at roundup time.

In addition to the cattle, the Blumes raised sheep and turkeys. Lloyd often rode among the brush and willows along the creek to move a wandering cow or steer. He wore leather chaps, jacket and gloves as protection against cuts and scratches. A pistol was carried as a necessary part of ranch life.

Lloyd's nephew, Milton Blume of Meridian, remembers the stories told of cowboying in the high country of Idaho.

Lloyd Blume on the family ranch near Morgan Creek below Challis. The picture was taken about 1930. He is about to mount his horse and run down a steer likely stuck in the thick brush in the background. Note the decorated leather chaps, jacket, and gloves. His Stetson at a jaunty angle and a pistol tucked inside the belt, Lloyd is prepared for any frontier activity.
Courtesy of Diane Garcia.

MACKAY WILDEST RODEO

The biggest summertime event in the Lost River Valley takes place every year during the fourth weekend in June. The little town of Mackay, with Idaho's highest Mount Borah a few miles from the town's center, calls itself "the most lofty incorporated city in Idaho." It originated in 1900 as a supply point for mines in the nearby mountains and it sponsors what is tagged as "Idaho's Wildest Rodeo." Street parties, parades, old-time western shootout, and dances are held along with the rodeo.

Mackay's Perks Bar is the central gathering point during the rodeo. "It gets wild and woolly during the rodeo with all of the genuine cowboys and cowgirls in town for the event," is the way the internet tells of Mackay.

The first rodeo was held in 1945 in a pasture near town owned by Albert "Hoot" and Leona Anderson. and more than five hundred dollars was raised for award money. Cliff Caldwell of Blackfoot won fifty dollars for placing first in each event of bareback and bull riding. Albert Quist of Arco was second and Louie Corgatelli came in third, and took a fifteen dollar prize for scores in bull riding and the bareback horse race.

Other winners included Vernon Porter, Bill Gay, Cliff Caldwell, Fred Thompson, Bob Scott, and Clyde Twitchell. The best bucking horse award went to Charlie Haight.

The fiftieth anniversary of that first event was held June 23–25, 1995 with a huge attendance. Downtown businesses no longer close and events are not quite the same in that buffaloes are not ridden, but it remains the biggest social event of the year. Among the constant supporters of the Mackay Rodeo Association for many years were Gerald and Bea Twitchell.

CLAYTON, MAY, AND PAHSIMEROI

The July 4, 5, and 6, 1935 rodeo at Clayton, southwest of Challis, was sponsored by American Legion Post No. 114. Jimmy and Pauline Nesbitt, outstanding trick riders, performed. Pete Grubb, world champion bronc buster, returned to ride for the home folks.

There was a unique feature of the July 30, 1927 rodeo at May, located about seventy miles southeast of Salmon and centered in the valley between the Salmon River and Lemhi mountain ranges. Homer Holcomb, circus and rodeo clown, drove a car from the Sanitary Grocery downtown to the rodeo grounds blindfolded. He drove at an average speed of twenty-five miles per hour and made it safely.

Everett Colburn produced the rodeo and provided stock for bucking contests, roping, and bulldogging. The event was a success and five new chutes, fence, and sprinkler were installed for the 1928 event. Thirty head of cattle, twenty bareback riding horses, and thirty saddle broncs were on hand to compete and entertain in 1928.

A rodeo billed as the Pahsimeroi was held on the Ziegler Ranch, fifteen miles south of May, on July 4, 1938 and again in

1939. A good crowd of neighboring ranchers and participants from other towns attended.

IDAHO BRANDING

Despite its recent flurry of growth, Idaho is still a sparsely populated state. Less than two million persons were counted during the last census, and while it is not known exactly how many cattle and horses live within the boundaries, it is expected that the animals would give the humans a real race in numbers. The 485 pages of cattle and horse brands, ranging from the A&A Cattle Ranch at Grandview in Owyhee County to Rachel Zumwalt at Stites in Nez Perce County and David Zweifel at Dubois in Clark County give an idea of the numbers of cattle and stock owners.

In early ranching days, a roundup was a social event accompanied by real labor with workers from each ranch rounding up cattle and herding them to a central spot. Each ranch sorted out its own animals according to the brands, branded the new calves and selected older cattle to be sent to market.

Stock branding was used to reduce loss by theft or wandering away. Workers for each ranch slapped its particular brand on all its animals. The code of the West was rarely broken in the matter of returning lost animals to the ranch by brand they carried. However, some dishonest operators tried to change the brand to look more like their own. Justice was swift and strong to anyone caught tampering with another's brand.

Animals are herded to a hot fire where red-not branding irons await the animal dragged into position on it's side or haunches. A tally is kept of the number branded and then registered with the Idaho Brand Board. The Brand Board is composed of five members, one of whom is chairman. A state brand office is maintained in Boise with district offices in Lewiston, Caldwell, Idaho Falls, and Twin Falls. Each office has two or more brand inspectors who are kept busy complying with the laws of the state. Recorded brands must be renewed every two years. If the

State Brand Inspector finds a conflict between brands of two owners, they may cancel the brand that infringes upon the one previously recorded. Charges are made for all branding activities as well as for certificates of ownership and transportation and annual inspection. The State Brand Inspector collects fees for the Idaho Beef Council, Idaho Horse Board, and Idaho Department of Agriculture.

Just a few of the thousands of Idaho brands are shown here:

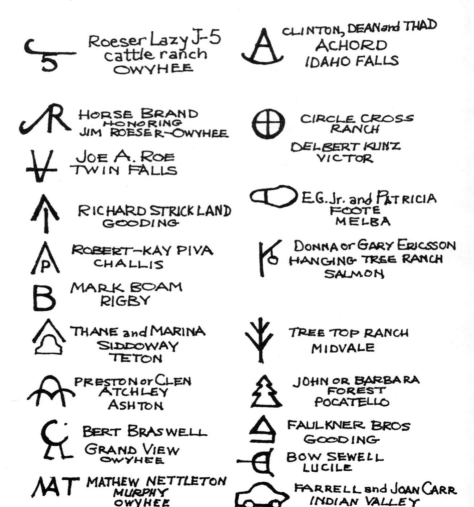

Roeser Lazy J-5 cattle ranch OWYHEE

CLINTON, DEAN and THAD ACHORD IDAHO FALLS

HORSE BRAND HONORING JIM ROESER—OWYHEE

CIRCLE CROSS RANCH DELBERT KUNZ VICTOR

JOE A. ROE TWIN FALLS

RICHARD STRICKLAND GOODING

E.G. Jr. and PATRICIA FOOTE MELBA

ROBERT—KAY PIVA CHALLIS

DONNA or GARY ERICSSON HANGING TREE RANCH SALMON

MARK BOAM RIGBY

THANE and MARINA SIDDOWAY TETON

TREE TOP RANCH MIDVALE

PRESTON or CLEN ATCHLEY ASHTON

JOHN OR BARBARA FOREST POCATELLO

BERT BRASWELL GRAND VIEW OWYHEE

FAULKNER BROS GOODING

BOW SEWELL LUCILE

MATHEW NETTLETON MURPHY OWYHEE

FARRELL and JOAN CARR INDIAN VALLEY

Artwork by Author.

Collegians Compete

The advance from bulldogger to banker was quite a leap, but Parker Glen Woodall made it with aplomb and several interesting stops along the way. Born to Idahoans James Parker Woodall and Kay Davis Woodall in Lexington, Nebraska, where his father was construction superintendent for Idaho's Morrison Knudsen Company, Parker remembers, "I went to nine different schools while in the second grade." Morrison Knudsen had railroad building contracts in Oregon, Wyoming and Montana during the World War II, when train transportation was critical to the nation. The senior Woodall and his family were kept on the move.

Wanting strong and steady schooling for their children, the Woodalls moved to a cattle ranch at Sweet, Idaho in 1945. It has been their home ever since. Sweet is a small village northeast of the county seat of Emmett and not far from the Payette River and Squaw Creek. To the north are the mountains and High Valley which provide some of the best cattle grazing land in the state.

J. Parker was a cowboy in his own right, born and reared in Horseshoe Bend, where the cattle industry was big. His wife was an accomplished horsewoman and a winner of the women's stake races held in Emmett. Her father, Chuck Davis was a cattle rancher at Jerusalem, near Horseshoe Bend. Her grandfather, State Senator Elmer Davis of Boise County, also announced the calf roping events at the Payette River Valley Cattlemen's Association meeting in Garden Valley. Parker G. became a calf roping winner.

When college time arrived, Parker Glenn enrolled at the University of Idaho and joined the rodeo club. It was automatic that he became one of the dozen on the stake race team as well as a calf roper. "We were known as the Vandal Riders in those days of 1957–1959, and it was organized in 1950. We had one 'home rodeo' each year and because we didn't have an arena, the Pomeroy (Washington) Pony Punchers let us have it in Pomeroy." It was long after Parker graduated that Vandal Riders realized their dream of holding the Idaho Western Classic Rodeo in the Kibbie Dome. It didn't happen until 1983.

At the tenth annual Northwest Junior Rodeo held in Lewiston, Parker was one of more than one-hundred student cowboys to participate. All of the prize money beyond expenses was donated to help other young people such as the Shrine Crippled Children's Hospital and the Lewiston Boys Club. Riding the horse named "War Bonnet," Parker participated in the championship bareback bronc riding and in the championship wild steer riding.

Parker went on to enter the field of education, serving from 1973 through 1977 as superintendent of the Coeur d'Alene school district. He became an organizer of the Northern State Bank and served as its president from 1979 until 1997, when it merged with Washington Trust Bank and he was named president of the North Idaho Region. His interest in rodeo and his Alma Mater Idaho is still proud and strong. The Woodalls are people to "ride the river with," constant in their friendships. J. Parker is still on his cattle ranch at Sweet and when asked when he plans to retire, his answer is, "Well, if I retired I'd want a few acres and a few cattle. And that's what I have here, a few cattle and a few acres."

UI RODEO CLUB

For nearly fifty years, the University of Idaho Rodeo Club has been touched by success and failure, budget battles and championships, support and disappointment.

The UI Club organized in 1950, one year after the National Intercollegiate Rodeo Association was formed. Thirteen colleges met to organize, adopt a constitution and bylaws. Soon all types

They called their group the Vandal Riders and they enjoyed pleasure riding, but competitive rodeos in the Idaho, Washington, Montana region found them ready to rope, ride, barrel race, and steer wrestle. The two hanging on to the prize saddle in the front are Parker Glenn Woodall and Jim Swain. Second row, left to right, are Bob Redmond, Howard Sturzman, Mary Wishard, Betty Keith, and Larry Holmquist. Back row: Terry Martin, Orville Sears, Bob Monroe, Brock Livingston, Clova Beck, and Forest Hall, advisor. *Courtesy of Parker Woodall.*

of Idaho students with a variety of majors and a love of rodeo, came together. Lois Lower, one of the first Vandal Riders, recalls the feelings, "As the Vandal Riders, we thought we could conquer the world, or at least win the NIRA championship." They didn't win the championship but did establish a strong foundation for a future of rodeo and friendship.

From the get-go, the national organization had financial problems. Sound leadership and corporate sponsors built the foundation which brought a growth from the original thirteen to an organization with more than two hundred member colleges and universities with more than three thousand members.

The National places emphasis on fostering team spirit through rodeo competition; encouraging the sport that has roots in the heritage of this country; giving high priority on academic as well as athletic ability; helping young people achieve higher education and become contributing members of society. The UI Club willingly subscribed to the precepts.

Lack of an arena in Moscow for several years took the UI Club's annual rodeo to Pomeroy, Washington and the Tammany Arena in Lewiston. When it was possible to relocate to Moscow's Latah fairgrounds, the club's reputation strengthened.

When the Idaho Western Classic Indoor Rodeo chose the Kibbie Dome on April 15-17, 1983, years of dreaming, diligence and dedication paid off. Roach Construction Company of Genesee worked with the club to transform the Dome into a fifteen thousand square feet dirt surface arena with pens and chutes. Chuck Stauber, club president, voiced the optimism felt among the members: "It will become just like football in the Dome."

Bob Tallman, renowned professional announcer, presided at the first Western Classic. His talents and the club's organization created a show that Dean A. Longgood, Blue Mountain Community College called, "The best production I have attended in twelve years of college rodeo."

It was a great show, but a financial disappointment. The expense tag was $65,254 and the Rodeo Club owed its University $44,000. So many accolades poured in calling the production a success, highly organized and classy, that the University approved the proposal for another the next year. Yet another well organized event in 1984 was in debt for about the same amount, forty thousand dollars.

Students who were more interested in other pursuits were highly critical. Mark Engberg was an angry architect student who wrote a fiery letter to the U newspaper, the *Argonaut,* after the first classic: "If this $104,000 were used to purchase more books for the library rather than dirt for the dome floor, we could be on our way to getting above the national library standards again." When the next year's event was approved and again a productive success but a financial failure, student headlines included, "Losses May Throw Idea of Dome Rodeo" and "Rodeo Rides Rocky Range."

Former club member and Pullman, Washington resident Gary Watson, wrote an impassioned letter for publication in *The Argonaut:* "For the past two years, the UI Club has produced one of the five largest regional collegiate rodeos in the nation." The voices of support seemed to have some affect, as the UI administration gave one last vote of confidence: the final Idaho Western Classic was in 1986.

Club officers that year were Otmar Hofsteader, Mike Lancaster, Mark Pratt, Molly Stowers, Lori Lancaster, Janice Harold and the Western Classic Royalty, Heidi Boehger, queen, and Mandie Duncan, princess.

Some athletes of any sport: golf, basketball, football, baseball, hockey, and others, have what others may consider "quirky" pre-game rituals. They are invoked or performed to help the athlete focus on the competition.

Students and spectators at a University of Idaho rodeo in the early eighties could have observed Marty Bennett of Rupert perform a ritual that seemed half-wild. He rapidly slapped his face several times, then kicked the air and stomped about in a small circle. This was followed by pacing up and down a straight path. When asked about his intricate psyching routine, he quite sanely said, "The competition is between you and the animals. A lot of this is just mental. You got to do what it takes."

In an interview with the *Daily News,* Marty said the ritual "Just gets my adrenaline going. It gets me away from the crowd." Whatever else it did, it secured for him the 1982 title of Idaho College Rodeo All-Around Cowboy. Before attending the University, he twice qualified for the high school national finals. He started bronc riding while in high school at Rupert.

As good sons have been saying about good fathers for centuries, Marty recognizes his father's influence and support with, "I owe most everything to him." Before moving to Rupert and while a student at Utah State University, the senior Bennett was a rough-stock rider. He encouraged his son's interest in rodeo, and Marty started bronc riding while a freshman in high school.

Because of its strong rodeo program, Marty first considered attending the College of Southern Idaho at Twin Falls, but he wanted the excellent pre-veterinary program at the University. Weighing his options, he felt he took the weaker rodeo along with the strong pre-vet program at the University. Even love for rodeo took second place to his desire to be a good student. He succeeded with a full credit load and 3.8 grade point average.

The five hundred dollar veterinary-rodeo scholarship he won made studying a must and he was as intense about studies as bronc riding. Strenuous as his studies were with not enough time for diligent rodeo practice, he was seeded second in the regional rodeo while a freshman. Marty said, "I always dreamed of being the best." His talent and ambition added a sparkle to the 1984 and 1985 rodeo clubs.

There is never enough money for College rodeo and it was in the midst of a series of funding battles that Marty was one more cowboy who proved what the club was all about—riding and dreaming of being first.

RICKS COLLEGE/BYU, IDAHO

When Mel Griffeth wants to pay a compliment to a fellow Idahoan, the finest thing he can say is, "He's a good ol' Idaho cowboy." Griffeth is not only a "good ol' cowboy" himself, but much of his adult life has been centered around horses, riders, and cowboys. He has been with Ricks College's biology department for thirty-seven years and he teaches a popular course called "Field Biology-A Horseback." If the weather is good on Tuesdays and Thursdays, members of the class mount their horses and ride to the Palisades. They have ridden as far as Yellowstone Park and the Teton Peaks.

"Our textbook is the great outdoors, written and painted by

the greatest of authors. And our challenge is to learn to read it," Griffeth uses as a descriptive for his teaching.

A splendid sense of humor comes through in conversations with Mel Griffeth. In telling how he became the coach for the Ricks College rodeo team, he laughed and said, "While sitting in the biology department office one day, two youngsters came in and said 'We gotta rodeo team and we need a coach.' I didn't even have a western shirt, but as soon as I agreed to take over the coaching duties I went downtown in Rexburg and bought a bolo tie and I was then a cowboy."

Seven years later, in 1970, Griffeth was named president of the National Intercollegiate Rodeo Association. He says that the success of the college rodeo team is directly related to the enthusiasm of the coach. There could not be a more enthusiastic teacher than Mel Griffeth. His students have garnered five national championships and the national bull riding title twice. Among his students is Lamar Roche now living in Parma, Idaho and running a cattle ranch of five thousand head. "When they become a national champ, they start thinking big and doing great things," he stated. Another student, Tom Clyde, a national steer wrestling champion now lives in Connell, Washington, in the Tri-Cities area and has a ranch of eight hundred head of dairy cows and four hundred head of beef cattle.

Cherry Stoddard (Sager) who won contests in break-away roping now has a family of eight and still competes after twenty plus years. She and her family make their home in Burley. Nick Baldwin who was a calf roping champion is now on the faculty at Ricks College teaching animal science. His son, Nathan, recently won the Rocky Mountain Regional Championship in calf roping and was one of the competitors at the Nationals in June 1999 at Casper, Wyoming. Joanne Coates (Roche) was a national champion at goat tying. Her husband is an agriculture teacher at Mackay High School and they run a cattle ranch there. Nicole Dansie qualified for the finals, but as they were slated to be held on Sunday and because of her spiritual standards, she would not

The Americanas, eastern Idaho's outstanding drill team brings glory and praises whenever the members and their mounts appear. With the horses' haunches clipped in a checkerboard pattern, snappy riding gear, and the riders erect, it is easy to see why this group brings fame to all of Idaho. The Americanas were awarded both the Presidential Sweepstakes and first place in the Equestrian Division in the 1991 parade in Washington, D.C. One parade watcher, noting the checkerboard pattern on the rumps of the horses, said, "They must have been born that way." A bystander called out, "You must feed them Rice Chex!" A picture perfect Capitol policeman said, "If they don't vote for you, I'm going to arrest them." Mel and Rama Griffeth are the leaders and both agreed that the most beautiful sight was when the group rode in formation in front of the Washington Monument.

Members have included Carlo Erickson, Tim McGarry, Michelle Robison, Marla Nef, Danya Klingler, Cheryl Findlay, Nikki Howard, Colleen Passey, Shantelle Robinson, Tracy Morris, Kathy G. Hawkes, Melvin D. Griffeth, Rama Jean Griffeth, Julie G. Lee, Melanie G. Schwendiman, David Schwendiman, Cady Williams, Katy Porter, Lois Mortenson, Mandy Mortenson, Shirley Perry, Lorie Jenson, Carla Erickson, Brenda Anderson, Becky Munns, Keith Munns, Brandy Albertson, Chantrie Burton, Megan Burton, Buddy Calderwood, Heidi Calderwood, Candice Drussel, Delbert Edstrom, Carrie Edstrom, Heidi Parker Edstrom, Bill Griffeth, Emily Hansen, Jolinda Hansen, Kathy Hawkes, Joshua Hawkes, Jared Hawkes, Whitney Hawkes, Tausha Henderson, Monica Hill, Adrian Jeppesen, Krista Meyers, Jud Miller, Anna Miller, Mindy Price, Laleene Ricks, Julie Saurey, Shanna Saurey, Tara Schwendiman, Ashlie Schwendiman, Vanessa Schwendiman, Sylvan Seely, Gail Seely, Shelly Seely, Sylvia Seely, Amy Thompson, Max Wade, Pam Warthen, Jody Warthen, Jaquie Whitmore, Kellie Whitmore, Tina Whitmore, Nicole Wilcox, Nikole Wren.

compete. Griffeth fields between fifteen and twenty to the championship category every year. He says, "Our prospects are good for more national winners and we often place in the top ten."

The Ricks College rodeo team had a program for thirteen years followed by a hiatus of ten. The college team is now back and participating in ten rodeos each year stretching from St. George, Utah to Boise. The annual rodeo at the college is held the last week in April and regularly attracts a standing room only audience at the indoor arena which seats two thousand. It is located at the Madison County Fairgrounds. The National Finals are held at Ricks College during the week with the award-winning events on Saturday night. Mel and his wife, Rama, have four daughters: Kathy (Jim Hawkes), Melanie (David Schwendiman), Julie (Kevin Lee), and Rama Jean (Kyle Christensen), and eighteen grandchildren. Melanie and Julie are Roman riders.

Five of the grandchildren ride with the Equine Precision Drill Team which he originated and has directed for fifteen years. The drill team is called "The Americanas" and was so named "To strengthen our culture with a large part of patriotism," Griffeth said. There are fifty members, all dressed in matching outfits of red and white and all riding black quarter horses. One twelve year old and several high school and college students ride Roman and each of the fifty riders carries an American flag. The Americanas have presented their precision drills and fancy riding in many places, including Calgary, Alberta; Cheyenne, Wyoming; Stockton, California; and Sun Valley, Idaho. In 1999 they appeared at least twenty times.

One of the great thrills for all of the riders was on the Fourth of July, 1991, when they trucked twenty-nine horses to Washington D.C. to ride in the parade. "We unloaded those horses right in front of the U.S. Capitol building and we spread good old authentic Idaho horse manure from the Capitol building down Pennsylvania Avenue to the White House," Griffeth laughed as he talked. The next time the Americanas go to Washington, D.C. to parade, they are going to ask Idaho's senior

U.S. Senator Larry Craig to ride with them because, "He is a good ol' Idaho cowboy."

COLLEGE OF SOUTHERN IDAHO

The College of Southern Idaho in Twin Falls is fortunate to have as the riding and rodeo instructor World Championship rider Shawn Davis, whose rodeo history is in the chapter on Champs. His teams and single riders and doggers repeatedly win in contests with other colleges and universities.

NORTH IDAHO COLLEGE

The passion for rodeo possessed by Michelle Holt, North Idaho College's last rodeo advisor, began when she was a small girl in Montana. For a Montana youngster growing up on a ranch, rodeo was simply a part of life. Upon moving to Idaho to become an English professor at NIC, it was not with any idea of becoming the rodeo advisor, but in the fall of 1995, a young cowboy who was also an English student approached the teacher and told her that he would be missing a couple of classes because of participation in the Professional Rodeo Cowboys Association events. In discussion with him, the professor learned that the student body would benefit from a College Rodeo Club. Her lifelong love of horses and people came together to give her the advisor task.

It became necessary for Professor Holt to return to Montana to be with an ill family member. This was a blow to the yet small, but growing club. The rodeo schedule for the students was a busy one with ten during the October-November and March-May schedules in northern Idaho, Washington, and Oregon. Fund-raisers kept the members busy during the off-season. The rodeo club was independent of the athletic teams, so private sources and the NIC Associated Students assisted the club operations.

Several of the members have gone on to four-year colleges and continued in rodeo. How the students felt about the advisor is summed up in a note the 1997 club president Cameron Rasor

North Idaho College students Cameron Rasor and Jesse Palmer calf-roping at Lewis and Clark State College Rodeo. *Courtesy of Michelle Holt.*

wrote on the back of a rodeo picture featuring him and another student, Jesse Palmer: "Thanks for all the time and money you have put into this club. Without you we would be nothing. Thanks again and good luck in coaching in the future. Sincerely, best friend and soon to be rodeo star, Cameron Rasor."

But until Professor Holt or someone like her appears on the NIC campus, the rodeo club is on hold.

HIGH SCHOOL RODEO

"High school rodeo gives students who are interested a chance to excel, a reason to improve grades, be part of a group, experience success, and improve self esteem." The words are those of Marvin Hansen of St. Anthony in eastern Idaho. He considers it a privilege to work with high school students of rodeo: "I have watched as they became district, state, and national champions. Some went on to become college champions and a few decided to become professionals."

Hansen has been involved with high school rodeo for more than thirty years during which many good athletes participated. He says, "I have seen students go from failing more than half of their classes to getting a grade point above 3.0, because they became involved in something in which they could excel. The same rules apply to rodeo as to any other high school sport. Those who do not understand the sport of rodeo do not realize the time, money, and effort these young people put into it."

High school rodeo in Idaho began in 1949, with a State Finals where participants could qualify for the National High School Rodeo. This involved only a few Idaho participants. The program grew rapidly and in 1960 the state divided into districts. District One runs from Salmon to Driggs; District Two, North Idaho south to a part of Boise; District Three, the Boise area; District Four, the Pocatello area; and District Five, the Twin Falls area.

Rodeo clown Jesse Heim of Kuna and Wilder risks life and injury to distract the bull from attacking the dismounted rider. So many of the top rodeo athletes begin their career in Idaho High School Rodeo, and this is another one of those success stories. Jesse began his career as a rodeo clown during high school. He went to clown school in California, then worked the high school and homeground rodeos until his graduation. Jesse now is a professional rodeo clown and bullfighter, with memberships in PRCA and ICA. *Courtesy of Tass and Greg Heim.*

As involvement increased, new Districts Six, Seven, and Eight were added. High school rodeo includes the following events for girls: cow cutting, queen contest, breakaway roping, goat tying, pole bending, barrel racing, and team roping. For boys: cow cutting, bareback riding, calf roping, saddle bronc riding, steer wrestling, bull riding, and team roping.

District Seven holds a contest to determine the academic rodeo team in the district. It is not uncommon for those with a 3.9 or 4.0 to compete. District Seven also has twelve rodeos held on six weekends. The top six contestants in each event qualify for state competition which has been held in Pocatello for the past several years.

Shane Morton

"We all rode in rodeo parades to represent our schools, and the cowboys and the hippies always had a fight at the State Rodeo in Burley. It was fun!" The words are from the mouth of Shane Morton of St. Anthony, one of the best of the Idaho High School Rodeo stars. Upon further inquiry about the cowboys and hippies, it was learned that the cowboys from out of town, always wearing their western gear, would show up in the downtown areas before the actual rodeo took place.

The youngsters hanging out in the downtown areas with their colorful, but different, costumes of baggy tie-dyed shirts and dragging pants, sandals and wearing their hair down over their shoulders or in a pigtail, could not resist letting their feelings toward the rodeo "squares" be known. Hence the fights that Shane and his buddies thought were "a lot of fun."

Involved in high school rodeo during the years of 1968 to 1972, Shane was a representative of District One. This included Idaho Falls, Salmon, Mackay, Challis, Arco, Mud Lake, Sugar City, St. Anthony, Ashton, Rexburg, Rigby, and Tetonia. Since then it has grown so large that it was split and is now District Seven, including Idaho Falls, Rigby, Rexburg, St. Anthony, Sugar City, Ashton, and Tetonia.

He qualified for the State Finals four years in bareback riding, calf roping, and bull riding; and he also qualified two years in team roping.

Only one rodeo was needed to qualify for State. The first year the rodeo was held in Mackay; the second, in Arco; the third, in Mud Lake; and the fourth, in Rigby. They now have six rodeos to qualify for State, and each contestant gets to compete two times at each rodeo. The District rodeos were produced by Phersons of Darlington, Hoggan Rodeo Company of Hamer, and Crystal Brothers of Rigby.

Shane was the All Around Champion at the Rigby Rodeo. He also qualified for two National Finals in Fargo, North Dakota, and Filer, Idaho. Along with Jerry Angell, and Bobby Remington, Shane won the team trophy, triumphing over forty-three other contestants from Arco, who had the largest team that year. St. Anthony High School still has the trophy.

Shane can only remember two queens from District One: Louann Campbell and Susan Maheras.

The High School State Rodeo, produced by Haslam Rodeo Company from Utah, was previously held in Burley. The past years it has been held in Pocatello.

Marv Hansen was the advisor and coach when Shane was enrolled in school. Shane described Marv as being a "most respectable man." In 1971, Shane was Student, District and State President of the Idaho High School Rodeo; Rose Johnson, Mackay, Adult District President; and Moe and Carol Sagers were adult State Presidents. All three are described by Shane as "very good leaders."

Admiration for Shane Morton is great in his hometown of St. Anthony and throughout the rodeo communities. And for good reason. He and his brother, Dirk, were pickup men at the Fort Hall Rodeo about 1970. The horse that Shane was riding was smacked by a bucking horse with a wallop so intense that both rider and mount were knocked end over end. Shane's neck and head were badly twisted and injured and he was hospitalized for months. Although unable to participate now, his love for and interest in rodeo remain strong.

COWBOYS AND COWGIRLS GO TO SCHOOL

Rodeo schools provide future competitors and champions for shows throughout the world. Idaho has a number and they are comparable to those at the universities and colleges. Toots Mansfield, winner of seven world championships, started the first one in 1954 as a calf roping school in Big Springs, Texas. A sixteen-time world champion rider, Jim Shoulders, started the first riding school in 1963 at Henrietta, Oklahoma.

Shawn Davis (see chapter 16) has run a topnotch annual school for years at the College of Southern Idaho, Twin Falls. He uses the CSI Expo Center for classes in hands-on practice. He brings in about 120 head of horses. Several have taken part in the Professional Rodeo Cowboys Association National Finals in Las Vegas.

Stock contractors also run some schools and hire cowboy award-winners to teach in their particular field. An old rodeo saying is, "The best way to learn how to ride a bronc, rope a calf or wrestle a steer is to just do it." In today's rapidly growing world, the opportunities are not as great as they once were, as neither facilities nor animals are as available.

Davis says that he was "Among the last of the cowboys to come up through the ranks without some kind of formal instruction. When I started there were maybe five hundred of us who tried to learn to ride broncs by trial and error. Of those five hundred, only five made it and only two or three, including myself, made it big."

That kind of learning, Davis believes, can be wrong. He and other school operators think that is why riding-training schools are needed. Bad habits are less likely to be adopted at a school and if a cowboy doesn't get it corrected, he may never end up in the money.

Professional cowboys who need to get back in shape after an injury or want a refresher course, attend the school along with the "tenderfeet" who want to learn from the ground up. Rodeo fundamentals are taught by Davis and longtime friend J.C.

Trujillo. Both learned through the school of hard landings. They use their own experiences and knowledge, instant replay videos, mechanical bucking machines and actual animals. They attempt to match the horse to the cowboy's ability and teach all about the equipment. "We stress safety. and how to handle the livestock in any situation," Davis says.

After learning on the first mount, the student is permitted to ride on all the horses he can take. Students also sign up for bull wrestling, saddle or bareback bronc riding. Rodeo contests demonstrating competitive pressures make up the graduation day events.

Strong People, Hard Lives

GOVERNOR-SENATOR-HORSESHOER

When Len B. Jordan of Grangeville was a candidate for the office of Governor of Idaho, his campaign manager, Bill Campbell of Boise, wanted to stress the facts that Jordan was a man who had spent hundreds of miles and hours on horseback and that he would be prudent with the taxpayers money. A poster was designed with a photo of the candidate in jeans, denim shirt and boots. Those miles on horseback had left him with enough of a bow in his legs to carry the whimsical caption, "He didn't get those legs riding a pork barrel." The sheepman, rancher, automobile dealer and state legislator went from the Governor's office

Len Jordan

to the United States Senate and was appointed by President Eisenhower to the International Joint Commission.

When the Jordan family lived at their "Home Below Hells Canyon," which Grace Jordan used as the title for her splendid book, at the Kirkwood Bar Sheep Ranch, they were six trail miles from the nearest road at Pittsburg and sixteen miles from the highway at Lucile. Son Joe said, "We used horses to get 'out' or the boat when it was running. Our sheep camps were supplied by mule packstring, both on the Snake River winter range and the Selway-Elk City area summer range, which was a twenty-four day trail for sheep and packstock, each way. Horse and mule shoeing was a major task. Dad did a lot of it as the combination of black-smithing and shoeing was hard, particular work."

Len Jordan was a particular man in all he did, ranching or government. Sharp-shod pack animals were a necessity, Joe pointed out and said, "Dad started with blank shoes and forged toe and heel calks sharpened to grip on ice." The ranch was located on a hillside too steep for cattle and the trails were too precipitous for flat-land horses. Much of the river trail was blasted out of the rock canyon walls, so the stock needed good shoes year around. Ace Barton of Riggins lived with his family at Sheep Creek and fondly remembers how Len would stop and spend the night at their place enroute from one sheep camp to the other "way over in the Selway country. We liked to see him coming."

The sensitivity and strong character of Len Jordan comes through with the story Joe told of his Dad's return to the ranch after they had sold it about 1940 to Bud Wilson. The Jordan's camp tender (packer), Del Catron, remained on the ranch. That autumn the new owner was away and Del became ill. Len Jordan returned to Kirkwood Bar from Grangeville and put winter shoes on the horses that had served him so well. "He was just not com-fortable," his son said, "with some strange shoer."

Years later, for a time, Len Jordan was associated with the Campbell family and their Circle C Ranch. It was not unusual to see the working cowboy herding cattle anywhere from New Meadows to the Snake River.

JOE STRAIN, WHIPMAKER

No, cowboys don't whip their horses. Yes, some cowboys buy whips because they like to crack 'em. Stage (Rhinestone) cowboys buy whips to use as props. Others who buy whips include western actors, jugglers, movie studios need them for mule skinners and bull whackers, cattle workers, gun spinners and trick shooters, stuntmen and those involved in martial arts. A whip gains a life of its own in the hand of an artist. With a twist of the wrist, the whip artist can snap a cigarette from the lips, encircle the ankle or waist of an assistant on stage, shred a paper held out from someone across the room. When they want the best or a special kind, they contact a talented and pleasant young fellow in Rathdrum, Idaho. Twenty-four year old Joe Strain who installed his whip factory in the daylight basement of his parents home has been at the self-taught craft since he was twelve.

At that age he had two years of learning and braiding leather, which moved him into plaiting (another word for whip braiding). He then "borrowed seventy dollars from Mom to buy a large cowhide." He carefully fashioned a couple of whips and sold them, using the money to buy more leather supplies. He was on his own and on his way.

Mark Allen is a dealer in western arena arts based in Las Vegas and when young Strain telephoned him to tell about his whips, Allen said, "I thought I was dealing with an adult, until I learned how old he was." He liked the whip Strain sent as an example of his work and ordered several to sell. Over the years, Allen has remained a customer and thinks "Joe will soon be one of the premier whipmakers in the world." A modest young man, Joe laughs a little and says, "Well, I don't know about the world. How about the best in Idaho?"

Northern Whip Company has one owner, one manager, one whipmaker and one salesman. All four are Joe Strain and he keeps very busy, but refuses to lessen the quality by speeding the process. He produces ten to fifteen whips a week, and they retail for three hundred dollars apiece. Special orders can go as high as seven hundred dollars. They can vary from short quirts to the fifty-footers favored by performers. Joe taught himself to crack a whip, even from horseback, and improved his technique by studying the film, *The Man From Snowy River.* He has become a master at whip demonstrations.

He purchased a machine to do the cutting for him, but soon went back to using his thumbnail and a box knife to cut the kangaroo leather strands more evenly and quickly. Among his hundreds of clients are such people as Bill Bowman, an honorary Texas Ranger who does trick shooting, gun spinning and whip cracking. Several rodeo queens have purchased Strain whips and there is a collection at the Will Rogers Ranch in California, where the son and grandson of the late comedian-entertainer do gun and rope spinning and whip cracking.

RAY HOLES, SADDLE MASTER

Other fine saddle makers listed in this book would have agreed that one of the best was the late Ray Holes of Grangeville area. No one could be long in Ray's presence without sensing that "here is an extraordinary human being who truly loves his fellow man." His daughter-in-law Ellamae Holes said, "When Ray would come into the shop as he was trying to retire, his presence just made people feel good. There was sort of an 'aura' about him that drew people." Perhaps because he went through the Depression years, or maybe he would have been that way had he been wealthy, but he never believed in charging an arm and a leg for his finely crafted saddles. He was willing to extend himself to help others. Years ago when a group of travel writers, editors, and photographers were traveling Idaho to learn what makes us "tick," Sunday was the only day they could be in Grangeville. Ray thought it no imposition to be called from the comforts of home to open his shop and demonstrate tooling a beautiful saddle design.

Ray made saddles at the family home ranch south of Cottonwood in 1934. They sold for sixty-five dollars and would go for many hundreds today. In 1936 he rented a building in Cottonwood for seven dollars and fifty cents a month. He and Lillian Baer were married and were able to rent a cold water flat for seven dollars a month. In the fall of 1939, they moved to Grangeville, and have operated out of three different locations, but always on Main Street. Somewhere along the way, he purchased a full-size model of a horse, which graced the large window front of the shop. It attracted attention from homefolks and travelers.

Numerous cowboys and cowgirls yet today boast of owning a Ray Holes saddle. From the start, Ray wanted to make saddles for the working cowboys from the Idaho hills and prairies that he knew from childhood. He stayed with them, although he took orders from others who stopped by and talked him into it. Such cowmen as Clark, George and Deward Gill, Roy Tumelson, Muggs Bentley, Ward Sewell, and others were proud of their working saddles.

During the years he operated the shop, Ray made over 3,000 saddles. His son, Jerry, who was raised in the business, and wife Ellamae, started buying the store in 1973. For a few years Ray was in semi-retirement and he and Lilian moved to a small ranch along White Bird Creek south of Grangeville. At last count, including the fine custom saddles made by Jerry, numbered 4,030 and the places of sale include: England, Germany, Italy, Belgium, South America, and Japan. On the fiftieth anniversary of Ray Holes Saddle Shop in 1984, they brought out a model named "The Dean Oliver," honoring Idaho's still-reigning World Champion calf roper.

For several years, Jerry and Ellamae traveled with a twenty-foot red trailer with "Ray Holes Saddle Shop" emblazoned on the sides. The trailer showed up at the National Rodeo Finals, the Cow Palace, Boise's Horse Exposition, rodeos and shows throughout the west.

A few years ago, Jerry and Ellame sold the saddle section of the businenss to friend and employee John Calhoun, who had been saddlemaker and shop foreman eighteen years. The Holes operate the western clothing and tack section and it is still the Ray Holes Saddle Shop.

LITTLE JO MONAGHAN

When Little Jo Monaghan died in 1903 at Rockville in Idaho's largest and most southwestern county of Owyhee, the undertaker discovered that the person who had ridden the Idaho ranges and was considered an expert at taming and riding bucking horses was not the cowboy that everyone had thought—but a cowgirl. This unusual story made headlines across the United States and even jumped the Atlantic Ocean to appear in the London newspapers.

Not enough history was known about her to have the exact dates, but it is believed that she arrived in Idaho in 1867 or 1868 (some sources date it at 1875) depending upon which publication is read. Before someone discovered she could tame a wild horse, she herded sheep and found work doing ranch chores. She always dressed in the clothing of a ranch worker and was accepted as one.

Nevertheless, Jo never stayed in the cowboys sleeping quarters, preferring the top of a haystack or curled up in a blanket. She removed herself from others as much as possible. A small person, standing five feet and two inches, she barely weighed a hundred and thirty-five pounds. She also had a high voice.

When people wondered why she falsified her gender, only guesses could be given. In her fine publication, *Idaho Women In History,* published in 1991, Betty Penson-Ward wrote, "My guess is that she liked the life. She had an identity. In a time when a woman had few career choices other than teaching, wife, or a prostitute, there was little difficulty for a male in finding a job (as a man). She could go into saloons. She could vote and serve on a jury, which many riders claimed she did."

Penson-Ward wrote that Little Jo was the star of the first western movie ever filmed west of the Mississippi. She rode bucking horses in Iowa for a film of Andy Whaylen's Wild West Show by Vitagraph Film Company. She was asked to do another film the next year but declined. Perhaps she was fearful that if she appeared too often her disguise would be uncovered.

One story has it that Jo had been driven out of her eastern home by parents who were mortified that she became pregnant. She is said to have left a baby son with a sister who raised him. At the time of her death, she owned several hundred head of cattle and horses.

The Champs

DEAN OLIVER

He stands six feet three inches tall, weighs a solid two-hundred pounds, and has a rugged face filled with character. Idaho's proudly claimed world rodeo champion Dean Oliver has a muscled body which he keeps in shape through working some horses and one-hundred and forty head of cattle while still managing to get in a few rounds of golf. Oliver stays so busy that the fat doesn't have time to settle around his middle. The large, capable hands that have tied thousands of piggin' strings around the heels of calves, are a good match for his long legs that stride across the living room in the Greenleaf, Idaho home where he and his wife, Martha, live, or out on the range in back of the house.

At seventy-one, he plays golf in the range of his age and enjoys it. He took up skiing for several years, but the necessity of a hip operation put a stop to visiting the slopes. The golf greens took skiing's place. When asked if it were true that he was the one who started the fad of wearing a cowboy hat while skiing, he said, "No, I don't know who did that, but I like to keep my ears warm."

Whether or not he knew it, Dean Oliver's boyhood was dedicated to preparing him to become a world rodeo champion. No one deserved the multiple honors more, before nor since, because no one worked harder. He knew calves and horses as well as any youngster in Idaho, and better than most in the nation. He knew the wiles and ways of the frisky calves. He knew his horses as well as he knew himself. He knew the strength and endurance of the animal, and he knew how to care to the needs of all three, cowboy, horse, and calf. When the time came to enter the larger arena of national rodeo, Dean Oliver was ready. He was strong, skilled and eager.

To Idahoans with generations of this rugged, outdoor way of life coursing through their veins, Dean Oliver is a genuine cowboy hero.

Oliver's many trophies and a large beautiful oil painting of him on his favorite quarter horse gelding, "Mickey," where Dean is about to rope a speeding calf, hang on the dining room wall in the Greenleaf ranch house. Attention is drawn to a large and handsome bronze of the same two subjects. The artist was Ed Hayes of Houston, Texas, who sculpted fifteen or twenty of the nation's top rodeo champions. The nameplate carries the simple message:

> ### The Dean of Ropers
> • **DEAN OLIVER AND MICKEY** •

Mickey was eleven years old when Oliver purchased him. "He was beautiful," Oliver said, "he weighed eleven hundred and fifty pounds and stood 14.3 hands high." The roper's roper went on to say that, "Teamwork between the roper and his mount is all important, and Mickey was a great one."

Admirers, broadcasters, and writers speak or write in superlatives when describing Oliver, the champion. "The cowboy's cowboy. He is simply the best. Dean is the Dean. The real McCoy. There's no one like him." Little matter who says it, nor the actual words; when it comes to a World Champion Rodeo star, the bottom line is that there is not a more-admired Idahoan than Dean Oliver. Others in this chapter come close: Dee Pickett, Harry Charters, Deb Copenhaver, Shawn Davis, Jackson Sundown, Burrel Mulkey, Harry Hart, Guy Cash, to name several. But Dean still reigns.

When a conversation happens to team Oliver and Pickett, the words can come out, "Those two. They are the Godfathers of Idaho Rodeo. They are always there, overseeing the youngsters, the newcomers on their way. They want to help when and where they can." That statement was not from anyone named Corleone, but from Idaho's former state treasurer Lydia Justice Edwards, who has a passion for rodeo and its advancement as the American sport.

Admiration for the rider/roper has no bounds and many there are who can recite the reasons why he is so high on the Good Guy list. He was born in Dodge City, Kansas (what better name could a cowboy have for his place of birth) on November 1, 1929, just days after the "Black Thursday," October 24, stock market crash on Wall Street and the ensuing Great Depression. The Oliver family moved to Nampa during the Depression and it became necessary for Dean to help support his mother after his father's 1940 death in a plane crash. Dean was one of seven children and possessed the courage and the desire and the strength to do what was needed. He soon quit school and went to work on a dairy farm, from early morning until after nightfall, seven days a week, for $175 a month. Those hard and long hours developed in him the trait of "never give up," which served him well in the rodeo arena.

The story of how he and his brother Vernon would sneak out of the house at night when everyone was sleeping and practice roping the neighbor's calves is a legend passed on to three generations of rodeo aficionados. Dean worked at whatever jobs were available and finally managed to buy a horse that was a tad on the wild side, kicking and biting until under control. The next big purchase was a calf with which to practice roping skills. Years later, in an interview he said, "I felt that rodeo was my only real chance of having anything."

"Rodeo rewarded him with more than he dreamed. He won the Nampa Rodeo championship ten years in a row. On the national and international basis, he was called "the greatest calf roper in the history of rodeo"; to have earned nearly a half-million dollars between his start in 1951 through 1972, a cool $455,464; and hold a world record eight calf roping

Dean Oliver, longtime World Champion calf roper, shows his speed and agility which are the reasons for his winning eight world championships. *Courtesy of DeVere.*

championships, compiles a mighty reputation. When he also competed in steer wrestling, he won the world champion all-around cowboy from 1963 through 1965, and held the record in 1969 for winning the most money in a single event in the year, $38,118. It was for calf roping. These were but a few of the state, regional and national awards he received over the years.

Dean's wife Martha (Reizenstein) is his greatest supporter and worked all the time he was in the process of becoming a world champ. They have five daughters, Sheryl, DeAnn, Nikki, Kelli, and Karla; the latter two are twins. There are five grand-children. Nikki also rides and excels at cow-cutting. She is married to the son of the late Jim Roeser of Caldwell. Jim was a champion saddle bronc rider.

The Idaho Centennial Homecoming magazine of one-hundred "people who make a difference" said of Dean Oliver: "When Oliver found the horse that suited his roping, there was no stopping him. He won eight national championships . . . still holds the national record in calf roping . . . 1962 through 1964, he won All-Around Champion for roping and bulldogging . . . was the first roper from the Northwest to win a championship. Over the years he won the Nampa Rodeo ten times in a row, even though 'your home town' is the hardest win. Today the kid who years ago snuck into the Snake River Stampede is on its board of directors."

DEE PICKETT

To be or not to be, a Dallas Cowboy or an Idaho Cowboy? That was the question for the multi-talented, athletic Dee Pickett of Caldwell back in 1977. Dee was twenty-three and already a standout performer on the football field and rodeo arena. The Dallas Cowboys and Seattle Seahawks were contacting his Boise State coach Jim Criner to learn if he could be lured to either team. They also kept in touch with Pickett, attempting to persuade him to go pro. In his mind, he tossed coins. Rodeo and football pros made about the same amount of money. The awards and rewards were great in both.

Finally, the mental coin toss flipped on rodeo! Both sports held generational strength for him. Pickett's great-grandfather, Cy Johnson of Nampa, was a money winner at rodeos throughout the northwest and touted as one of the few great bronc busters in Boise Valley. This was before and during the twenties. He was awarded a saddle at the prominent Pendleton Roundup. Johnson got his start at the 1913 wild horse roundup-and-ride in Nampa, the forerunner of the Snake River Stampede. Two qualified for the final ride, Bob Foster and Cy Johnson. Pickett's great-grandfather came in second.

Sixty-five years later that the great-grandson was named

rookie of the year in professional rodeo, an award given to the cowboy who wins more money in two or more contests than any other first-year performer. The first half of the year 1978 he won only $1500, but came on strong in the last half with a total of $30,140. This qualified Pickett for his first National Finals Rodeo in team roping, and he fell short by nine hundred and fifty dollars to qualify for calf roping. The home newspapers, the *Idaho Free Press* of Nampa and the *News Tribune* of Caldwell on July 16, 1979, extolled his skill, with: "Pickett's future among the ranks of the professional rodeo cowboys is ripe with promise. Of the twenty-three previous rookie winners, ten have gone on to become world champions."

Of those ten, four were Idaho champs: Harry Charters of Melba, Jim Kornell of Salmon, Bob Robinson of Tuttle, and Jim Steen of Glenns Ferry. More would follow. When Pickett joined the Professional Rodeo Cowboys Association, Coach Criner admitted that he had always known that Pickett, who had won his first saddle at fourteen as all-around champion of the Caldwell Little Britches Rodeo, would likely choose rodeo over football. "He was always up front about his love of rodeo and I was on hand for his first contest in the arena." Criner said that Pickett had the same commanding appearance on the football field that he did in rodeo, and said, "Dee will be a winner in rodeo for a long time to come. The sport of rodeo is lucky to have won him."

As a boy, Pickett had much exposure to football. His father, U.S. Marine Dick Pickett, played on the Marine team. After three years on the University of Idaho football team, Dick joined the Marines. Dee was born in San Diego and his dad put a football in his hand by the time he was toddler, hoping he would become a player. When Dee was seven, they moved to Nampa, where he first experienced horses and rodeo. His uncle, Bill Johnson, a calf and team roper in the Idaho Cowboys Association, took him into the arena and taught him how to ride and rope.

The next year he was only eight, so fibbed about his age and said he was nine in order to compete in the junior rodeo in

Baker, Oregon. He didn't win, but was pleased with a buckle for being the youngest contender in calf riding and roping and in the breakaway contests.

That fall, young Pickett started playing touch football with his fourth grade classmates but the coaching by his dad and his own ability soon elevated him to the fifth and sixth grade teams. He played half-and-quarterbacks. For several years he didn't need to make a choice between the two athletic loves, and he enjoyed and excelled in both.

The same year he won all-around champion at the Little Britches Rodeo, he was starting quarterback for the Vallivue High School. He remained the football starter all four years. He won the all-around high school rodeo championship twice, was state high school team roping champ twice, participated in the National High School Rodeo Finals twice and one year won a go-round in the calf roping contest.

He felt that high school football was first with him, but he noted that he didn't like it when he had to miss the late summer rodeos because football practice was underway. His feats on the gridiron were earning him bids from several northwest colleges and after making several recruitment trips, signed a letter of intent with Brigham Young University in Utah. Rodeo was a jealous competitor and he didn't like leaving for the university when he was leading in calf roping in the Idaho Cowboy Association and there were six more rodeos to go that season. He wanted to defend his title, but he carried out the intent of the letter and went to Provo. Four days later he was very homesick and couldn't quit thinking about rodeo going on without him. He went home and finished the season. Again he won the calf roping title.

His plan to attend Boise State University was foiled by eligibility rules compelling him to first attend a junior college for a semester. He transferred back to BSU in the spring and to no one's surprise was the starting quarterback that fall. In next to the last game, Pickett suffered a knee injury so severe surgery was

required. It was not successful and another operation was scheduled. He missed the first three fall games. Guess who led the
team to the Big Sky conference championship when he did get
his hands on the ball? You're right, Pickett.

During the spring and summer he did a lot of thinking and
announced that he was not going back to the university for his
senior year, but was going to become a professional cowboy.
Years later in March 1985, when the Professional Rodeo
Cowboys Association annual rodeo banquet presented him
awards of cash, an engraved silver and gold buckle, hand-tooled
saddle and a year of free airline tickets, as the world champion
all-around cowboy of 1984, he tearfully told the huge Denver
crowd, "I look back and remember that time when I turned my
back on something I was a lot better at (football). If I had known
that it would turn out like this, I would have slept a lot better."
He went on to say he thanked God for his championship and he
hoped to be a good representative of the sport of rodeo. As every
Idaho rodeo aficionado knows, he has been superb.

He won the all-around by earning more than one hundred
and twenty-two thousand dollars in the 1984 team roping and
calf roping events, taking in more dollars than any other cowboy.
His teammate was Mike Beers, also of Caldwell.

When Idaho's Centennial Commission published the 1990
book, *Here We Have Idaho* in 1990 and listed biographies and
color photos of one hundred "People Who Make a Difference,"
two happy, laughing cowboys astride their handsome horses
were featured on the back cover: Dee Pickett and Dean Oliver.
Dee's biography told of his marrying Brenda Lee, who was Miss
Rodeo America in 1983. The couple logged over one hundred
thousand miles on their pickup in 1989 while he roped in more
than one hundred and ten rodeos.

MIKE BEERS

Mike Beers and Dee Pickett pooled their skills and knowledge as rodeo ropers to build a formidable team. Mike joined the

ranks of outstanding cowboys in 1984, when he and Dee won the world championship team calf roping contest.

In the 1985 contest they finished out of the money, but tied for fourth in team roping in the winners list for the year. They opened a roping school in Caldwell and had all the students they could handle.

In team roping, the partners back their horses on either side of the chute and wait for the steer to break out. While whirling lassoes overhead, they give chase. The header throws first over the steer's head and turns his horse aside while turning the steer's rear to the heeler who circles his rope and watches for the perfect time to toss the lariat just above the ground and under the steer's hooves. Tricky business. Then he tightens the noose around the legs. That is "head and heel."

When he received his honors for the world championship team roping during the Pro Rodeo Cowboys Association awards banquet at Denver on January 8, 1985, Mike Beers told the huge audience that it had been a good year for him and Pickett. He said, "Three good things happened this year. I won a gold buckle, bought my own place (in Caldwell), and I'm getting married on March 11." That was the day he married Bonnie Breck.

The 1998 *ProRodeo Cowboys Association Media Guide* lists Mike Beers as one of the top 15 Team Ropers (heelers). In 1984, Mike earned the status of "World Champion Team Roper," and in 1997, he placed tenth in the "All-Around" category. Coming from Powell Butte, Oregon, Mike is described as: Height: 6-2; Weight: 210; Events Worked: Team Roping, Calf Roping, Steer Roping; National Finals Rodeo Qualifications: (16) Team Roping 1980–87, '89–91, '93, '97 (invited '88, '92); Calf Roping '81, '83, '85; National Steer Finals Rodeo Qualifications: (1) 1992; Born May 4, 1958 in The Dalles, Oregon; College: Blue Mountain Community College (Pendleton, Oregon); Family: wife, Bonnie; sons, Brandon, Joe; Other Occupation: none; Special Interests: roping; Professional Rodeo Cowboys Association Membership: 1980; Achievements: Colombia River Circuit All-

Around champion, 1985, '87–88, '91–95, Team Roping champion, 1981, '83, '85, '88, '91–92, Calf Roping champion, 1981, '95, Steer Roping champion, 1986, '88, '91, '94, '96; Coors Chute-Out Team Roping champion, 1984; National Intercollegiate Rodeo Association/College Nationals Finals Rodeo Team Roping champion, 1978; Oregon High School All-Around and Team Roping champion, 1977. His 1997 earnings were $50,851 and career earnings at that date were $1,265,790.

JACKSON SUNDOWN

The year was 1911. The place: the Pendleton, Oregon, Roundup. The rider was a fifty-year old cowboy with the intriguing name of Jackson Sundown. He was twice the age of most of the other bronc-busters and twice as good. He was riding a vaulting, springing, sunfisher with the unlikely name of "Angel." He was the Indian of whom the Nez Perce tribal members were the most proud. His history was amazing. With the long braids tied under his chin, this six-footer stayed on the bucking horse to capture the World Championship that year.

Jackson Sundown decided that he would take one more ride in the contest at Pendleton. During the 1915 roundup he came in third and was thinking about retiring when friends helped him make up his mind to have another go. He packed his buffalo-skinned tepee and his cowboy gear and went to Pendleton. He was so popular that from the get-go, roars of support came with every jolting jump that Angel made. Riding in the grand finals against Rufus Rollen of Claremont, Oklahoma, and Bob Hall of Pocatello, both of whom were also applauded, it was apparent that Jackson Sundown was a favorite and the crowd went wild when he was named the winner. As Rollen and Hall were eliminated from the contest, the crowd rose to its collective feet, shouting, "Sundown—Sundown!" As the shot was fired to bring the ride to an end, the applause was thunderous. The slim, modest and almost shy fifty-year old Nez Perce Indian became Champion of the World. He had used his old range saddle, as always. When the handsome leather-tooled prize saddle was awarded and he was asked what he would like to have engraved on the silver plate, he asked that his wife's name be inscribed.

The new World Champion was invited to ride again at a special performance held in 1917 in Lewiston with Idaho Governor Moses Alexander as the guest of honor. It was a proud day for Governor Alexander and Jackson Sundown, both of whom had gone through hazardous days as young boys and shown great courage after growing into manhood. The Governor thoroughly enjoyed this part of the wild west he chose for his home and felt genuinely honored to be a special guest at a rodeo.

Born in Bavaria on November 13, 1853, as the youngest of eight children, Moses Alexander immigrated to the United States in 1867. He moved in with a sister in a Jewish neighborhood in New York City and found it difficult to learn English where Hebrew was still the principle language. He sold newspapers, did odd jobs for merchants, and moved to Chillicothe, Missouri, to help in a store operated by his cousin. He showed a real talent for merchandising as a salesman. He needed to learn the English language in a hurry and after work studied not only English, but history and the U.S. Constitution. He became an avid reader of newspapers and that reading was a major influence in shaping his political beliefs. When his cousin died, Alexander became a partner and within a few years, sole owner of the store. In 1891, he was heading for Alaska when he heard about Boise, Idaho being a fine place for investments. He checked out the town and bought a former saloon and converted it into a men's clothing store. The business prospered and within the next few years, he opened stores in many neighboring towns. He was mayor of Boise and reorganized lagging city departments, passed anti-gambling ordinances and worked at making the capital a modern city. He later became governor and promised a platform of economy. One newspaper, the *Owyhee Avalanche* editorialized, "If Governor

Alexander is successful, he will be far greater to the people of Idaho than his biblical namesake (Moses) of Bullrush fame was to the children of Israel, and our state will be the modern Land of Promise."

It was not without problems that Governor Alexander served as governor. A bill which would make Idaho a prohibition district aroused such passion that his life was threatened if he signed the measure. Acting like an Idaho cowboy would, he did not seem disturbed and the signing went on as planned. He was a patriot and became active in sending the Idaho National Guard to the Mexican border and it included his only son, Nathan. When Germany announced a policy of unrestricted submarine warfare on January 31, 1917, and President Wilson severed diplomatic relations and asked for a declaration of war, Governor Alexander advised the President that the recently demobilized Idaho militia was ready to respond to any call.

Little wonder that Jackson Sundown was proud and eager to perform at a special rodeo for such a man as Governor Moses Alexander.

The horsemanship of the Nez Perce was envied and admired throughout the Indian nation. It was from these Nez Perce warriors that Jackson Sundown learned to ride. He rode his own Appaloosa pony from the time he could walk. By the time he was eleven years old, the five bands of the Nez Perce Indian Nation swept through Idaho, fleeing over the Lolo Pass into Montana. They were hotly pursued by U.S. Army troops commanded by General O.O. Howard. Sundown and other boys were hiding under buffalo robes when the Army troops made an early dawn attack on the Indian encampment, August 9, 1877, at the Battle of the Big Horn in Montana. Although the tepee in which they were hiding was set on fire, the boys managed to escape.

The Nez Perce continued the flight toward Canada where they expected to join with Sioux Chief Sitting Bull. An early snow on September 30 at Bear Paw made it easier for the cavalry to again swoop down upon the Indians. Young Sundown was one of the Nez Perce who escaped from that fight, and he did so by hiding himself from the soldiers by clinging to the side of his horse so that it appeared riderless. He was, however, slightly wounded and had no blankets nor food. He continued to ride north and eventually reached Sitting Bull's Camp in Canada.

He remained there for two years and then went to the Flathead Indian Reservation in Montana. On the Flathead he gained an early reputation as an outstanding rider. It was about 1900 that he moved to Culdesac, Idaho, and built a log cabin on the land allotment secured. He married a young widow of his tribe and became a father to her two small sons.

The late George Greene spoke often of the fame that Jackson Sundown brought to the little town of Culdesac which lies at the north side of White Bird Hill. He became known as a winner in the Culdesac annual roundups and by 1914, the top riders refused to sign for a contest with Sundown, knowing they would be beaten. They told Al Fonberg, the roundup manager, that they would not stand a chance against him. Among those riding at Culdesac were Red Gaskill, Harry Pruitt, Red Pruitt, Sol Henry, the Picher brothers, Lee Kelly, Talian Redheart, and George Wicks. As he did not have competition for the bucking contest, Fondberg hired him to give special demonstration rides during the three days of the event. He received fifty dollars a day and was much admired by the crowds.

Jackson Sundown was a friendly man and enjoyed telling the tales of his life to young boys and any others eager to hear them.

He died in 1923 of pneumonia and is buried at Mission Creek near Lapwai. Old cowboys, historians, and tourists who have knowledge of his championship stature often ask directions to the place where he is buried.

A. Phimister Proctor, a nationally famous sculptor, did a statue of Jackson Sundown in 1916 and exhibited it several times in European shows. It now is on permanent display in the RCA Building in Radio City, New York City.

DEB COPENHAVER

A rancher, cattleman, instructor and inspiration to many cowboys, Deb Copenhaver was the World Champion saddle bronc rider in 1955 and 1956. Eighteen years later his son, Jeff, became the World Champion calf roper. In 1992, Deb's name was enshrined in the National Cowboy Hall of Fame in Oklahoma City. In 1993, he was honored by the PRCA in Colorado Springs.

He was born in Wilbur, Washington January 21, 1925, and his first rodeo ride was at Kellar, across the Columbia River. "I sure liked it," he said. He worked hoeing weeds to make money enough to buy a pretty sorrel mare he called "Tooty" and kept her for a long time before selling. Years later he went to the Pendleton Roundup and saw a board member riding "Tooty." The former and current owners became friends.

Deb lost in his first bareback contest in 1940, but won bronc riding the next year. In 1942 he went into military service with Seabees Construction, a branch of the Navy. He built bridges, landing strips and necessary buildings. Returning in 1945, he moved to the Post Falls area and bought a place in the hills below Signal Point. He attended the little church at Pleasant

Deb Copenhaver of Post Falls displays bucking bronc champion form at the big Ellensburg, Washington rodeo. *Courtesy of Oscar Steinley.*

View. Years later when he was holding meetings for the "Cowboys for Christ" movement in Cheyenne, he said, "I remembered the Pleasant Valley Church and the great times we had there." He sold the small ranch in 1960 and bought another on the Liberty Lake side of the mountain.

In 1946, in Calgary he entered the amateur bronc and wild steer contests and won a "day money" prize of three hundred dollars, which he split with others. In 1953, '55, and '58, he won as high as thirty-five hundred dollars as the champion bronc rider. In 1952, '53, and '54, he came in second to Casey Tibbs. "It got to be an absolute obsession with me to win that title," he said. In 1955–56, he spent four and one-half weeks at Madison Square Garden and rode nearly every day, with a double performance on weekends. It was worth the effort. Deb said that Pete Grubb, "a great Idaho cowboy," was his traveling buddy to Madison Square Garden. Other Idahoans at the Gardens at the time were Bob Robinson and Dean Oliver.

Deb is now raising cattle and has fifty head of cows and eight brood mares at his ranch in Creston, Washington. He also preaches the gospel at Creston and is invited to speak at many churches throughout the area.

Deb Copenhaver of Post Falls shows several prize saddles he has won.

BOB A. ROBINSON

World Champion steer wrestler Bob A. Robinson of Tuttle proudly wear the belt buckle which came with the prize. He first broke into rodeo in 1957 and won the Rookie of the Year award for steer wrestling. He turned pro that Labor Day and made several outstanding wins. He went on to the Cow Palace where he won the all-around trophy. Bob stayed with it until winning the grand prize. The award came from steadily placing at rodeos of

Bob A. Robinson of Tuttle, one of Idaho's finest and most admired cowboys, rides on "Tight Rope" in 1953 in El Paso.

Bob A. Robinson has a gold World Championship buckle for finishing at the top of all steer wrestlers. He first broke into pro rodeo in 1957, won Rookie of the Year award, and won the dogging at the Cow Palace. He was fired with a competitive spirit that became his trademark. All of Idaho joins Rockland, where he was born, in pride for Bob and his many awards. This is his 1960 NFR appearance. Harry Charters is hazing for him. *Courtesy of DeVere.*

all sizes. He did win some hefty prize money at major rodeos along the way: $1,085 at Denver; $1,903 at Houston; and $1,650 at the finals. By the time 1960 rolled around, it took three pages for the IBM report on his winnings.

Bob was a four-event man and as a result, often was listed on the championship lists. The Rookie of the Year award was established in 1956 and from the beginning, winners were predominantly steer wrestlers. In 1959, the Idaho image was enhanced when Harry Charters of Melba dashed into rodeo fame with his unusual style. In 1964 yet another Idahoan, Jim Steen of Glenns Ferry was selected as the beginner showing the most promise. Steen was showing signs of becoming a champ when he performed in local rodeos in 1963, but he broke his leg and was unable to ride for several months. During that time he did a lot of thinking and decided to resume rodeo as a professional. It was his good friend, Bob Robinson who coached Steen as he worked his way to the winning of the Rookie of the Year award.

BURREL MULKEY

Burrel Mulkey was, is, and always will be the hometown hero in Salmon, Idaho. And for good reason. Burrel was born a cowboy, worked and rode horses all his growing-up years, started rodeo competition in 1928 and retired at the top of the heap in 1948. Burrel competed in hundreds of rodeos in what was now considered the early-days of rodeo. He carried home many awards, trophies, and winning purses. He reached the peak when the Rodeo Association of America named him World Champion bronc rider in 1937.

From an excellent publication called *Patchwork: Pieces of Local History,* compiled and written in 1992 by Salmon High School's Honors English III class, with Michael Crosby, instructor, and Beau Weber's by-line, readers learn all about Burrel's career. He learned to ride on the family cattle ranch situated along the Pahsimeroi River in Lemhi County, more than one hundred miles from his birthplace at Clyde.

In a March 6, 1986 interview with the *Challis Messenger*, Burrel told of his long ride herding the family cattle. "I was just a timid kid when my folks pulled out (from Clyde to the Pahsimeroi Ranch) for the new place and left my brother and me to winter out the cattle and bring them over to the ranch in the spring. When the time came, my brother set me up with camp supplies and an ol' blue roan and helped me start the cows on the way and then left. Well! I was scared to death. 'Fraid I wouldn't find the way, that the cattle would get away or that any bad thing I could imagine would happen to me. Well, I trailed all those cows all those miles, something like over a hundred, and when we broke over the divide between the Lost River and Pahsimeroi, I blubbered like a baby. When I came in sight of the new homeplace, I just swelled up, straightened my back, held my horse with his head high, and I put those cows through the gate like I'd done it a hundred times."

He had won his spurs and right then, it could be predicted that one day this boy would be a champion.

In the twenties, he rode for cattle companies in both the Pahsimeroi and Lemhi valleys, improving his skills as he chased, raced and herded. Dick Coleman recalled riding with Burrel for about three years when they worked for the Wood Livestock Company. The company had near three thousand head of cattle and Burrel worked with Jim Egge, the foreman who later became sheriff. In the thirties, the family moved to Salmon Bar and later ranched on Carmen Creek.

When they moved to the Pahsimeroi, Burrel and his siblings rode horses to school. Burrel didn't continue with schooling, but while there, learned enough to be described by Tom Richardson: "Even though he didn't have a high school education, he was a fair hand at writing and spelling." In Roberta Green's article in the *Challis Messenger* March 6, 1986, reminiscing on Burrel's life, he was quoted as telling of riding horses to school, and "We'd milk the cows and do the chores, then get down there to the schoolhouse and get it over with. I didn't go on with my education, but I helped put meat on the table and helped my sisters go to college."

Dick Coleman told a story of how another good rider, Pete Grubb, entered rodeoing. Dick and Burrel were going to the roundup at the little town of May, where they also attended dances and horse races. They rode their horses up to the school-house where from their saddles they could look into the window. Dick's horse wouldn't move up to the window, so he climbed on behind Burrel. Dick said, "The kids were liking it pretty good, but the teacher (who became Dick's wife) wouldn't even look at us. Pete Grubb was there, supposed to be in the eighth grade. He came out and got on his horse and came with us. That was the end of his schooling."

Living and working in both the Lemhi and Pahsimeroi valleys, Burrel spent so much time on a horse that when he began rodeoing he was a natural. Dick and Burrel did some riding at the Ziggler place and on Sundays would go to Charlie Snook's Ranch to ride bucking horses. Snook built chutes and Burrel liked riding horses that they thought no one could ride. He started competing in small rodeos at Hayden Creek, Agency Creek, and some of the ranches. He soon moved on to the larger ones.

Pete Grubb, the cowboy they liberated from school, was entering other rodeos and one day in 1928, came by the Edwards Ranch where Burrel was working in the corral. Wearing bright new rodeo regalia, fancy shirt and pants, new boots and Stetson, Pete made an impression on Burrel when he said, "This is peanuts, Mulkey. Come with me on the rodeo circuit. They pay a lot more money and we'll see new country and court new girls, to say nothing of rubbing elbows with the greats in rodeo."

Burrel finished his work, grabbed his clothes and paycheck and they struck out for the rodeo at Mountain Home. Burrel, then twenty-four, entered his first saddle bronc contest and won second. On to Ogden, Utah, where he competed against experienced riders and placed third. In an interview with the *Challis Messenger,* March 6, 1986, "I will say from the first time I crawled on the competition horse at Mountain Home, I went right on winning. It's all in how to square a horse and how to take your rein.

"We paid our own entry fees and travel and housing expenses. Some of the wives stayed home and worked most of the time because they believed in their husband's careers. What most of the public did not know was that we had to win to eat, and only four could win in bronc riding once or twice a week. Those who didn't win borrowed from the winner until the next week."

That was during the Depression years, and Burrel reported, "About the time I started rodeoing the country was in a mess. Grub lines and people out of work. We never made much, but we didn't stand in lines, either. None of us went hungry."

Along with always eating, Burrel and Pete found a source of ready cash. Following the afternoon shows, they tried out new bucking horses, testing how well they bucked. They were paid five dollars a head and at the end of each show had pockets stuffed with five-dollar bills.

Burrel and Pete left the Pahsimeroi rodeoing together. Later Burrel traveled with Guy Cash, Floyd Sterns, Nick Knight, and Floyd Stillings. Idaho rodeo towns during Burrel's early days included: Salmon, Challis, Stanley, Sun Valley, Mackay, Soda Springs, Mountain Home, Nampa, and Caldwell. Floyd Stillings, one of the best riders, took a liking to Burrel and admired his riding style. Stillings said, "Travel with me and I'll show you the ropes and make a champion of you." Stillings made good on his word and started Burrel thinking of rodeo as a profession and "was more of a father to younger cowboys and kind of rode herd on us."

Dick Coleman credited the good bucking horses in the Salmon area with giving Burrel a "leg up" when he got into the big time. "They had just as good horses as they had at any of the other rodeos. A lot of big outfits bought their bucking stock right here. Mackay and Stanley and other small towns had bucking strings and put on rodeos," Coleman said.

Burrel won at nearly every major rodeo and at Ogden five years in a row. A saddle so heavily mounted with silver that it must have weighed more than he did was the prize when he won the Northwest Championship at Pendleton. Other wins included Madison Square Garden, Boston Garden, Calgary, Fort Worth, and Chicago. The Madison Square Garden Rodeo ran for thirty straight days, and he competed there for twelve years in a row, being a contender for the top championship at each one. He won more than seventy rodeo championships in the United States and Canada.

When he won the Rodeo Association of America's world champion bronc rider for 1937 and the all-around championship the next year, the amazing thing was that it was for riding in just one event. The word is that the association then changed the rules so that winning had to be in at least two events. The *Idaho Press Tribune* in a July 12, 1981 interview reported: "It was almost impossible but not quite, and in 1938, short, husky saddle bronc rider Burrel Mulkey of Idaho won rodeo's highest title by just riding saddle bronc."

He was installed in the National Cowboy Hall of Fame in Oklahoma City in 1965 and the Kern County (California) Elias Hall of Fame in 1970.

As happens to many cowboys, Burrel had his injuries, but said, "I healed up easy." Let him tell about it: "I was only hurt once at Mackay. That day the cowboys who had won bronc or all-around had to ride an old horse they had for this event. I saddled up in front of the grandstand. It had been raining, and just as I stepped up, he reared back, slipped into a hole and fell. The halter broke and he fell again. I was underneath him. He hit me in the head, with the weight mashing my head in, knocked my eye down my face and filled my face with gravel. I was out of it for fourteen days and never rode for a year. But I got over it.

"I had my neck broken by being bucked off at Butte, Montana. Didn't know it was broken until I tried several times to

get up and fell back on the ground. In three weeks I was riding
with a cast. I had my legs broken a few times, also my collar-
bones. But I healed easy."

On June 26, 1940, when Burrel was thirty-five and Mernie
Silicz of Kernville, California, was twenty-two, they married. She
was of pioneer stock and her father a cattle rancher. Their daughter Myrna was born in 1946. He openly told people, "We sure
loved that little girl. She never gave us a minute's trouble. She just
soaked up all our lovin' and paid it back a hundred fold." Lucky
little girl. Blessed parents. She grew up on their ranch at Lake
Isabella in California, attended college and became a teacher.
Myrna married David Sweeney and their daughter, Natalie, is
Burrel and Mernie's only grandchild.

The ranch was where he spent the rest of his life. He gave
up rodeo, but never his interest in horses and was employed as
brand inspector by the Department of Agriculture. Later he
worked for a cattleman and land developer at Lake Isabella.

Burrel was a likable and happy man. He enjoyed all kinds
of people and while he thought he was the luckiest man in the
world to make a living doing what he loved to do—rodeo—he
never regretted quitting when he did. "I had seen too many of my
good friends keep trying past their prime. It was heartbreaking. I
couldn't bear to watch them." He attended reunions of the old-
time cowboys at the National Finals a few times and kept in
touch with many of them.

Dennis Coslon, a Salmon rodeoer, won a silver belt buckle
at a rodeo in California and said a little old guy came up to him
and said, "Hey, kid, I want that belt buckle." He told the Idahoan
that he wanted to show it around and let people know that
Salmon, Idaho, still produced saddle bronc riders. As they talked,
the young rider learned he was visiting with Burrel Mulkey and
said that he, "Was one neat old man."

Burrel Mulkey died at seventy-eight at Lake Isabella on
November 24, 1982. He was seventy-eight. His wife said, "Just
before he died he said to me, 'Mernie, it was a great life . . . the

best part was making a living for us doing the kind of work I loved."

PROUD TO BE A CHARTERS

As a boy, Harry Matthew Charters wanted to be a calf roper, but the first prize he won at the first rodeo he attended, was champion of the wild cow-milking contest. It was at the little town of Horseshoe Bend on the Payette River.

He was born April 16, 1925 at Nampa. When they felt he was old enough, his parents bought a horse, considered fast by the standard of others in the area, and while learning to ride, thoughts of rodeo entered his head. Harry was a tall and well-built youngster and the horse seemed small to him. He continued to ride on the family farm learning to handle ropes along with the horse.

"I never had a good lariat rope, just old worn out ones, but I kept at it and roped whenever I could. Usually Dad's calves. I remember one he had just bought at the Nampa sale yard. I got a rope around its neck and the horse ran off with that calf and drug it down below some rocks and peeled it up pretty bad. I never had nerve enough to tell Dad what happened until years later."

Charters finally entered rodeo as an amateur, won the cow-milking at Horseshoe Bend, and signed up for others on the weekends. He participated in two or three a year, improving his skills at each. He joined Tom Conroy on a trip to New Mexico and made a horse buy of "Badger," a Hancock he described as "a great, big, stout horse that I used all through the amateur years." Idaho rodeo goers will remember "Badger" and Charters as a glued-together team winning most contests.

At last, Charters had an arena where he could practice and started bulldogging. He won third at a professional rodeo in Nyssa, Oregon, but remained an amateur. "I could win money as an amateur, if I didn't win too much. I won money at both Nampa and Caldwell and they started raising cain about it. I really didn't have any intention of going professional at that time, but I got to winning more money and enjoying it. I spent a lot of sleepless nights wondering if I wanted to go professional. I knew it meant a lot of travel. I would like awake at nights thinking, 'Do I want to be a big duck in a little pool, or a little duck in a big pool?'

"Finally, in the fall of 1958, I decided I would go professional and sent for my card. I had won about three saddles at the Idaho Cowboy Association finals, and went right on to Jerome and ended up winning the All-Around at the first Rodeo Cowboys Association event I had ever attended. I was thirty-two, considered old for a cowboy and it should have been about the time I was quitting."

The next year he won both Rookie of the Year and the World Championship in steer wrestling. "That's one record," he said, "I don't think they will ever break. Most all these rookies are eighteen or nineteen years old and I was thirty-three." He was attending a rodeo every week, sometimes two or three. When the Nampa Rodeo was on, he would fly back and forth to compete in Salinas (California), Nampa, Salt Lake, and Ogden at the same time. He rode the horse, of other cowboys in the other towns. In turn, that owner would ride Charters' horse when they competed at Nampa. It is a common practice among rodeoers.

Although he won the World Championship only once, he was runner-up in 1963 and came within $137 of winning it again. And likely would have except for a broken leg. He was beaten out by Tom Neesmith of Oklahoma, described by Charters as "a real fine cowboy." About that time Charters said, they "just didn't figure we northern cowboys had much chance with a timed event, because we couldn't practice in the winter time. But, of course, Dean (Oliver) won roping several times, and he broke that tradition. And I really wanted to win that, because I always wanted to be able to say, 'Well, the northern cowboy with a broken leg can beat the southern cowboy.' "

Charters couldn't remember how many times he had made

it to the finals in calf roping. He went to the national finals three or four times and was in the all-around at third or fourth a couple of times. Out of the more than three thousand members, only the top fifteen in each event go to the national finals.

He worked the Caldwell Night Rodeo and won the calf roping trophy in 1968. As he accepted the trophy, Henry Christian approached and said, "Harry, don't leave. Looks like you may win the all-around." Charters laughed and said, "Hank, if I win the all-around I'm going to quit." Christian just laughed at him, as though he'd heard that a thousand times from cowboys, Charters remembers, and added, "But I had thought about quitting all the traveling, quitting rodeo. And so I end up winning the all-around, and I took my trophy and rode out. And I never went back. So, that made another record that'd probably be kind of hard to beat. I won the all-around the first RCA Rodeo I went to, and the last one."

HARRY HART

From a ten-year-old roping goats at the family homestead on the east Pocatello bench to thirteen years of performing at New York's great Madison Square Gardens Rodeo as a champion roper and bulldogger was not a dazzling giant leap for Harry Hart. Rather, it was self-disciplined, steady, day-after-day practice, persistence, and performance. Hart was born in 1905 in New Jersey and first saw Idaho in 1914 when his parents looked for a suitable home in the west. The bench homestead later became a part of the two thousand acre ranch where Hart ran one hundred and fifty head of cattle. He also leased one hundred and sixty acres of rich flatland on Fort Hall Indian Reservation to grow hay.

Learning to rope the "offensive smelling" goats just for the sport of it, had much to do with developing the champion roper. Goats are nimble of foot, supersonic in speed, and slippery as greased lightning. From goat roping to one of the best calf ropers in the country was a natural for Hart. Only he knew the hours dedicated to practice. He developed a string of roping horses and selected the best and most adaptable for the arena's race against time.

He knew the horse's judgment must match that of the roper if they work as a precision team. When the rope is thrown, the speeding horse must judge the split second to stop short, keeping the rope taut, while the rider leaps from the saddle, runs down the rope, throws the calf and securely ties three legs with the piggin' string he clinches between his teeth. All this in a matter of seconds. The tie must hold after the roper raises hands in the air to signal "mission accomplished."

Harry Hart's husky broad shoulders, strong arms and legs, belied his quickness in riding, roping and bulldogging. From his first entry in the 1927 Cokeville, Wyoming, rodeo he began a string of wins that included Butte, Montana, Blackfoot, and the then-famous "Henry's Stampede" near Soda Springs.

He was a natural who instinctively knew what to do in rodeoing, even down to the gear that best suited him. Most early cowboys used the old rawhide ropes. Later ones used nylon. Hart used what was known as yacht line, originally developed for hauling huge and heavy sails on yachts. It came in eighteen hundred foot lengths, all of one strand, from the Plymouth, Massachusetts Cordage Company. He gave it a description that also applied to him, "tough and reliable."

By May 1980, in a first-rate interview with Lena Anken Sexton in the western edition of the magazine *Acreage,* Hart said, "They have shortened the rope now, because of the really fast horses. We used about twenty-one feet when I was roping. We didn't want to take a chance of the rope busting, so in the steer roping the rope was used only once." He explained that steers used in the earlier rodeos were "Pretty big. A lot of guys couldn't throw those big fellows. We used to rope calves bigger than some of the steers they bulldog now."

Hart was asked to perform with a group scheduled to rodeo from May through July in London, England. Harry took his own horses from Pocatello to Cheyenne, thence by train to Montreal,

Canada, and by ship from there to London. He chose to travel with his animals on the stock boat, rather than the passenger ship. Three escort steamers, one in the lead and two at the rear, accompanied the ships down the St. Lawrence River during a wild and surging ocean storm. The escort craft dropped completely from sight during the heavy swells and rollers. Hart admitted to being thoroughly seasick, but "the horses took it easy and got fat" during the voyage. Pumps worked night and day to empty the hold of water. After they landed in England, the shipping officials admitted they had struck a rock in the river.

From 1930 through 1945, Hart missed only the World War II gas rationing years of 1942 and 1943 in competing at annual Madison Square Garden rodeos. In 1939, he rode away with two of the biggest awards, World Champion steer wrestler and Rodeo Cowboy of America. Hart also won what he considered a small fortune that year. The $7,000 he won looms larger now, when it is realized that boots sold for $6.95; a ten-gallon wide-brimmed and high-crowned hat (the kind Tom Mix wore) $4.95; the ever-worthy blue jeans $1.95; and a snappy bandana tie for thirty-five cents. Hart remembered that the $18 boots he wore sold for $150 in 1980. As the rodeo world reached the year 2000, some fancy boots have reached that amount in dollars. He also remembered that good roping horses could be bought for about $600 in the 1940s and 1950s and "a great one for up to $2,500."

Like many old-time cowboys, he longed for the days when he rode the range all morning, had a bit of lunch, and then cranked up the Model T or started the Model A and drove to the rodeo.

GUY CASH, SR.

When anyone openly admired the way Guy Cash of Grangeville could remain in the saddle with a rip-snorting bucking, whirly-gigging horse beneath him and asked, "Isn't riding those bucking horses hard on you?" His answer was, "Riding them isn't hard on you, it's the ground that tears you up." His son

Guy Jr. remembers being with his dad at the National Finals Rodeo in Oklahoma City years ago when they met an old time rodeo cowboy friend. He said, "Cash, I was just talking about you. I told someone you were the most 'ground shy' bronc rider I'd ever known." Guy Sr. was mighty hard to buck off.

Whether or not they are attracted to rodeo, hometown Grangeville residents remain proud of Guy Cash, who died in November 1985. The most illustrious of all the local riders and the youngest of the four rodeoing Cash brothers, Guy was born August 17, 1902, on the Salmon River breaks, west of Tolo Lake and Grangeville to pioneer parents, John Charles and Eliza Ellen Cash. The local newspaper, the *Idaho County Free Press* announced his birth with, "Born to John and Ellen Cash, a nine pound Democrat." He was the youngest of eight children and the brother of cowboys Walter, Manford, and Eddie. The parents arrived on the Camas Prairie with an immigrant wagon train from Indiana and settled on land stretching to the foothills near Tolo Lake, where all four of the future cowboys were born.

Named a several-times champion at Grangeville Border Days Rodeo, Guy went on to become a world class bronc rider and bulldogger. His first success in the bigtime came in 1924 when he garnered a second in the Northwest championship in Pendleton, vying against riders from Idaho and neighboring states of Oregon and Washington. He then competed around the circuit, from Los Angeles to New York City and from Ottawa, Canada to El Paso, Texas. His rodeo career spanned twenty years and the glory days were from 1929 through 1941.

Two of his most illustrious wins were the All Around Championship cowboy at the Pendleton Roundup and the North American bronc riding championship at the Calgary Stampede. Several prominent wins included the bronc riding championships at Nampa's Snake River Stampede, Caldwell Night Rodeo, and events in Elko (Nevada), Los Angeles, Spokane, and a number of others.

In 1925, when only twenty-three and in his first full year in the arena, Guy won the all-around champion award. He had placed in the money in an Oregon rodeo, and was feeling flush enough to buy a new car and head for the big time in Cheyenne. He arrived so late that he entered only the wild horse event, but not steer wrestling. This proved to be a technicality that later cost him the title he had won on points in the bronc riding. That fall at Pendleton, Guy won the all-around world championship. During those days, the cowboy who received the big money at Cheyenne and Pendleton was automatically declared the world champion all-around cowboy. A well-known rodeo winner, Bob Crosby, challenged the award because Guy had entered only one major event in Cheyenne. Crosby's challenge was upheld and the award was taken away. It was possible to win the biggest purse but not the prize. Guy Jr. said, "Dad always said, 'this was the biggest mistake in my rodeo career.'"

Guy Jr., reports that one of the more interesting contests which was won by his dad was at Elko, Nevada in 1928. There the six finalists in bronc riding rode the last horse until it quit bucking. "Dad drew a horse called Major Bowes (the Major Bowes radio contest show of entertainers and their acts was a wildly popular one back then) and that horse bucked for nearly two minutes." Guy Jr. went on to explain that two minutes of bucking full speed around the arena is a lot different than the eight seconds they currently ride. In the early career of Cash Sr. horses were larger and stouter than today and the equipment was less uniform. Rides were for ten or twelve seconds, and in some rodeos such as Elko the contestants were to continue their final ride of the event until the horse quit bucking. The eight second rule came in after World War II. Along with winning the contest, he was awarded a five hundred dollar silver mounted saddle.

GUY CASH OF IDAHO
WINS BRONK RIDING TITLE

was the front page banner headline on the July 15, 1939 edition of the *Calgary Herald*. A part of the text reported: "Climaxing a

20-year career of rodeo competition, Guy Cash of White Bird, Idaho, captured the North American bucking horse riding contest at the Calgary Stampede this afternoon. A record crowd saw the thirty-seven-year-old make a great ride on "Charlie Furman," a rough old outlaw, to retain a margin of points he had established in the preliminary and semi-final contests."

A fine photo with the story quoted: "Guy Cash said just after the draw for the finals, 'this thing isn't won until the last horse is ridden'," and then went on to put up a thrilling display of horsemanship to win the North American bronc riding championship.

One of the truly "touching" moments of the champion's life came at the final award ceremony when he shared the spotlight with Helen Keller, the famous and admired writer and educator who became deaf and blind at nineteen months from a severe illness, and received such training that she graduated from Radcliffe College cum laude. Before thousands of rodeo enthusiasts, Miss Keller asked to feel Champion Cash's face, so she "could know what a Champion Cowboy looks like."

In traveling the circuits, cowboys and girls participate in, or hear of, so many funny or ridiculous happenings that they collect a lifetime of stories. Guy liked to tell of the trip he, Burrel Mulkey and Pete Grubb of Salmon took to New York City in 1928 to ride in the huge Madison Square Garden Rodeo. Pete, described as "a bareback rider par excellence," had a strong streak of fun running through his entire being. Back home in Idaho, he picked up his mail at the post office in the little village of May, in the Pahsimeroi country. When Pete was registering at the Garden, he was asked where he was from. "Pahsimeroi, Idaho," he replied. "How do you spell it?" He solemnly said, "M-A-Y."

One of the things Pete and Burrel liked to do was to amuse or confuse the hurrying New Yorkers. All duded up in their cowboy outfits they would hunker down on the sidewalk anyplace in downtown Manhattan, stretch their necks and stare upward, open-mouthed and wide-eyed at the tall buildings. This brought no end of amused glances from the sophisticated New Yorkers passing by. Many of them hesitated and stared at the cowboys. Little matter that all the cowboys had to do to see towering heights in their own Idaho backyards was to glance at the mountain peaks of eleven-to-more-than twelve thousand feet in the Pahsimeroi (Lost River) and Lemhi ranges.

All four of the Cash brothers, Walter, Manford, Edward, and Guy, were active in rodeo. Edward died at an early age, but the other three were honored at different times as Marshal of the Grangeville Border Days. Guy was Marshal in 1965.

Idaho champs were recipients of so much publicity in towns and cities around the circuits that the state could not have afforded to pay for the favorable comments.

After retiring, Guy Sr. acquired rodeo stock and produced shows in the northwest. He was a leader in forming the annual amateur rodeo in Riggins. He served as sheriff of Lewis County, ranched in the Nez Perce and Craigmont areas and helped his wife in a shop she had in Nez Perce. He often traveled to Oklahoma City in December to watch the National Rodeo finals.

His death came in November of 1985, and a splendid monument denotes the gravesite in Grangeville's Prairie View Cemetery. His name is recorded with that of other famous cowboys in the National Cowboy Hall of Fame in Oklahoma City.

SHAWN DAVIS

If there is a "typical cowboy champion," he'd be Shawn Davis of Twin Falls. Typical in that he worked many hard years to become a professional and then the best saddle bronc rider in the world. He was industrious and trained diligently, but suffered the broken bones and near-death experiences of the roughest of cowboy life. The three-time world champion saddle bronc rider has been described as "never eats, never sleeps or relaxes, there is always something going on in his life," and most of it is connected to rodeo. He also holds morning workouts with his race horses.

Davis hailed from Montana and competed in all the large

rodeos and many small-town events. He eventually became equine instructor for the College of Southern Idaho in Twin Falls. At the same time he was the coach of the CSI rodeo team as it built into one of the outstanding college programs in the United States. He operates saddle bronc and steer wrestling schools in Twin Falls. He and his wife, Zena, have raised a son, Zane, a two time College National Finals Rodeo All-Around champion.

In 1965, Shawn Davis, then listed as from Whitehall, Montana, was the national champion in saddle bronc riding, collecting a purse of $25,599. In 1967, he again placed first in saddle bronc at the nationals, with a win of $25,277. Also, he placed fifth in the important All-Around Cowboy with an additional purse of $25,406. In 1971, he came in fourth in the national saddle bronc championship, gaining $17,471.

In 1969 at Thompson Falls, Montana, the horse being ridden by Davis made a leap and flipped over backward, landing on Shawn and breaking the rider's back. It was necessary for the doctors to fuse the vertebrae and he was out of action for months. While driving from a Wyoming elk hunt with cowboy friends and heading for the San Francisco Rodeo in the old Cow Palace, driver Pete Gay attempted to pass a truck and the car lurched into the ditch. Both rear tires blew and the car turned over. Shawn then suffered an injury to his knee. In 1975, while he was riding in saddle bronc competition at Cheyenne, Wyoming, another horse fell, landing over his right leg and breaking the lower shin bone. Fearing further damage to his sciatic nerve, doctors fused the vertebrae.

FRANK McCARROLL

Because his beautiful and talented wife, Bonnie, won so many championship trophies and awards, international recognition and her untimely rodeo death brought highly publicized sorrow in many lands, Frank McCarroll, a rodeo champion in his own right, did not receive as much "ink" as he deserved. He would be the last to complain, for Bonnie's success was a joy to

Frank McCarroll shows his championship style in downing the bull in a matter of seconds at an early Weiser Roundup. Frank and his wife, Bonnie, were both champions and brought great rodeo acclaim to Idaho. *Courtesy of Weiser Museum.*

Frank. Wherever Bonnie rode, Frank was nearby. On at least two occasions he saved her life.

IN THE MONEY

Idaho's champions were in the money in many categories for years. Included in an incomplete list of years, riders and awards are: 1962 Dean Oliver won first place in calf roping and took home $27,756 and second in all-around cowboy, winning $29,989. Harry Charters won second place in calf roping, winning $16,016, which brought him into fourth place as all-around champion and an additional $22,694. In 1963, the Oliver-Charters duo were at first and fourth as all-around champions. Oliver won $28,375 in roping and $31,329 as an all-around champion. Charters won $25,149 as an all-around champion. In 1964, Dean Oliver won all-around champion and won $31,150, also winning $23,591 for calf roping. He was considered the favorite bull rider. Ken Stanton of Weiser appeared on the RCA roster with the ninth spot in the all-around champion with a win of $20,492. He was also the fourth place bull rider, which

brought him $12,899. In 1965, Oliver won the all-around cow-
boy again! He also won the purse of $33,163 and a second place
in calf roping, which brought him $23,687. And, again, Ken
Stanton won third place and $15,823 from bull riding, which
moved him into the fifth-place slot as all-around champion and
$25,787. Another name to become well-known to Idahoans, that
of Shawn Davis, of Twin Falls, listed then as being from
Whitehall, Montana, won first in saddle bronc and $25,599. In
1966, Dean Oliver took second in both calf roping and all-
around champion with a purse of $24,208 and $34,290. Ken
Stanton took fifth in bull riding with $11,929, and sixth in all-
around champion, winning $23,904. In 1967, Shawn Davis took
first in saddle bronc with $25,277, and he also took fifth in all
around champion with $25,406. In 1968, Shawn Davis took first
in saddle bronc with $22,697 and ninth place in all-around
champion, winning $27,015. Dean Oliver took fourth in calf rop-
ing and won $19,733. In 1969, Dean Oliver took first in calf rop-
ing with $38,118, and a third place all-around champion with
$39,081. Ken Stanton went back to ninth in the all-around cham-
pion and won $25,612.

In 1970, the only Idaho winner brought the town of Salmon
back into the forefront. He was Bill Kornell, winning $16,902 as
the fourth-place winner in bull riding. In 1971, Shawn Davis,
took fourth in the saddle bronc and won $17,471. In 1972, Dean
Oliver took third in calf roping and $25,358. Dean Oliver placed
second in calf roping and $23,697, and Jeff, the son of Deb
Copenhaver, listed from Seaside, Oregon, took fourth and
$21,837 in 1974. In 1975, Jeff, now listed from Spokane,
Washington, took first in calf roping with $34,628; and he also
took ninth in all-around champion with $34,670. Royce Smith of
Challis took fifth in bareback and won $28,261. John Davis of
Homedale took seventh in bull riding and $18,681. Darrel Sewell
of Lucile took fifteenth in steer wrestling and won $12,837.
Twelve Californians out of fifteen listed teams roped in 1975,
which had grown from only five, all Californians, in 1974. In

1976, Royce Smith of Challis, fifth in bareback and $2,485. John Davis of Homedale, thirteenth in bull riding at $585. Jeff Copenhaver of Post Falls and Spokane, fifth in calf roping at $3,450. In the same year, Dean Oliver eleventh in calf roping at $1,169.

Jim Roeser rides "Baby Face" in the tenth go round at the NFR in Dallas, 1959. *Courtesy of DeVere.*

Fifty Years of Champions

Dodge National Circuit Finals

All-Around Champions
Dean Oliver, Boise   1963, '64, '65
Dee Pickett, Caldwell   1984

Steer Wrestling
Harry Charters, Melba   1959
Bob A. Robinson, Rockland   1960

Team Roping
Dee Pickett, Caldwell   1984

Saddle Bronc Riding
Deb Copenhaver, Post Falls   1955, '56

Calf Roping
Dean Oliver, Boise   1955, '58, '60, '61, '62, '63, '64

Queens and Cowgirls

Western history is filled with women who were more than capable of contending with the wilderness experience. They dealt with the Indians, helped clear and till the land, insisted on building schools and churches as soon as the family homes were up, and raised their families right along with the garden, the chickens, and horses. Always there were horses. Usually the entire family learned to ride. The girls were not an exception and as rodeo evolved so did the women riders. Idaho had its share of those who rose to stardom in the sport. Many became champion riders.

Fancy duds and ten-gallon hats make the cowgirls standouts at an early Weiser rodeo. They competed in the bucking contest.
Courtesy of Weiser Museum.

Dolly Mullins and Mildred Douglas, each with a foot on the back of the other's horse, show judges in the flag-draped stand and viewers below what two trained trick riders and horses can do.
Courtesy of Weiser Museum.

The bareback bronc, with all four feet off the ground, is proof positive that Jan Edmonson of Garden Valley deserved to win the All Girl Rodeo at Murphy, Idaho. Jan clung to the mount despite his airborne plunges during a wild ride. *Photo by Gregg.*

Putting on chaps can be a problem, especially when they belong to a six-foot tall friend. Susan Beckman (now Susan Roghani, rural Meridian) borrowed the chaps, bell, spurs, gloves, bull rope, boots. . .and entry fee to ride in the Idaho Girls Association event in 1974 in Council. At a later event, at Murphy, the rope slipped on her rain-washed, sand-covered steer and she came home with two broken ribs. Two days in the Weiser hospital took care of the problem. It also ended her career.
Courtesy of Joy Beckman.

'Way back in 1917, Weiser held some of the biggest roundups in the area. Mildred Douglas waves her hat as "Bright Eyes" bucks off across the arena. *Courtesy of Weiser Museum.*

BONNIE McCARROLL

Bonnie McCarroll's first memory of what the future held for her as a world-champion bronco rider was that of her mother on horseback and carrying Bonnie in her arms as they rode over their vast Idaho rangeland. Riding the range, breaking wild horses, entering and winning arena events until she became one of the country's most decorated queens was the life of Bonnie

Courtesy of Freita P. Holsted

McCarroll. The log cabin where Bonnie Treadwell was born on September 29, 1929, was smack-dab in the middle of her grandparents' two thousand acre cattle ranch in High Valley south of the little town of McCall on the shores of Payette Lakes. The number of horses and cattle nearly equaled the number of acres on the ranch and gave Bonnie every opportunity to ride and form a colorful vision of her future as a bronco buster. Her grandparents joined the parents in unqualified encouragement. By the age of ten she was an excellent rider. In that talent she followed her mother, an experienced horsewoman.

One of Bonnie's earliest thrills in the saddle was on a mustang (wild horse) that her mother was taming. The animal appeared to be gentle and Bonnie pled to ride. As soon as she was in the saddle, "He gave a start and away he went down the mountainside just as hard as ever he could run." As she recalled he ran over rocks and fallen timber for nearly a mile, but she held on and finally pulled him to a stop. Then she headed him

When cowgirls were permitted to ride bucking broncs, they often "bit the dirt." In this now famous photo, Bonnie McCarroll is thrown from "Silver" at a Pendleton Roundup. Although often cited as the photo where she received fatal injuries, this picture was shot much earlier. "Silver" appears to be taking a walk on his hind legs.
Courtesy of Weiser Museum.

back to the ranch where her family was anxiously waiting. Even at age ten, that ride was so exciting that it was a harbinger of what she would do with her life. By the time she was fourteen she could ride nearly any unbroken horse on that gigantic ranch.

When she finally persuaded her reluctant father to let her ride one of the wildest, he handed her the reins and said, "You are a girl so we'll give you two reins instead of one." As she mounted the bronc he began to act, she said, "Like a wildcat," and she was able to hang on for about five seconds. "All at once I seemed to grow wings. Up, up I soared and even turned a somersault, and the earth seemed about ten miles below. I went to sleep and when I woke up I was in bed." Her father said, "You loosened up on your knee grip. Don't do it again or you'll hurt yourself." Never again did she loosen her knee grip.

Soon she was riding in the Idaho State Fair at Boise. Ed

McCarthy owned the string of horses performing at the Fair and
Bonnie convinced him that she should ride one of the bucking
broncs after the show. She remembered that she managed to stay
on top of a tough little bronc called "Bear Cat." She put on a fairly
good ride until "Bear Cat" bucked against the barn wall, stumbled
and fell. Nearby cowboys dragged her from the saddle. She was
badly bruised and shaken. Even so, she made up her mind right
then that she would never quit riding until she became a champion. And a champion she became.

It was at the Idaho State Fair and Rodeo at Boise where she
first met the man who became her husband, Frank McCarroll.
She and some of her friends were complaining that the arena
events were unusually dull. "When suddenly an angry steer came
bellowing out of the chute and went charging across the field
with two men galloping after it." The man who dove from the
saddle to the head and of the steer and bulldogged it within thirty
seconds was Frank McCaroll.

The year before Bonnie and Frank were married in 1916,
she signed on for her first professional rodeo in Vancouver,
British Columbia. She was then sixteen. She rode six different
horses in as many events and won second place. During the final
ride, the horse she had been assigned fell on her and she was so
badly bruised that she was unable to walk for two weeks. In true
cowgirl style she felt that despite the injuries she was well on her
way to becoming the champion she had set as her goal.

She won first place and the women's world championship
bronc rider trophy at the Madison Square Garden Rodeo in
1922. The next year she was back in New York for the huge
rodeo at Yankee stadium. Awed fans returned for five consecu-
tive days to watch the Idaho rodeo star conquer a string of the
wildest mustangs without a mishap. She continued her series of
world championship bucking contest wins at Cheyenne Frontier
Days besting ten other cowgirls. She continued to ride "slick."

Bonnie realized how dangerous rodeo could be and remembered her closest call with death in 1923 in the Detroit, Michigan

stadium. A horse extremely hard to handle had been given her and she did well until the ride was nearly over. As the bronc neared the wall the pickup rider (whose job it is to catch and hold the bucking horse when the event is over, permitting the rider to dismount), thinking the horse might hit the wall and fall, grabbed the reins from Bonnie and jerked so hard that the bronc lost his stance and fell to his knees. Bonnie was thrown loose from the saddle and, in falling, loosened her grip while her right foot was still in the stirrup. Her foot flew up, caught the spur behind the cantle board in back of the saddle, locking it tight. In the meantime the horse regained his feet and started bucking and kicking, again dragging her by one foot. The pickup man was still holding the reins, trying to stop the bucking bronc, and manage his own mount all at the same time.

As Bonnie's head neared the ground, she threw out her hands to protect her face and managed to grasp the tail of the pickup man's horse and held herself up from the heels of both horses. Within seconds several cowboys including Frank rushed to her rescue and freed her foot.

When Bonnie was seventeen in 1916, the McCarrolls were married. Years later, in one of her last interviews she said, "I have won the championships at Chicago and Cedar Rapids, Michigan, making me a winner at every worthwhile rodeo ever pulled in the world." No cowgirl could have realized any greater ambition. It was in 1924 that the McCarrolls were invited to perform before the King and Queen of England, as well as before the Queen of Spain and her twin daughters, in Wimbledon stadium. Bonnie came away with the World Championship Cup won in the international cowgirl bucking contest, a portion of the seventy-five thousand dollar prize money and England's prestigious Lord Selfridge trophy.

Bonnie McCarroll was Idaho's first woman national rodeo champion, and so accomplished that she made the sport look much easier than it was and twice as exciting. Her abilities lead other women riders into the profession. She was riding slick in the 1929

Pendleton Roundup on the afternoon of September 19 when her
horse was knocked down by the horse of her pickup man. She was
hurtled back and forth, and finally thrown free when her horse
stumbled and fell. The numbed crowd gasped when she landed on
her head and suffered multiple injuries. She was rushed to the
Pendleton hospital but never regained consciousness. She died on
Sunday evening, September 29. Her rodeo champion husband, her
mother, Mrs. Alice Beaumont of Boise and her brother, Ike D.
Treadwell, were with her during the final hours of her life.

Newspapers throughout the country joined Bonnie's friends
and family in mourning her death. Both the *Boise Capital News*
and the *Idaho Statesman* carried banner headlines. One photo caption read, in part, "Her accomplishments in rodeos throughout the
world have carried the fame of Boise to distant lands, and her
home city has been a deeply interested spectator of her courageous ten-day fight for life in the Pendleton hospital. This was to
have been her last year in the saddle, her husband, Frank, having
at last gained her promise to quit the rodeo trail which made both
of the McCarroll's famous." Mementos of her rodeo life buried
with her included a prize golden pin of a steer head with diamond
eyes. The pearl-gray sombrero she wore during her final ride,
along with the boots and spurs were placed on top of the coffin.

Freita P. Halsted of Boise is often contacted for information
on Bonnie and memories are still vivid. She told Pam McLary,
also of Boise and now associated with the Cowgirl Hall of Fame,
that she thinks often of Bonnie's house at Third and Broad
streets. She remembers Bonnie's handsome palomino Montez
and the excitement the neighbors experienced when rodeo stars,
including Tom Mix and Yakima Canutt, came to visit the
McCarrolls. When Bonnie assured Frank that she would retire
from rodeo and settle down, building began on their Spanish
style home on Crescent Rim Drive. It was still under construction
when she died and later became the home of Gordon and Nelle
MacGregor. The site now holds the impressive home of Velma
Morrison and John Hockberger.

Hundreds of newspaper and magazine articles have been and are continuing to be published about Bonnie McCarroll's life and death. Most of them state that many changes for America's rodeo cowgirl began with her tragic death. It is cited as the major factor in bringing an end to women's bronc riding contests. Carrie Singleton writing in *Northwest Magazine,* July 11, 1976, ended her article "The Powder Puff Buckaroos," with: "The last Cowgirl Bucking Championship was held in 1929. The death of a popular cowgirl, Bonnie McCarroll—due to injuries suffered when she was thrown in the bucking competition—brought to a close one of the most captivating events in the history of the Pendleton Roundup."

Bonnie now rests in a silent grave in Morris Hill Cemetery not far from the spot which she and Frank chose for their home. From the first bench overlooking the Boise valley she loved, the cemetery is a place visited by hundreds of people each year. Many walk by the simple granite headstone lying flush with the grass that bears the simple message: "Bonnie McCarroll 1899–1929." Most do not give the headstone a second glance.

But once in awhile a visiting old-timer to whom rodeo is a large part of Idaho will tip his Stetson as he pauses at Bonnie's grave in silent salute to the greatest cowgirl.

MABLE STRICKLAND

In all the rosters of outstanding rodeo cowgirls, Mable Strickland was always at or near the top. She was that rare cow-

Mable Strickland, wife of Hugh Strickland, also an outstanding rodeo performer, was popular on the many circuits they rode. She competed with the best in bucking bronc riding and trained her horse in performing many tricks. *Courtesy of Weiser Museum.*

girl who vied against the cowboys in steer roping. Not only was she a tough competitor, but often the winner. Official records were not kept before 1929 and much of her riding history has been lost in the shuffle. Under the heading "Pips and Chips" by Art Jones in the *Deadwood* (Black Hills, South Dakota) *Magazine* of April 2000 appeared: "Had official records been kept prior to 1929, Mabel Strickland would have won more world titles than any of her contemporaries. A proficient bronc and steer rider, trick rider and steer roper, Mabel performed for twenty years at every major rodeo in the country, attracting large crowds whenever she appeared. She was only thirteen when she began her twenty-five year career in Walla Walla, Washington, and made her first Pendleton appearance at the age of fifteen."

She was born Mable Delong in 1897 in Walla Walla, where she spent her childhood. From the beginning, horses were a big part of her life. Her father was a boot maker and she met many cowboy patrons in his shop. Her father put her on a horse when she was three, and she was determined that was where she wanted to spend much of the rest of her outdoor life. While still a tot, she became fascinated with rodeo and all its trappings. From thirteen she studied trick riding and by sixteen was winning prizes. When she graduated from Walla Walla High School in 1916, she entered rodeos as a relay racer in Boise, Idaho Falls, Pendleton, and other towns.

Through the rodeo route she met handsome Hugh Strickland of Idaho and they were married in 1918. *(See Chapter 16.)* They traveled together while both were riding the rodeo circuits and during their free time from rodeo were at home in Fort Worth, Texas, with their daughter, April. Hugh suffered a fatal heart attack in 1941. Soon thereafter Mabel left rodeo. After WWII, she married a Spokane cattleman, Sam Woodward. They later lived in Arizona and she became involved in the National Appaloosa Horse Club which had headquarters in Moscow, Idaho. It was January 3, 1976 that the outstanding cowgirl and horsewoman died at seventy-nine in the Buckeye, Arizona hospital.

Mabel was petite and pretty and nearly every article written about her mentioned that she was attractive. Her cowgirl outfits were worn with a flair for style. Standing only five feet four inches and weighing 112 pounds, it was apparent that she was "born to the saddle." Mabel was popular with the other riders as well as the rodeo goers who packed the grandstands when it was known she was performing. In 1927, she was selected as queen of the Pendleton Roundup, an unusual recognition for a champion rider. Many years later, in 1973, she was the first cowgirl to be named to the Pendleton Roundup Hall of Fame. She was then seventy-six years old.

Her photo and name grace the walls at the Cowgirl Hall of Fame in Texas and the Rodeo Hall of Fame in Oklahoma. During the rodeo off-season she moved to Hollywood and appeared as a stunt rider in films or doubling for stars. She appeared in the film *Rhythm on the Range* with another part-time Idahoan Bing Crosby, who owned a home at Hayden Lake for many years.

Mabel was the only cowgirl to appear on the souvenir cover of the program for the Cheyenne Frontier Days. Roping the steer in only twenty-four seconds at Cheyenne in 1925, she broke the world record and was named Cowgirl Champion. In 1923, at Cheyenne, she won the relay race and bucking horse contest. In the relay, riders raced around the track at lightning speed, leapt to the ground, saddled a fresh horse and at full gallop rounded the track for a second time. She was also named champion of the bucking horse contest.

JANET ALLEY YOUREN

Any mother can understand why the mother of Janet Alley Youren of Crouch, Idaho, wanted her to quit roping, barrel racing, bronc and bull riding. Even before one learns that Janet suffered injuries such as a broken nose (ten times); broken cheek bones (eight times); all but one of her ribs broken; a broken back; collapsed lung; bruised heart; skull fracture; and dislocated shoulders. But, Janet said she felt vindicated with her rodeo passion when in 1993 she became the first Idaho woman rodeoer to be inducted into the National Cowgirl Hall of Fame. She is in good company with just two other Idaho women receiving that honor: Sacajawea, the Shoshone guide for the Lewis and Clark expedition, and Gertrude Maxwell, an Elk City outfitter, horse trainer, and rodeo participant. Sacajawea was named in 1977 and Maxwell and Youren were inducted together in 1993.

"My mother told me I should quit when I was on the top instead of going down to the bottom. No one knew that I would stay on top for so long," she said. The National Cowgirl Hall of Fame was located in Hereford, Texas, for many years before moving to Fort Worth.

In the 1970s in Idaho, the women's amateur rough stock competition was dying. Youren made up her mind that the only way she could compete as she had been doing since she was twelve, was to turn professional. Janet became one of the nation's top competitors, winning the women's world bareback bronc riding title in 1991 and in 1987. She was runner-up for that title in 1992 and 1993, and has had eleven other runners-up in bronc and bull riding. She put as many as three hundred and fifty thousand miles on her truck in two years as she crossed the continent to ride in rodeos that led to the World Finals in Guthrie, Oklahoma. That was where she was named to the Hall of Fame.

Janet quit riding bulls after thirty-one years of competition, and then focused on bareback riding.

She has a riding school for girls at Garden Valley, to teach those who want to learn to ride rough stock. They come from as far away as Australia. She teaches the youngsters how to jump off a bucking horse toward the center of the arena and away from the fence, and how to avoid being struck by the pickup men on horses. Janet speaks from first-hand knowledge when teaching how to avoid the very injuries she has suffered over the years. She tells the girls to, "start rolling before you hit the ground. When you are still, the animals can get a real lick and kick on to you."

More than twenty-five years ago, Janet's father was the producer of a rodeo which featured the first all-girl event. Her mother of eight children, four girls and four boys, taught all of them to become experts at rodeo. She smilingly reported that her children were born "between rodeo seasons," and during the season she packed them into the truck and drove thousands of miles to events all over America and Canada.

MISS RODEO IDAHO

Idaho's Miss Rodeo contest has been in place for years and grew to a first rate pageant in 1956 at Caldwell, remaining there for eight years. It then moved to Twin Falls and later returned to Caldwell. Several in Twin Falls County again became interested in holding the event along with the fair and rodeo in Filer. Dean and Alma Vickers and Jack Windsor drove to Caldwell and met with the rodeo committee and suggested the contest be moved. Caldwell was not too interested in retaining the event and national coordinators of Miss Rodeo America approved the move to Twin Falls.

Mr. and Mrs. Tom Shouse were taking over the managership of the fairgrounds and became enthusiastic about the contest. Gene Hull was manager for many years. He was followed by Mr. and Mrs. Bob Harvey, Carla Dennett, and Sheri Prescott. The contest was moved again in 1996, this time to Nampa. The contest is held the third full week in July in conjunction with the Snake River Stampede. Contestants must hold a current Rodeo Queen title within Idaho.

Kendee Hess

During 2000 Miss Rodeo Idaho was Kendee Hess of American Falls. Her parents are Mr. and Mrs. Mike Hess. The pageant coordinator is Sandi Johnson of Nampa.

The winner at Nampa advances to the Miss Rodeo America contest in Las Vegas, Nevada, held in conjunction with the National Finals Rodeo each December. Idaho is tied with Texas for having the most Miss Rodeo Americas.

Selbi Ann Board

The "third time is the charm" held true for Selbi Ann Board of Hailey. She hung in there while trying to win the Miss Rodeo Idaho crown. After two failed attempts, she was crowned at the Nampa Stampede in 1998, and became the 1999 Miss Rodeo Idaho. The first holder of the title from Blaine County and surrounding area, she was the second young woman to win in all categories: speech, poise and personality, rodeo knowledge, horsemanship, and most photogenic. Her prizes included ten thousand dollars in scholarships, a fine-tooled saddle, and a horse trailer. Selbi Ann is twenty-three years old and a fifth generation native of the beautiful Wood River Valley. She feels there could be no better place to grow up. "My family still owns land that was homesteaded by my ancestors. I take pride in knowing that my family was involved in the early logging, ranching and Basque history that helped inspire my community and make it an exceptional place to live," she said. Upon receiving the honor, she paid tribute to her parents, Linda and Don Selbi, and others in the family.

The scholarship could not have come at a better time, as she graduated from Wood River High School in 1995 and studied special education at the College of Southern Idaho. Then came a year off to travel throughout the country promoting Idaho and rodeo. Another among the superb young people who want to assist less fortunate people, she dedicated her year of travel to helping the handicapped. The experience from which she speaks was working as a volunteer at Hailey's Sage Brush arena teaching the physically challenged children how to ride. Selbi Anne said that it was an inspiration to watch the children with difficulties learn to ride with confidence and gain self esteem. She wants to get more girls competing in rodeo and was eligible for another competition for herself in November 1999, in competition for Miss Rodeo America in Las Vegas, Nevada. She is attending Boise State University and majoring in communications.

Chris Holmes

Chris Holmes was chosen Miss Rodeo Caldwell in 1973 and became Miss Rodeo Idaho in 1975. She entered the Miss Rodeo America pageant that year and advanced to second runner-up. Her young life was filled with horses and at age seven was a member of Eh-CAPA (which is Apache spelled backwards). The group of youngsters perform like a drill team for various functions. Chris rode with them until she was eleven. At age nine she competed with Little Britches rodeos and from 1970 to 1973 she participated in high school rodeos.

Later she entered the Futurities top ten and emerged in the finals of all but the first. She won the fourth in barrel racing in the Big Futurity in Phoenix, Arizona. She and her cowboy husband, Greg Holmes, raised and trained futurity colts. Greg was a saddle bronc rider and won first in the Idaho Cowboy Association Rodeo in 1981.

Chris was ICA champion barrel racer in 1997, winning more than five thousand dollars. In January 1997 her main horse, Gold Coast Flyer, fell on concrete in Odessa, Texas, and was body sore at times. Yet she placed at El Paso, Phoenix, and Denver and was among the top twelve in WPRA standings to qualify to enter at Houston.

Chris and Greg are a team and train and develop every horse together. They have horses for sale and emphasize matching horse with rider.

Margaux Edwards

As Miss Idaho Rodeo in 1997, Margaux Edwards dedicated herself to serving as the best possible ambassador for the sport of rodeo and liaison between the public and the professional rodeo participants. She announced at that time that she firmly believed in preserving rodeo as the unique part of our western heritage. She was and is a proponent of educating others on the proper and humane treatment of animals.

She was born October 17, 1974, in McCall to Frank and Lydia Justice Edwards and lived in the small ranching community

Congressman Butch Otter, Miss Rodeo Idaho Margaux Elizabeth Justice Edwards, and Miss Caldwell Night Rodeo Theresa Maher visit with Ty Murray, leading moneymaker in Rodeo USA, at the Bullarama held at BSU. *Courtesy of Lydia Justice Edwards.*

of Donnelly. She has two sisters, Alexandra and Dawn, neither of whom have taken to rodeo. In Donnelly Margaux learned the importance of hard work along with family and community values. As she grew she never failed to attend the rodeo held in nearby Cascade each summer. Working on Paul and Gretel Kleint's ranch for seven summers and riding with their daughter Kathy, brought her into contact with horses. The girls spent several summers at Rodeo Cowgirl Camp. The Kleints treated her as another daughter and taught her riding and care of the animals. Margaux had a favorite horse, Harley, and they both enjoyed driving a large herd of cattle. "When I wasn't busy as Miss Rodeo Idaho, my favorite place to be was herding with Harley." Together, they enjoyed breakaway calf roping, trail rides and team penning.

Margaux studied pre-veterinary science at the University of Idaho before transferring to Lewis and Clark College and changing her major to education. While at Lewis and Clark she rented pasture for her horse so that she could ride in the evenings and weekends. She maintains her interest in Friends of Rodeo, an organization dedicated to ensuring humane treatment for rodeo animals, and active in the Fellowship of Christian Cowboys.

Tiffany Novak

The first announcement of eighteen-year-old Tiffany Novak when she became the 1999 Miss Teen Rodeo Idaho was, "I am dedicated to serve as an ambassador for the sport of rodeo. I firmly believe in promoting rodeo as it is a unique part of our western heritage. I will strive to be a positive role model for the younger generations. Our youth needs to be educated and given goals to work for in life. We need to show them that they do not need drugs nor alcohol." The daughter of Tom and Valerie Novak of Nampa was crowned during the Gooding Fair and Rodeo on August 15, 1988.

Tiffany was a member of the Snake River Stampeders riding group and performed at the National Finals Rodeo in Las Vegas in 1997. She also belonged to the Idaho Girls Rodeo Association and 4-H Club, where she qualified for both State and National horse judging.

Tiffany plans to further her education toward a degree in business management or in the medical field. She is currently a certified nurse's assistant.

MISS RODEO AMERICA
Dorothy Alexander

Dorothy Alexander of Boise long ago subscribed to the belief, "If you build it, they will come," and proved it was applicable to the Miss Rodeo America contest and pageant. With outstanding success directing Miss Idaho and Miss America events about thirty years ago, she was invited to judge Miss Rodeo America at the annual National Finals Rodeo in Las Vegas. At that time there were only twenty-two contestants and the board members were cowboys, farmers and ranchers who could not devote much time to that event. In fact, plans were being made to shelve the pageant.

Dorothy thought it a huge mistake to drop an event with great possibilities for rodeo. She was impressed with the "all-around American girl" representing the states. She wrote the board urging it not to drop the contest, stating that the caliber of the contestants was high, and that the college scholarships offered was an incentive to the girls to go on to school.

The upshot was that two of the officers flew to Boise and asked her to direct the pageant. She accepted and dedicated her-self to building the sport and set about securing western sponsors to provide hats, boots, clothing, saddles and trophies. She remem-bers, "My first new sponsor was Wrangler and they are still. McDonalds furnished three huge and beautifully outfitted buses to transport the contestants to all the meals, entertainment, and planned functions."

During the twenty-five years Dorothy devoted herself to the pageant and its contestants, she traveled between Boise and Las Vegas at least five times each year to organize meals, entertain-ment, hotel housing, horses for competing, and announcers. She has nothing but praise for the help received from friends to chap-erone and judges for the interviews, horsemanship, appearance and personality. Her friend Velma Morrison of Boise who has operated a California horse ranch and raised thoroughbreds for years, says, "No one knows more about rodeo than Dorothy and it was a joy to serve as a judge for her."

Dorothy did not resign the position until each state had a contestant and a director. She is especially proud of the generous scholarships given to the winners and runners-up in each cate-gory. In telling of the pleasure in watching the girls gain poise and self-assurance, she said that many had never been out of their home state and that they formed lifetime friendships.

Dorothy and her husband Jim have moved to Pittsboro, North Carolina, but return often to Idaho.

Joni James

When Joni James of Jerome won the 1990 Miss Rodeo America title at the Lazy E Arena in Guthrie, Oklahoma, November 29, it was after six days of tough competition, She set another record in that never before had a daughter followed in her mother's footsteps in receiving the title. She credited her mother, Karen James, the Miss Rodeo America for 1962, as being of the greatest influence in achieving the title.

When Karen won, she was an Idaho State College student and Joni won after graduating the previous may from Boise State University in Boise, with a bachelor degree in biology and a minor in secondary education. Joni, then twenty-three, led the field of forty other contestants in horsemanship, personality, speech and appearance.

Her stated goals were to help barrel racers earn equal money and to assist in extending the sport of rodeo to extend beyond the boundaries of the United States. She became an enthusiastic promoter of rodeo as she toured the country, stating, "I will never leave rodeo. My mom told me over and over that she wouldn't trade her year as Miss Rodeo America for the world."

Prior to the national competition, Joni was named the 1988 Dodge National Circuit Finals Rodeo Queen and the 1989 Miss Rodeo Idaho title. She had high praise for the Pocatello Rodeo committee, "If it hadn't been for the DNCFR, I don't think I would have ever been Miss Rodeo America." Her mother's comment was, "Every mother would like to see her daughter follow in her footsteps, that is only natural. To have the dream come true is something very, very special and personal."

Shelly Williams

It is the night of the 1998 National Finals Rodeo and the Miss Rodeo America Pageant in Las Vegas, Nevada, the town of glitter, glitz, and gambling. But, of far greater importance, to the performers and viewers, than the flashiness of the casinos to the performers and viewers is the year's final rodeo competitions with its own excitement, pride, and splendor. It is sponsored by the prestigious Professional Rodeo Cowboys Association in the Thomas and Mack Center. With an attendance topping seven hundred thousand for ten performances and prize money rolling near four million dollars there is no question about the sport of rodeo and where it stands today in American entertainment.

Shelly Williams of Kuna, Idaho, has just been crowned Miss Rodeo America to reign all of 1999. With her crowning, Idaho and Texas are tied at six in the number of Miss Rodeo America Queens. Utah is second with five. The tempo is expansive, upbeat, and joyful as Shelly meets with proud and happy friends and relatives in the hallway. She is basking in the warmth and affection, when a tall cowboy strides to her side, leans over and gives her a hug and says, "Congratulations, Idaho. You make us proud." He is Butch Otter, then Idaho's Lieutenant Governor and now the First Congressional District's member of the U.S. House of Representatives. "That was so nice of him," Shelly said, "and his office donated the Idaho flag for the pageant. The flag of every state which has a competitor is flown during the pageant. I was proud of Idaho."

Congressman Otter has been participating in rodeos for years and continues to rope and ride in as many as twenty in Idaho alone each year. He was right on the money when he said to Shelly, "You make Idaho proud." Shelly Williams is an unusual young woman who will continue to make Idaho proud long after her rodeo awards and trophies become a part of the decor of her home. She is lovely to look at, well spoken, well mannered, hard working, and eager to get on with a rodeo career. She is also primed to keep the strict regime necessary to finish an education and keep in the trim physical shape necessary to be a top barrel racer.

May 9, 1974, Shelly was born in Phoenix, Arizona to Jim and Beverly Williams, now of Kuna, Idaho where they have about forty acres of land. The Williams have a second daughter, Nicole, also a rider and a business management student at Boise State University. She is married to her high school sweetheart,

Ryan Kirtley. Nicole participated in a number of Peewee and Junior rodeos.

Shelly has fond memories of visiting the Pawnee City, Nebraska, farm of her grandparents, John and Lila Williams, and her own family moved to Nebraska in 1982. "We had a real menagerie of animals: horses; sheep; and pigs included. In January 1984, when I was about twelve, we moved west to Boise and the next year to Kuna." Both parents were good riders and it was a great day for them when they could give their daughters horses. Jim gave the girls riding pointers when they were starting.

A handsome Arabian/Quarter Horse, a sorrel mare, was her favorite and she named her "Razana." Shelly's voice softens as she talks about that consumate riding horse: "I learned Eh Capa bareback riding on her when I was thirteen. There were thirty-six of us kids in Eh Capa, all riding bareback and jumping. In the middle of the performance, we take off the reins and operate by leg pressure and voice command. It requires dexterity and Razana was wonderful. She was so beautiful with four perfect stockings and a blaze down the front of her face. She wasn't ill or anything and yet she died in January, 1999."

Her current horse is "Goose," a Palomino paint of sixteen hands and 1200 pounds. He is described by Shelly as being enormous. When he was a colt, he was cuddled so much that he thinks he should still be petted and snuggled even though he has grown to be a huge horse. "He always lives up to his name and when he walks behind you he nudges you in the back end," Shelly said. In other words, he "gooses" those who get ahead of him.

High praise is given to her riding coach, Janis Wroten Meek, as a superior leader with talent and ability to inspire the young-sters to continuing improvement and skill. Janis Meek was a Snake River Stampede Queen in the mid-seventies.

Shelly won so many competitions that it would take an entire chapter to list all of them. She won her first competition in the Idaho Girls Rodeo at Nampa in 1990. From there she was in a veritable whirlwind of rodeo, competing in one a month. In 1994, she was named the Caldwell Night Rodeo Queen, going on to the Portland Rose Parade and the first place trophy as "best in the parade." Caldwell Night Rodeo sponsored her at the Pendleton Roundup. In 1995, she became the Meridian Lions Rodeo Queen and in 1996, reigned as Riggins Rodeo Queen. "That Riggins rodeo is such a fun one," she said, "and I ran barrels there." Shelly is partial to running barrels and excels in it. May 1997 found her leading the grand entry at Twin Falls Western Days, where professional bull riders show their stuff at the Filer fairgrounds.

The first Miss Rodeo Idaho to be crowned in the new arena in 1997 and to serve in 1998, the tempo for Shelly accelerated even further. She made appearances in ten different states and still regrets that she had to miss three of the PRCA rodeos in Idaho. She attended all others, but "I had to miss Coeur d'Alene, Salmon, and Grace because I had other invitations on their dates." Then came the coveted crown event, the 1998 competition for the PRCA's Miss Rodeo America and Shelly Williams was crowned. In addition to being tied with Texas for the most national winners, Idaho claims the only mother-daughter team to ever carry the title. Karen Lavens (James), 1961–62, and her daughter, Joni James, 1990–91, of Jerome.

A 1992 graduate of Kuna High School, followed by two and one half years of study in communication at Boise State University, Shelly is now studying public relations, communication, German history, and language at the University of Nevada, Las Vegas. Along with her national queen title she was given the scholarship. German study holds a special interest for her as she was one of eighteen Kuna High School students to exchange visits with a similar group from Germany for a six-weeks study program. They stayed for a summer with German families in Reutlingen, about an hour's drive southwest from Stuttgart.

What would she like to be "when she grows up?" Shelly laughed at the question and said, "What I would love to do is

work with the sports channel on ESPN and TNN cable, inter-
viewing athletes and others involved in rodeo." She has no intention of giving up rodeo and hopes to make it to the national final
in barrel racing. To do so, she must be one of the fifteen top
money winners. To qualify for entering, she hopes to compete in
the Houston Livestock Show, Denver, Reno, Caldwell, and
Nampa and win the Columbia River circuit year-end average at
Pocatello.

When she wins, Idaho will be joined by the rodeo world in
being proud.

MISS RODEO USA
Kimberly Dawn Williams

Idaho rodeo is rich with inspirational stories. One of the
most dramatic and exciting is that of Kimberly Dawn Williams of
Twin Falls. Born with a genetic deficiency that left her almost
deaf, she met many problems in her young life and sometimes
felt that she could not compete in the hearing world. The inspir-
ing thing about Kimberly Dawn was that she never stopped trying. That attitude of fortitude found her prepared for the top of
the horse world when she was named Miss Rodeo USA. In 1996
she was named Miss Rodeo Idaho and went on to compete in the
Miss Rodeo America contest. That time she won fifth place. In
1998 she competed again for the top title and won. She was
crowned on January 17 in Oklahoma City, Oklahoma. Since then
the pageant which is a part of the National Finals Rodeo has been
moved to Las Vegas.

Her name was added to the glamour of the history of
national queens dating back to 1955. The pageant has taken
giant strides in numbers and prestige. Miss Rodeo America
makes hundreds of appearances as she serves as a goodwill
ambassador for the professional rodeo sport and it was reported
that Kimberly Dawn was one of the most inspirational.

Born to Dave and Kathy Williams who have normal hearing, Kim and her brother, Kevin, both possess the gene that

robbed them of most of their hearing. Mother Kathy said Kimberly at four years was already riding when they learned she had not been understanding language. They enrolled her in the Idaho School for the Deaf and the Blind in Gooding. While attending classes she lived with close friends, Denise and Don Gill, who remain involved in rodeo and devoted to Kimberly. Denise was a former state director of Miss Teen Rodeo Idaho and Don was an advisor for the Gooding High School Rodeo Club.

With added attention given by the Gills, by the time she was nine she decided she would like to be a rodeo queen. From then until fourteen she won many riding contests, giving up most of her social life to do so. Few people who meet her recognize her lack of hearing. She is an expert at lip reading and uses the latest in high-tech hearing equipment. She pays close attention as others speak and is complimented for her charm and humility.

When successful in rodeo on local and state levels, Kimberly decided to enter the Miss Rodeo USA contest. The rest is history and continues the story of her determination to overcome all handicaps. Being queen for the entire country involved much travel in behalf of the International Professional Rodeo Association. She enjoyed promoting rodeo and proudly wore the Western gear, including the big prize buckle. Her cowgirl hat was emblazoned with the queen's tiara.

RODEO QUEENS
Barbara Renner

Rodeo queens and their princesses are important to the excitement, color and pageantry that go with the show. They are happy, wear big smiles and perform beautifully on their horses. They represent their home rodeos at other functions and in other towns. While another type of "Queens of Rodeo" are those women who devote a good part of their lives to managing, operating, arranging, hiring, directing and assisting with rodeos.

Barb Renner of Coeur d'Alene was one of the best of the fair and rodeo managers in the minds of those who know her, also one of the few women to hold the title for so long. Those who watched all that she did to grow rodeo, think of her as being seated on a diamond-studded saddle on the most beautiful of all white horses. They recognize what she has done for all of North Idaho and that they are the beneficiaries of her hard work and helpfulness. When the North Idaho Fair and Rodeo came to an end along with the month of August 1998, so did Barb's lengthy career as Fair manager.

The *Coeur d'Alene Press* paid editorial tribute on August 24, 1998 with the heading RENNER'S SERVICE MUST BE HONORED. The writer pointed out that her resignation is, "marking the end of a period of unprecedented growth and success and the North Idaho Fairgrounds has seen remarkable improvements and the fair itself has become the region's premier summer attraction. Her success has brought personal recognition from her peers, including election to the presidency of the International Association of Fairs and Expositions."

The editorial went on to suggest that a record crowd show up for the final day as an unofficial "Barb Renner Day." They did.

In 1963, wanting something with a bit more zip than trail riding, Barb Renner joined Claudia Steinley and LaVonne Witter in organizing the Saddelite Drill Team. Other young women wanted to join and put their horses through the paces of snappy drills. In short time they were appearing at many Northwest rodeos, including Cheyenne Frontier Days and the Omak Stampede.

Ann Marie Weeks

Another mother-daughter rodeo queen story is Ann Marie Weeks, the 1991 Pocatello Frontier Rodeo Queen for 1991 and her mother Bernice Weeks of Malad. Her father is Grant Weeks. Ann Marie was queen of the Malad Rodeo and her mother held the same title exactly twenty years previously. "It was the first time in Malad's history a daughter followed in her mother's footsteps," Bernice said. Ann Marie said she "started riding when I was about six months old and never stopped." She was a member of the Malad High School and the Fourth District high school rodeo associations at the Idaho finals three years running. She was in junior barrel racing when she was four.

During the last round of competition in the Miss Rodeo Idaho contest in September 1990, her horse fell and Ann Marie suffered a broken shoulder. In spite of the injury she ranked fifth and won the Miss Congeniality contest.

Gertrude Maxwell

Beyond Grangeville to the east, along the Clearwater River where the Indians camped, is the historic little town of Elk City. From that village came a well-known packer, guide and school-teacher who loved rodeo. Gertrude Maxwell was born in the high mountain country three miles northwest of Elk City on June 30, 1908, at the very time her father, Oscar Maxwell, was fording streams to reach Dr. Shinnick. Baby Gertrude arrived at the home before they did.

A Nez Perce Indian family, the Pierre Corbetts, was camped nearby and swam their horses across the runoff to see the new baby. She was one of the legends that grow up around horse peo-ple. The story includes being a rodeo queen at a young age, and recognition again at the end of her horse career.

Gertrude learned to ride while a toddler and lived her life around horses. "Like most teenagers with horses, I considered myself a bronc rider," Gertrude wrote in *My Yesterdays in Elk City*. "I was at a Kooskia rodeo without my parents and in those days they saddled the broncs in the arena. They turned a small bay mare loose with a 'would-be-cowboy' aboard and he didn't stay long. I had watched the horse rear up and he bucked straight and with good rhythm. I made the mistake of saying I could ride that horse, so someone ran to the announcer and told him what I had said."

The announcer yelled out that they had a girl who was going to attempt to ride the animal that had just thrown a man and if she could actually ride him she would get twenty-five dol-lars. "I had made my brags," Gertrude said, "and I couldn't chicken out then. Much more boldly than I felt, I walked up to where the horse was standing blindfolded with a gunnysack. The attendants wanted to hobble my stirrups but I said, 'Nuthin' doin', I'll ride him clean or not at all.'"

She rode until he quit bucking and someone grabbed his lead rope. Gertrude was enjoying her success and receiving the prize money when, to her surprise, her parents appeared. "Right there before the very crowd that had been cheering me, Mother gave me a most unmerciful tongue-lashing and topped it by using her knee to kick me in the posterior." Although mortified to tears, Gertrude remembered she still clutched the prize money.

Over the years, Gertrude owned bucking and packing horses. Of one, she wrote, "Laddie, a beautifully built palomino gelding, was about the most worthless saddle horse I ever had and, along with his other shortcomings, he was 'barn sour.' I always said he was like riding a Guernsey cow." She owned many horses, with a given name for each. One called "Bud" had been "bucked out" from a professional rodeo string and had a way of rolling his skin which made him hard to ride.

When she taught school in Lewiston, she took three horses with her. She boarded them with a farmer in Lewiston Orchards so she could give riding lessons on weekends. She eventually went into the business of outfitting, packing groups into the back-country. Of one trip she said, "We saw lots of wildlife, elk, deer, a few moose, and one bear that the horses smelled. We almost had a rodeo!"

In 1937 Gertrude was selected as the rodeo queen for the Border Days annual rodeo in Grangeville. Forty-two years later, she was given a greater honor as Grand Marshal at the Fourth of July Border Days Rodeo. She was presented the 1979 silver buckle for her cowgirl belt, riding all three-parade days on a fine horse loaned by the Homeseys of Kooskia. She thought being queen was great, "but I believe being Grand Marshal was more fun," she laughed.

Cassia County Queen

Among the queens of the Cassia County Fair and Rodeo was Ruby Parke (Kalensky) of Declo. The first one to serve, she was chosen in 1937 by the fair board members. The system of selection was based on riding ability, appearance, poise, personality, and skill. This criteria is still used. Mrs. Kalensky said that at that time she was a "typical teenager" and loved adventure as well as horses. She was born on a ranch north of Declo as the tenth of eleven children of Anson and Julia Parke. Five of her eight brothers became professional jockeys as well as trainers of thoroughbreds.

Duties of the queen include riding in the parade, opening the stampede each night, and marching with the Cassia County Posse in the Grand Finale. She remembered that it rained during her reign but that fair attendees turned out in great numbers and all of the activities took place, including twice daily parades, horse racing each afternoon, and the stampede every night. She appreciated being queen at that time, stating that the challenges for queen contestants in modern days are much greater.

Lewiston Roundup Queens

Roundup Royalty for Lewiston at the September 8, 9 and 10, 2000 events were Queen Jennie Bullard and her princesses Brooke Howell and Jackie Alboucq. Royalty is chosen from those girl riders between the ages of sixteen and twenty-one. The contact person is Rick Truby of the Roundup Association.

Well-known for riding abilities and adept at making a good impression for the Lewiston area and its roundup were the Queens from 1935 through 1947: Dorothy Brock, Rhea Richardson, Mildred Shepherd, Betty Jean Tippett, Arlene Johnson, Margaret Reeves, Julie Gibson, Linda Lou Butler, Barbara Tippett, and Mardell West.

Those chosen from 1948 through 1957: Mary Jane Brier, Joan Wittman, Molly Staley, Mary McDonald, Marjorie Hauger, Patricia McMonigle, Joan Luedke, Arlene Maynard Worley, Betty Jo Roberts, and Molly Melcher.

From 1958 through 1978, all with wide smiles, snappy

Stetsons and stylish outfits, include: Susan Cox, Mary Beth Wishard, Sylvia Nolt, Susan Duthie, Bette Ellis, Sharon Poston, Diana Schmidt, Linda Heimark, Kris Sheppard, Janice Nearing, Charlotte Rice, Terry George Reeves, Barbara Frost, Tammy Pennick, Polly Boren, Marjorie Chinchinian, Mickie Schmidt, JoJean Hinkley, Linda Burke, Janene Connerley, and Laurie Olson.

Karen Manser was the queen in 1980, and followed, through 1997 by: Ann Buratto, Carla Capps, Bobbette Ewing Franks, LaDawn Dodd, Jill Bothum, Charla Caufield, Karen Tippett, Stephanie Wagner, Debra Ferguson, Christine Clark, Jennifer O'Toole, Lori Meehan, Meredith Anderson, Tami Saleen, Jenny Marie Harris, Wendy Broyles, and Dani Ingram.

In 1944, when Julie Gibson was invited to be queen of the Roundup it was necessary for her to ask for a leave from Paramount Pictures, Inc., where she was under a seven year contract. She was known in Lewiston as Camille Sorey, daughter of Mr. and Mrs. Grover Sorey. She graduated from Lewiston High School in 1931.

Riggins Queens

With no queen chosen for 1959 and 1960, the crowned heads of the Riggins Royal Rodeo Court from 1947 through 1958 are: Joan Taylor Clay and Janie Spicklemire of Riggins; Edith Paul Keeler of Grangeville; and LaVern Derrick Wiley and Dollie Carrey Gills of Riggins.

From 1962 through 1983: Louise Johnson, Kooskia; Sharon Jackson, Stites; Linda Campbell Knoeber, New Meadows; Sharon Taylor Sickles, White Bird; Marilyn Campbell Perry, New Meadows; Sondra Endicott Hinkley, Riggins; Penny Stephens Van Wassenhove, Middleton; Sue Ellen Smith, Meridian; Janet DeVeny, Riggins; Terri Whiteman Knight, Riggins; Tincy Heath Wilson, Grangeville; Carol Baker Jones, Kooskia; Sue Whiteman Stewart, Riggins; Vicky Swedbloom Duvall, White Bird; Marty Spicklemire Clay, Riggins; Kandy Mocaby, McCall; Carrie Whiteman Dunham, Riggins; Gayle Gill Hagler, Riggins; Dee Marek Fredrickson, Riggins; Donna Close

Grush, Lucile; Donna Gill Medley, Riggins; Vicky Heath Smith, White Bird; Tracey Cole Tucker, Grangeville. No queen was listed for 1984.

From 1985 through 1999: Tamie Bowman, Riggins; Jill Lamb, Grangeville; Julie Christensen, Deneen Lammey, Lisa Herrera, Jill Gossi, Kahe Blessinger, Judy Henderson, all of Riggins; Theresa Maher, Emmett; Amy Paul Aiken, Grangeville; Brooke McKuskey Shelley Williams, Caldwell; Leslie Wolery. For 2001: Amanda Butler, Kuna.

Weiser Valley Rodeo Queens

From 1923, Queens reigned at the rodeos in Weiser. Records are not found for the years 1925 through 1931 and 1936. Jean Couper in 1923 was followed by Georgia DeVaul, Wilma Fisher, Melba Brown, Ellen Anderson, Doris Ballard, Claudia Keithley, Joyce Fraser, Carol Ramsey, Dorine Cartwright, Dorothy Dickerson, Lucille Allen, Marty Walker, Darlene McGinnis, Maxine Kelley, Tensie Rowan, Lela Coats, Carol Irby, Jeannie McVay, Beverly Ledington, Sharon Cary, Diana Thorson, Karen Bumgarner, Ginger Tarter, Marilyn Higgins, Linda Mastrom, Sandy Cutbirth, Vicki Maddox, Tara Johnson, Cora Smith, Judy Legg, Lynn Coski, Ann Legg, Rebecca Leslie, Jody Walchel, Chris Doherty, Dixie Wiggins, Cindy Sawyer, Darla Campbell, Karen Kelley, Cindy Johnson, Julene Grunke, Terry Gosse, Kimberly Kelley, Jackie Panike, Sue Chandler, Shari Whiting, Jennifer Chandler, Lonnie Owen, Becky Backus, Kassie Graham, Megan Kersey, and Leslie Woolery.

IDAHO HORSE QUEEN
Kitty Wilkins

The only cows on her ranches were there for the purpose of providing milk and beef for the many ranch hands, thus Kitty Wilkins could not rightly be called a "cowgirl." But, she kept busy building a gigantic herd of horses. Back in the mid-60s, the author interviewed Lee Strickland, the Wilkins foreman of several years. Lee's brother Hugo, known as Hugh, became an "award-winning cowboy." Lee was eighty-five at that time and tough as leather. His mind was vivid with memories of the many years during which he knew and worked for Idaho's queen of the thundering hooves.

At that time Lee was living in a modest white frame house near the Owyhee Junction at Nyssa, Oregon. He talked easily and lengthily about the woman he referred to as "Miss Kitty."

The Wilkins family moved to Boise in 1867 from Pataha, a wide spot in the rode just south of Lewiston, where Kitty's father, John R. Wilkins, built the first house in the vicinity. After three years at Boise a move was made to Tuscarora, Nevada and a large ranch was acquired and stocked with thousands of head of cattle and horses.

Kitty joined her father and later her brother in horse raising. Strickland remembered that all of her hands were skilled in horsemanship, riding, roundup, lassoing, and branding. Whatever related to horses they could do.

"Miss Kitty" owned about four thousand horses and eventually built the herd to eleven thousand. This included wild ones then roaming the ranges of Idaho in uncountable numbers. The Owyhee Mountains and the head of Bruneau Creek was the range for her stock, in addition to Wilkins Island, where the home ranch was located. It was not quite an island but located on land at the fork of the Bruneau near Jarbidge Mountain. There was also a winter camp and several branch camps along the Snake River. The Wilkins' range spanned about eighty miles, all the way from Grandview south to the Nevada line and from east to west up to fifty miles.

Kitty sold hundreds of horses at a time. One sale to the United States Cavalry, Lee recalled, was of five hundred. The sale was so satisfactory to both sides that it became a huge and regular event. She had a contract with the Army's Cavalry to furnish twenty-six train carloads of twenty-six animals in each, for a total of 676, every two weeks. While she never rode in a rodeo, the Cavalry contract called for the horses to be broken-to-ride before shipment. So, her cowboys, roped, tamed, and rode bucking broncs every day, creating virtual rodeos on the ranches.

The Strickland brothers broke hundreds of horses for the Wilkins outfit. Kitty demanded the best in horseflesh and owned Percherons, Morgans, Normans, and Hambeltonians. She bought one Morgan stallion considered to be the best in the country. Using imported stallions, hundreds of mares were bred and colts were added to the huge bands.

Lee Strickland, still solid as a rock at an age when most were sagging in a rocker, said, "When us Strickland kids went after a herd of horses, we got 'em. We could ride a horse one a hundred miles a day and not hurt him, either. There was real horses then. Better stock . . . better bred and used more." He went on to say, "If you mistreated a horse, Miss Kitty's temper would come wide open and you never did that again. She'd say, 'dirty scum of the earth,' to any people she was vexed with." He reminisced about the lush and beautiful bunch grass that looked like a grain field, "I'll say it was beautiful. It was belly-high to the horses. That bunch grass hay sold for forty dollars a ton in Jarbidge. Cut right on the mountainside and horses would eat every bit of it."

Surely, Kitty was a favorite of her father John Wilkins and learned all about horses by going with him to horse sales in various areas throughout the country. She later sold primarily to buyers in the Midwest and East, taking care of and accompanying many large shipments to Omaha, Chicago, St. Louis, and Sioux City. Beautifully dressed for the events, she did her own auctioneering at many destination points. Hundreds showed up to hear her extol the virtues of the animals and generate excited bidding. There was one shipment out of Mountain Home of twenty-six stock carloads for which she hired as many as forty men to round up, cut out stock from the range and drive them the seventy-five miles from the ranches and buildings on the Bruneau River.

Along with all her abilities at handling horses, shipping and auctioneering, Kitty was a classy dresser. She wore custom-made riding outfits and for special events had pretty dresses. Newspaper photographs show her wearing both western-style or feathered hats. Small wonder, she became a favorite of photographers and reporters where she appeared at the horse sales. Tourist development bureaus in any state in the Union would today pay thousands of dollars for the favorable publicity which she brought to Idaho.

There remains a difference of opinion on whether or not she rode conventional or side saddle. Her old foreman, Lee Strickland, insisted that she never rode anything but side saddle. Others say she rode western. It does not seem realistic with the many miles and thousands of horses that she did not, at least a part of the time, use a western saddle. Any opinion at this day can only be conjecture.

Even Father Time rode a galloping bronc on the Wilkins' Ranch. As Miss Kitty grew elderly there was a final sale of the gigantic herd of nearly eleven thousand head to the King Brothers of the famed Texas King Ranch. Lee Strickland reminisced about gathering six hundred and fifty dry mares and geldings for the final delivery. He said, "They was the prettiest things you ever saw and we trailed them six hundred and fifty horses through Oklahoma and down to Texas. We put 'em on the trail and drove right through American Falls. There was about fifteen men riding, and we sold and traded some of the horses as we went along. After that, every two weeks we shipped five hundred until all eleven thousand had gone to Texas."

MUTTON BUSTIN' WORLD CHAMP

"I wouldn't trade my title for anything," declared seven-year-old Teresa Farrens, daughter of Dock and Nancy Farrens of Pocatello, when she rode into the 1990 Dodge National Circuit Finals Rodeo Mutton Bustin' championship. The Edahow elementary school pupil set a new DNCFR arena record of 78 points in capturing the world title. She admitted the ride was "kinda scary and exciting, but when I was done I kissed the nose of my sheep." She giggled as she told of practicing by riding on the backs of her dad and older brothers, as well as the sheep they had at home. She was a three-time qualifier and to win was so exciting that she wants to be a veterinarian and marry a farmer and take care of his animals.

Adonis of the Arena

He's trim.

He's slim.

He forks a horse like he was born to it. And for all practical purposes, he was.

And as Katie Brodie of Hayden Lake says, "He is the best darn dancer in Idaho!"

He is C. L. "Butch" Otter, who, on November 7, 2000, was elected to the United States Congress from Idaho's First Congressional District. He was lieutenant governor for fourteen years and previously he served in the state legislature. Never was it difficult to know that he is a genuine Idaho cowboy. Neither is it difficult to understand that for his horse ranch north of Boise he borrowed the television series title "Lonesome Dove" for its name.

Idaho's newest cowboy Congressman C.L. "Butch" Otter is "ready in the hold," awaiting his turn for the team roping event. This was at Cambridge in 1997, and was followed by other rodeos in nearby Council and McCall. The former Lieutenant-Governor rides in many rodeos each summer.

He was born to Bernard Joseph and Regina Buser Otter. His father, a journeyman and electrician, goes by the name of Ben. Butch was born May 3, 1942, and while still a toddler, was put on horseback.

It also stands to reason that Butch Otter was delivered by Doctor Elizabeth Munn of Caldwell, who was a cowgirl in her own right. One rodeo season during the Caldwell Night Rodeo, doctor Munn was riding in the parade preceding the spectacular event when a motorcycle policeman rode alongside her horse and called out that she was needed for an obstetrics emergency at the hospital. He reached up and lifted her down from the horse onto the back of the motorcycle and they raced to the hospital.

Butch Otter weighed in at eleven pounds and three ounces. He was the sixth of nine children, five girls and four boys.

The Otter children grew up on farms and ranches where horses were needed to run the operations. Butch remembers that

Butch Otter entertains at the GOP State Convention in Lewiston, 1994.

he was, "Always compelled, even as a youngster, to ride the wild colts and steers just to see if I could do it. I entered my first home-town rodeo in 1963 in Council. I didn't win anything. But I got some bruises and a black eye and learned a lot. I loved rodeo even when I kissed old Mother Earth. The crowds cheering and all of the excitement. It is wonderful."

In 1978, Otter started entering roping contests in local rodeos and "play day" events. He continues to compete as he nears the big six-oh. He rode in twenty Idaho rodeos in 2000. In 1981, by invitation of his brother-in-law Don Simplot, he joined the "Granddaddy of all Trail Rides," the Rancheros Visitadores in Santa Barbara, California, where he was voted the "Outstanding Maverick of the Year." That year he won several rodeo events and became permanently hooked on riding and roping.

In 1988, Otter became a member of another cowboy group called Tejas Vaqueros (cowboys) in Kerrville, Texas. Again he was named the "Outstanding Maverick" and was the only Idahoan participating. He has roped in Idaho, Nevada, Montana, Colorado, California, Arizona, Texas, and Louisiana.

In Idaho in 1988, he participated in rodeos at Meridian, McCall, Cambridge, and Payette, which had started rodeo just four years previously; Homedale, Bruneau, Caldwell, and the Garden Valley Rodeo, sponsored by the Payette River Cattlemen's Association. Crouch and Kuna were others. He found himself participating in two competitive ropings a week during that season. A colorful character whether legislating or rodeoing, Otter entered a wild-cow milking contest and another rider, Dick Parker, who was announcing the events, took the opportunity to praise his agility and ability as a legislator and a cowboy. A reporter wrote, "Dick Parker gave an election speech for our Lieutenant Governor Otter while a wild cow stood on his back."

Otter and his former wife, Gay Simplot, are the parents of John S., Carolyn, Kimberly, and Corinne. On April 22, 1998, they became grandparents when John Clement was born to John S. and Sheila. John S. Otter is working in a marketing position in

Melbourne, Australia, and his father made a trip there in October 1997, to run with his son in a marathon.

For several years, Otter handled international marketing for the J. R. Simplot Company and became well acquainted with the overseas markets. As lieutenant governor, he worked to expand Idaho state's products to other states and countries, leading missions of manufacturers, growers, and producers. Before becoming lieutenant governor, when he served in the state legislature he was known as a strong supporter of small and large business. During all this time he has maintained his interest in rodeo and at every opportunity, he rides one of his horses across the acreage of Lonesome Dove Ranch.

The ranch is also the site of the Gem State Rodeo operated by Ron Scott and Rick Nichols. The children who learn to ride are invited to participate in the rodeo. The rodeo is family oriented and a governing rule is that one parent must also take part. Gymkhana events include: pole bending, tire, spud and barrel racing.

The Old Timer

Colen H. Sweeten Jr. is a native of the Curlew Valley in Southeastern Idaho. He earned his spurs as a caring, warm-hearted, and talented cowboy poet. His poetry shows that he writes and recites well because he was a natural cowboy on the ranches and rolling hills of the Curlew. He has never missed a meeting of the National Cowboy Poetry Gathering in Elko, Nevada and has given so many readings of his poems in so many places during the past half century, that it is impossible to list them.

In his 1996 volume *Hoofprints and Heartbeats,* another writer and reciter of cowboy poems, Michael Martin Murphy of Ranchos de Taos, New Mexico, composed the Foreword. Michael wrote: "It's absolutely essential that the writer of good cowboy poetry has had close contact with the lifestyle for some time. That's what gives it that special flavor . . .. The recent glamour attached to cowboy poets has caused a lot of posturing, but poets like Colen have held their place by being themselves."

Michael told of an incident a few years ago when he asked Colen to get up on the stage with him "in a highly professional entertainment setting. With his simple but hard-won values and loving (as opposed to sarcastic) humor, he received an ovation usually reserved for 'polished' performers. But it was his lack of polish that they loved the best. . .. He is not jealous of other artists . . . because there is no one else like him."

Colen speaks for many old cowboys, cowgirls, and rodeo fans who love the sport in his poem:

OLD TIMER

There's a cinch ring and a latigo
Hanging from the trunk
Of the Chevrolet my neighbors say
Is my smokin' pile of junk.
But it's fair time once again
And there's a rodeo in town,
So if I can get that junk fired up
I think I'll ride on down.

There's lot of dust on my J.B.
And a big dent in the crown,
But its been hangin' in the closet
Since last year's show shut down.

Ya see these red boots I'm wearin'
That I keep just for luck?
I won 'em in the finals
When a saddle bronc could buck.

And this wild shirt that Mary gave me
Seems to be gettin' kind of tame,
I wore it when they put me in
The Cowboy Hall of Fame.

Say, I could tell the buckin' style
Of every bronc I ever sat.
And it was a lot more fun to ride 'em
When you could fan 'em with your hat.

But I'm too old to ride tonight,
I'll leave it to younger hands,
I've got a complimentary ticket
For the best seat in the stands!

It's American. It's action. It's colorful and exciting. It's great and glorious. And in the summers of our various discontents with all the new entertainments, it provides a connection to the past.

It's Rodeo Idaho!

Yippee Ti Yo.

Bibliography

Books

Beautiful Bonner, The History of Bonner County, Idaho. Marylyn Cork, Project Director. Dallas: Curtis Media Corporation, 1991.

Canutt, Yakima with Oliver Drake. Stunt Man: *The Autobiography of Yakima Canutt.* Norman: University of Oklahoma Press, 1997.

Chedsey, Zona and Carolyn Frei, Editors. *Idaho County Voices.* Grangeville, Idaho: Centennial Committee, 1990.

Cole, Heidi Bigler. *A Wild Cowboy.* Cambridge, ID: Rocky Comfort Press, 1992.

Conley, Cort. *Idaho For the Curious.* Cambridge, ID: Backeddy Books, 1981.

Corgatelli, Kathy. *Idaho's Wildest, Mackay Rodeo's Early Years.* 1995.

Dobie, J. Frank, Mody C. Boatright, Harry H. Ransom, Editors. *Mustangs and Cow Horses.* 2nd Edition. Dallas: Southern Methodist University Press, 1965.

Elsensohn, Sr. M. Alfreda. *Pioneer Days in Idaho County,* Volume I. Caldwell, ID: Caxton Printers, Ltd., 1947.

Encyclopaedia Britannica. Volume 19. Chicago: Encyclopaedia Britannica, 1968.

Forbis, William H. *The Old West: The Cowboys.* New York: Time-Life Books, 1973.

Hanley, Mike with Ellis Lucia. *Owyhee Trails: The West's Forgotten Corner.* Caldwell: The Caxton Printers, Ltd., 1988.

Idaho Livestock Brand Book. State of Idaho, 1994

Idaho Poets and Writers Guild. *The Idaho Story, 1967.* Iona, Idaho: Ipas Publishing Co.,1967.

Jordan, Teresa. *Cowgirls: Women of the American West.* Lincoln, Nebraska: Bison Books, University of Nebraska Press, 1982.

Lawrence, Elizabeth Atwood. *Rodeo: An Anthropologist Looks at the Wild and the Tame.* Knoxville: University of Tennessee Press, 1982.

Kesey, Ken with Ken Babbs. *Last Go Round: A Real Western.* New York: Viking, 1994.

Larrison, Earl J. *Owyhee: The Life of a Northern Desert.* Caldwell, ID: The Caxton Printers, Ltd., 1957.

Mack, Beth. *The History of Weiser Roundup.* Weiser, 1993.

McDowell, Bart. *The American Cowboy: In Life and Legend.* Washington, DC: National Geographic Society, 1972.

Nelson, Marjorie L. Ramey. *Footprints on Mountain Trails.* Arco, ID: The Arco Advertiser, Inc., 1992.

Penson-Ward, Betty. *Idaho Women in History.* Boise: Legendary Publishing Company, 1991.

ProRodeo Cowboys Association. *1994 and 1998 Official Professional Rodeo Media Guides.*

Robertson, M.S. Rodeo: *Standard Guide to the Cowboy Sport.* 2nd Edition. Berkeley, California: Howell-North Books, 1965.

Savage, Candace. *Cowgirls.* Berkeley, California: Ten Speed Press, 1996.

Shadduck, Louise. *Doctors With Buggies, Snowshoes and Planes.* Boise: Tamarack Books, Inc., 1994

_____. "Kitty Wilkins, Queen of the Thundering Hoofs." *The Idaho Story,* Volumes I and II. Iona, Idaho: Idaho Poets and Writers Guild, 1967.

Youngdahl, Kristi M. *The Arams of Idaho.* Moscow, ID: University of Idaho Press, 1995

Newspapers and Other Publications

Caldwell *News-Tribune*
Coeur d'Alene *Press*
Idaho Free Press (Nampa)
Idaho Post Register
Idaho State Journal
Idaho Statesman
Northwest Ropers News and Rodeo News
ProRodeo Sports News
Salmon *Recorder Herald*
Spokesman *Review*
The Circuit Rider (Cowboy Chapter of Christian Athletes)

Rodeo material, Collections of the Idaho State Historical Society

Salmon High School Honors English Class. "Patchwork: Pieces of Local History." July, 1992.

Skaar, Sarah Henson. "Cowboy Days" and "Salmon Cowgirl's Pro-Rodeo" *Out West,* May/June, 1994.

Index

319